Fictional Meals and Their Function in the French Novel
1789-1848

The period from 1789 to 1848 in France represents the golden
age of French gastronomy, the apex of interest in and
consciousness of food. The July Monarchy (1830-48) coincided
with the supremacy of bourgeois culture and values, the rise
of the novel of manners, the growing consciousness among the
Romantics of the artist's social mission, and the Christian
Socialist movement. This book is an examination of the alliance between food and literature epitomized in certain
novels of the period.

Professor Brown studies the theme of food and eating in
Balzac, Sand, Sue, Hugo, and Flaubert, examining the meal
both as primary sign-function and as mimesis. His approach
may be broadly described as semiotic, though not in the
sense of a formal semiotic enquiry; it is his aim to uncover
the 'semiotic texture' of fictional meals and their range
of meanings rather than their formal properties or relations.

He attempts to explain why this period in France witnessed
a momentous surge in the number of fictional dining episodes,
to relate the alimentary discourse in the fiction of this
era to the prevailing bourgeois ideology, and to demonstrate
how fictional meals function as cultural and narrative signs.

James W. Brown is a member of the Department of French at
Dalhousie University.

Fictional Meals and Their Function in the French Novel

1789-1848

JAMES W. BROWN

University of Toronto Press

Toronto Buffalo London

© University of Toronto Press 1984
Toronto   Buffalo   London
Printed in Canada
ISBN 0-8020-5605-9

University of Toronto Romance Series 48

Canadian Cataloguing in Publication Data
Brown, James W. (James White), 1942-
   Fictional meals and their function in the French novel
   1789-1848

   (University of Toronto romance series, ISSN 0082-5336; 48)
   Bibliography: p.
   Includes index.
   ISBN 0-8020-5605-9

   1. French fiction-18th century-History and criticism. 2.
   French fiction-19th century-History and criticism. 3.
   Dinners and dining in literature.
   I. Title.   II. Series.

   PQ657.B76 1984   843'.7   C83-098873-4

This book has been published with the help of a grant from
the Canadian Federation for the Humanities, using funds provided by the Social Sciences and Humanities Research Council
of Canada, a grant from the Publications Fund of University
of Toronto Press, and a grant from Dalhousie University.
Portions of this book have appeared, in earlier versions,
in the *Romanic Review* and the *USF Language Quarterly*, for
which permission is gratefully acknowledged.

For Bibiana,

whose love has lifted me higher ...

ACKNOWLEDGMENTS

I am especially indebted to my close friend and colleague,
James R. Lawler, for his numerous suggestions and meticulous
reading of my manuscript in its final stages. I would also
like to thank my former mentors, Frank Paul Bowman, Robert
K. Bishop, and Lucienne Frappier-Mazur, with whom I first
discussed the topic of food in literature as a graduate
student at the University of Pennsylvania. All offered valu-
able insights on the subject as well as help with various
stages of the manuscript. To my friend and former secretary,
Yvonne Landry, I owe a special debt of gratitude for the
endless hours she spent preparing the final manuscript. My
sons, Jim and Michael, for their patient understanding and
loving support, deserve a very special acknowledgment.
Finally, I wish to thank my mother and father for having
introduced me to the pleasures of French culture and for
their ceaseless encouragement.

CONTENTS

INTRODUCTION

Although the question of critical perspective for this study will be taken up in more detail in subsequent pages of this introduction, some general notions about critical approaches to the culinary in fiction merit attention at the outset. Fictional meals are above all literary signs: consequently, they are subject to the same kinds of analysis as any other literary phenomenon, and, to varying degrees, they have interested major critics of all persuasions. Mikhail Bakhtin, the socialist critic, made an extensive study of banqueting in a work on Rabelais (*Rabelais and His World*, translated by Helene Iswolsky, Boston: MIT Press, 1965); Jean-Pierre Richard assumed a phenomenological posture in examining the food thematic in relation to sensation (*Littérature et Sensation*, Paris: Editions du Seuil, 1954 and *Proust et le monde sensible*, Paris: Editions du Seuil, 1974); Roland Barthes devoted several essays to the semiology of the meal in contemporary France (*Mythologies*, Paris: Editions du Seuil, 1957) and has also proffered a short semiotic analysis of alimentary codes (*Eléments de sémiologie*, Paris: Editions Gonthier, 1953 and 1964).

The critical approach to fictional meals adopted for this book may be broadly described as semiotic, though not in the sense of a formal semiotic enquiry. I shall not endeavour to reduce the meal sign to mathematical or logical formulations, nor shall I propose to devise semio-structural models of fictional dining episodes. Such procedures, while obviously

in need of elaboration, would be useful in a monograph on
a specific author - Flaubert immediately comes to mind because of the structural and thematic importance of meals
and eating in his total opus - but they would severely restrict the study of the semantic range and functions of
fictional meal scenes in general. Like most signs, the
literary meal is arbitrarily motivated; as such its signification is determined largely, but not exclusively as we
shall see, by the intentions of a particular novelist. Moreover, it is precisely this range of meanings, their semiotic
texture as it were, which I shall attempt to describe and,
where possible, to interpret in this book. Finally, because
the general meal complex in fiction (here defined as the
total semiotic discourse associated with food and the act
of eating - types of food consumed and food symbolism, for
example, the psychological dynamics of eating, and manners,
customs, and rites pertaining to the table) models itself
on actual nineteenth-century eating practices, it will be
necessary to describe the historical context from which the
fictional meal evolves and which provides the background in
which it is presented in nineteenth-century French novels.

The Historical Context: Repast and Revolution

The alliance between food and literature epitomized in the
nineteenth-century French novel bespeaks the passage, in a
semio-historical sense, from the meal as an extratextual
cultural entity to the intertextual phenomenon of the meal
as a narrative sign. So vast was the impact of the Revolution of 1789 on the culinary codes of the French, so great
the cleavage between eating mores under the *ancien régime*
and under the *nouveau régime*, that it would be impossible
to discuss the fictional meal without first sketching the
background and the circumstances from which it emerged.
Furthermore, it is essential to affirm that in any given
culture the meal structure reflects social organization to
such an extent that it may be considered a microcosm of a
particular society at a specific moment in its history.[1]
  Prior to 1789 social hierarchies within French society
were signalled by *la cuisine noble*, or *la grande cuisine*
as it was called, whose very title connotes superiority,
differentiation, and exclusivity. During the *ancien régime*
people ate either very well or very poorly. The distinction
between the nobility and the people was abundantly evident
at the table, so much so in fact that we may describe *la
grande cuisine* as a unique gastro-culinary institution.

Distinguished and secluded also was the very locus of eating
- meals were taken in royal residences, *hôtels particuliers*,
and *salons*, for restaurants as we know them today did not
exist. Refined they were too beyond comparison, prepared by
master-chefs in residence and served only to the gentry. By
contrast, the people enjoyed none of these privileges of
caste: theirs was a problem of procuring food, not one of
preparing to perfection and indulging to excess. Under such
conditions food naturally came to symbolize leisure and
prosperity on the part of the nobility, hard work and poverty
as regards the masses. Given the importance of eating, and
eating with dignity, in any man's subsistence, it is not
surprising that the Revolution began with a cry for food,
nor that the royal family became known as 'le Boulanger,
la boulangère, et le petit mitron.' Social disparities under
the Old Regime were often transformed into gastronomical
metaphors and were later used by novelists, though the metaphors have no claim to originality. Figuratively speaking,
the aristocracy devoured the people under the *ancien régime*;
hence the metaphor of social and economic consumption which
could be nullified only by reversing the social structure
of the nation by means of a revolution and thus producing a
shift in identity from 'eaten' to 'eater.' In many respects
the Revolution of 1789 was an endeavour of the lower classes
to become equals at the table and to partake fully of the
earthly bounty. Moreover, in view of the symbolic and metaphorical potential of food and eating, it seems only natural
that the Revolution would commence with eating festivals:
the table throughout history has been an excellent stage for
the propagation of political ideas.
  The Revolution of 1789 fathered a gastronomical revolution
which transformed the entire culinary system in France as
well as the socio-cultural connotations of that system. Among
the immediate changes subsequent to the Revolution was the
establishment of communal eating festivals in 1790, the first
of which commemorated the Fall of the Bastille. Food and
eating thus became intimately associated with social equality,
which was itself symbolized in the concept and practice of
commensality. A similar proliferation of banquets will again
occur in times of distress: first, 'Au début de la Monarchie
de Juillet, quand les libéraux comprennent leur infortune
et la tragi-comédie de 1830, les banquets distribuaient la
communion des espérances et de la haine' (Aron, 340); then
again, prior to 1848, when the Guild movement became inimi-
cal enough to the government that it placed an interdiction
on workers' banquets and thus impeded the spread of socialist

ideologies. Another immediate consequence of the Revolution
of 1789, albeit a somewhat unexpected one in a period of
duress, was the eating frenzy which occurred during the
famine of 1793. This seemingly contradictory behaviour describes a kind of sublimation on the part of the revolu-
tionaries, the sudden seizure of rights and properties
figuring as an overcompensation for previous privation occasioned by hunger and hardship. Almost inevitably, a second
gastronomical metaphor, related to but even more horrendous
than the first, emerges: the social scene with its gluttonous eating and vile bloodbaths invites comparison with an
act of cannibalism; it comprises a kind of ecstatic and perverted sensuality which results from human sacrifice and
which figures as the symbolic devouring of the enemy.

The Revolution of 1789 also prompted a series of gradual
social transformations which would eventually pervade French
culture and history to such an extent that they continue to
reign today in the form of the myth of bourgeois cuisine.
Foremost among the mythologies born of the Revolution and
maturing during the Napoleonic era was gastronomy. No longer
considered only as substances and markers of personal preference, food and taste now become marketable products in
the economic circuit controlled by the bourgeoisie - com-
modities subservient to the same laws of production, distribution, and consumption as any potentially profitable
merchandise - vogues subject to the same fluctuations of
whim which instantaneously promote or demote other such ar-
tifacts, as, for example, those of high fashion. The mythologization of cuisine and gastronomy, then, forcefully attests to the rising semiotic status of the meal: naturally,
a socio-cultural sign of such magnitude would eventually
find its way into literary works whose aesthetics were in
part governed by the exigencies of social realism. The novel
of manners could not eschew the depiction of meals without
doing irreparable damage to the very aesthetic and social
criteria on which it was based.

The events leading to the mythologization of cuisine are
conveniently echoed in the rallying cry of the French Revolution, 'Liberté, Egalité, Fraternité,' for the Revolution
doubles as an attempt to realize and conretize this edifying
slogan at the table. In a democratic society equals sup together. How propitious and appropriate, then, the appearance
of the first restaurant in France in 1782,[2] how fortunate
that a public eating house should be established wherein the
abhorred practice of segregated dining had been abolished
in favour of commensal dining! Although restaurants would

not multiply until after the Revolution, they served as
ideological prototypes for the principle of commensality.
The Bourgeois, who enjoyed a rising economic status during
the Empire, could now dine at a table adjacent to an aristocrat, making the act of consumption so conspicuous as to
become a sign of prestige and wealth in itself. Quickly
seizing upon the levelling function of the table, the bourgeoisie designates it as the locus of assimilation and social rapprochement, a countermeasure against the spatial
diffusion created by the *hôtel particulier* and a symbol of
the social and epicurean decentralization which dining in
restaurants would eventually produce. Finally, the Bourgeois,
not only as a frequenter of restaurants but also an an entrepreneur who owned and directed many of these establishments, democratized and politicized the meal: there was now
a restaurant or café to fit every pocketbook in Paris and,
expectedly, eating establishments, and even certain foods,
became associated with specific political affiliations and
factions. Amidst all this culinary activity the Bourgeois
was in control of the myth-making process: the medium in
which he chose to express the myth was gastronomy; the language selected for codification of the myth was verbal discourse, non-fictional at first, then fictional.

As regards the discursive context, reference should be
made to the great gastronomes of the post-revolutionary
period who, conjoining their enormous epicurean knowledge
with an equally magnificent verbal artistry, were instrumental in transforming culinary practices into written discourse. During the first decade of the nineteenth century,
for instance, Grimod de la Reynière's *Almanach des gourmands*
shaped the evolution of French cuisine and it also helped
it to endure by diffusing new recipes upon the public. By
1825, with the appearance of Brillat-Savarin's *La Physiologie du goût*, food had become closely allied with science;
one historian of cuisine describes this marvellous gastro-
manual in the most gracious of terms: '*La Physiologie du
Goût* would be the Bible of genuine gastronomes, the chef
d'œuvre of the Science of Good Food, the most glorious
monument to the Art of Good Eating ' (Guy, 122). Exaggerated
as the encomiums may be, they nevertheless reveal to what
extent the art of eating had been codified, for an aphorism
by definition is a laconic and often witty statement of a
universal truth; French gastronomy had officially reached
its apotheosis by 1815, its sovereignty extending throughout all of Europe.

The ascension and perfection of gastronomy affected not
only the culinary domain and the repertory of extant recipes,
it also provided the impetus for change in areas closely associated with the table, ultimately generating new codes of
etiquette, rites regulating service, locus of the meal, and
seating protocol. In brief, the entire complex of events
and activities related to eating underwent a new semiosis
which reduced the space between the act of eating and the
act of creation and turned the meal complex into a sort of
poetic language rich with cultural and ideological connotations of its own.

In the nineteenth century the aesthetization of food and
meals corresponds to Jakobson's now-classic definition of
poetic discourse in which the emphasis shifts from the content of the message to its form. Food is no longer viewed
as sustenance alone; it acquires a semiotic status and becomes a highly motivated social sign. Gastronomical trea-
tises, and indeed most nineteenth-century French novels,
attenuate the denotative value of food in their discourse
in order to accentuate its connotative value. The term *gibier*,
for instance, obviously denotes game, but in the post-
revolutionary period it connotes equality because prior to
1789 it has been associated with the aristocracy and the
hunt. Many other types of food came to signify something
beyond their normal range of meanings; as Paris gained ascendancy over the rest of France, it developed its own cuisine, and, as a result, certain kinds of food began to signal the dichotomy between the capital and the provinces.[3]
Foods were thus transformed into geographical metonyms: the
most classic example of this metonymical extension would
undoubtedly be Emma's wedding feast in *Madame Bovary*, where
le père Rouault synecdochically appropriates for his table
the culinary riches of his native province of Normandy.

Perhaps it would be fitting to discuss the last important
transformation related to food which the Revolution eventually precipitated by linking it to the most 'eloquent' of
all the dishes comprising Rouault's menu: *la pièce montée*.
In view of its elaborate culinary stylization and aesthetization, standing as a monument of gastronomical architecture,
la pièce montée graciously symbolizes the attempt to transform food into a work of art. As a logical extension of the
semiosis wherein the fruits of nature are pressed and re-
shaped into new forms, moulded so to speak and recreated as
culinary chefs d'œuvre, the role of the chef changes from
that of artisan to artist, possibly the most successful and
appreciated of all artists, for his creations have an appeal

which no other artistic medium shares. His is an art truly designed for immediate consumption, an art whose literal, if not literary, purpose is to please and edify. It is no wonder, then, that either because of its inherently aesthetic qualities or because of its capacity to signify socio-cultural phenomena the meal finds its way into so many nineteenth-century French novels.

The Semiotic Universe of the Meal

In view of the recent proliferation of semiotic theories and methodologies centring on literature in general, and narrative in particular, it would seem essential to begin this discussion by defining my own approach to the subject of fictional meals. Semiotic in this essay refers to the relationship between the literary sign (here designated as the fictional meal complex) and the cultural context wherein the sign is born and which invests it with meaning(s). I fully concur with the observations of D.W. Fokkema, for example, whose own concepts coincide largely with those of Kristeva and Lotman, that 'Any so-called autonomous interpretation of a literary text that does not take into account its function in the larger socio-cultural context must fail.'[4]

In considering the socio-cultural context in my discussion of meals as narrative signs I will undoubtedly be faced with objections from the more formalistically oriented semioticians. The first criticism which comes to mind would be that of my neglecting to examine the fictional meal in its literary specificity, that is, as a narrative sign, structure, or aesthetic entity in so far as it operates *only* at the level of the literary text. I considered such an approach, then abandoned it because it would ultimately result in a descriptive grammar of fictional meal scenes which, though needed, could easily be subsumed by a general theory of narration such as the one Genette postulates in *Figures III*.[5] Furthermore, I have tried to avoid a reductive synthetic approach since it would hardly do justice to such a verbally sumptuous and expansive topic as food and meals in fiction.

Secondly, and more important, a purely formal description would fail to account for the non-fortuitous link between actual meals as semio-cultural entities and fictional meals in their function as metonyms of French society in general during the period from 1789 to 1848. The manner and degree in which the *hors-texte* generates and predetermines the *en-texte* will be taken up in detail shortly. In the meantime it should be stated that an analysis which endeavours to

explore the interrelation between social and narrative
structures as they are actualized in the real and the fictional meal respectively must also follow the basic premise
that a coded semantic component is operative in the historical text and that this component will subsequently be
transformed into a literary structure.

Finally, some justification of my own analytical procedures
seems warranted at this point. Vague and as yet undefinied
as the space between the *en-texte* and the *hors-texte* may be,
it is nevertheless possible to reduce this space, if not to
eliminate it entirely, by focusing on a specific set of historical phenomena or realities such as food, clothing, or
gestures, to name but a few, which have been transcoded into
fictional constructs. Moreoever, the practice of transcoding
(i.e. writing) presupposes the existence of a semantic matrix, a something-to-be-transcoded, which bypasses the notion
of food as material or narrative substance. Clearly, food
nourishes, but it also signifies. If this were not the case
in an historical as well as in a fictional sense, then there
would be no reason other than a purely structural one to
include meal scenes in a narrative (the meal is an excellent
organizational device). After all, fictional characters do
not 'really' exist, so they do not 'really' eat, no matter
how copious and delectable the meal described by the narrator. On the other hand, psychological realism as practised
in the novel of manners, for example, might demand that
characters dine at regular intervals and in a prescribed
manner, but adherence to such narrative conventions only
serves to confirm the fact that the fictional meal is mimetic and that its generative base lies outside of the text
proper.

It would thus seem appropriate for practical purposes
that a semiotic analysis of fictional dining episodes be
centred on an era and on a body of literature in which food
and meals played a primordial role both historically and
fictionally. The period from 1789 to 1848 in France best
fulfils all the conditions for such an analysis because it
represents not only the Golden Age of French gastronomy but
also the apex of interest in and consciousness of food, as
has previously been demonstrated. Turning now to more specific semiotic notions, I should like to discuss some of
the criteria and practices upon which a semiotic enquiry
might be based. To begin with, although much of this semiotic matter has become common knowledge it would be prudent
to reiterate that such phenomena as meals could be viewed
as non-semiotic to the extent that intention to signify is

deemed a necessary condition for a definition of the sign.[6]
However, that fictional meals belong to an intentional encoding procedure is fully confirmed by their verbal status
as most readers conversant with semiotics well know, and
this because all verbal constructs in narrative exist as
signs by virtue of the fact that they operate in and through
language.

On the basis of these elementary principles we may assume
that two critical enquiries are possible and are, in fact,
determined by Saussure's now widely accepted definition of
the sign as consisting of a *signifier* and a *signified*. The
first enquiry would focus on the meal complex as *signifier*
or *signified* only and would proceed to describe its function
in a given narrative. But that would bring us back to an
elaboration of the formal characteristics of meal signs
which we already abandoned for reasons previously mentioned.
The second enquiry would centre on the dialectic between
signifier and *signified* which, of necessity, takes us outside of the text and forces us to postulate the existence
of a semantic structure which governs the encoding procedure
both in history and in literature. Fully cognizant of all
the risks involved in such a task, I believe that the second
kind of enquiry would be more propitious because the meal
sign operates simultaneously in the literary text and in
the larger cultural context; indeed, it is the cultural context which determines the semantic boundaries of the fictional meal.

In conformity with my stated intention to describe the
dialectic between *signifier* and *signified* for a given meal
complex, my next step would be to examine the primary codes
which govern the organization and signification of the act
of eating. The transformation from meal-as-phenomenon to
meal-as-sign relies on two fundamental extratextual codes
which generate several systems of social and narrative subcodes. The first is pre-linguistic, relates to the universals of eating, and results from the psychodynamics of eating; the second is coded in language, manners, or rites,
pertains to the particulars of the meal situation, and derives from the sociology of eating practices. Each of these
codes, which for want of a more specific terminology I shall
refer to as psychogenetic and sociogenetic respectively,
will now be taken up in detail.

The universals of eating correspond to the psychodynamic
aspects of the gustatory act, or to that pre-linguistic mental space wherein semiosis occurs as the transformation of
the instinctual into the symbolic. Semiotically speaking,

appetite constitutes what one gastro-critic has called 'le degré zéro de la conscience culinaire';[7] it is a basic bio-logical signal for the organism and, as such, it may be described as pre-semiotic since hunger obviously belongs to the non-intentional mechanism of stimulus/response. Secondly, appetite attests to, and even comes to symbolize, the space existing between subject and object, between 'me' and the 'world': by eating, man ingests and incorporates the world-object. Appetite, moreover, always signals a real or symbolic emptiness, it always confirms the nothingness separating objective from subjective being. This ontological dichotomy imposes its structure on man's mental space in the form of desire and fulfilment, a structure whose metonymic extension would contain the semes 'absence' and 'presence.' In Freudian terms appetite is equivalent to the specific desire to reduce and annihilate, if only temporarily, the space between 'me' and the 'world.' 'To be is to eat and be eaten,'[8] according to Norman O. Brown, a neo-Freudian for whom the world exists as food: 'Identification, introjection, incorporation, is eating. The oldest language is that of the mouth: the oral basis of the ego' (Brown, 165).

Appetite, or nothingness experienced, initiates a process of symbolization modelled on the act of eating, which itself figures as the conversion of an absence into a presence, or at least as the reduction of the space between the desiring subject and the object of his desire. The journey from remoteness to intimacy is none other than the paradigm of orality imposed on all communicative acts. The oral chain is cast in early infancy when the child's first contacts with the world (mother) take place during nursing. The practice of nursing generally leads to sensuality and sexuality in so far as it generates feelings of proximity, warmth, and reassurance, all of which prevail at mealtime and which will later become part of the positive affects associated with eating. For Freud, as everyone knows, orality and sexuality form links in the same developmental chain, yet both may be subsumed in the larger category of transactions or contacts between 'me' and the 'other'; both constitute the most direct and intimate forms of communication with the world. Consequently, the act of eating becomes the archetype of intercourse, both sexual and social. Because in the ritual of eating man engages himself in intimate contact with the world, the complex of events associated with eating are raised in human mythologies to the level of the cosmological.

Communication and contact in their most exalted forms
come to be known as divine communion; the rapports between
food and the gods have always existed. 'Pourquoi les dieux
furent-ils toujours présents à la table des hommes? D'abord
parce que les aliments, morceaux d'univers ingérables,
sources de vie et de plaisir, portes ouvertes sur l'intimité
du monde, sont les moyens les plus naturels pour accéder au
divin caché dans la structure des choses, voire sont les
gîtes favoris des dieux, les morceaux de leur corps qu'ils
donnent aux hommes élus.'[9] Eating is sacred; the world is
food; God is comestible. Man's desire to eat parallels his
desire to know; to partake of the flesh of the gods is to
have divine knowledge, to be one with the world. Under these
circumstances it is not surprising that the vast majority
of ritual practices and ceremonies develop a semiosis and
a symbolization based on eating,[10] nor is it coincidental
that certain types of food have the capacity to alter consciousness. The spiritual function of wine in the Dionysian
festivals comes immediately to mind in this respect.

Even in its solitary form, then, eating represents a communicative act. From the semio-linguistic viewpoint it re-
creates the primordial language, the one instance of communication in which no dichotomization of the sign occurs, for
food *is* the world-object, paradise regained, the locus of
unity wherein the *signifier* and the *signified* are consub-
stantial - hence the eucharistic rites in which Christ himself is transformed into food. In the original act of eating
praxis precedes semiosis: I eat the world and the world eats
me. But eating is also a social act and an initiation into
the world. Through its complex of associations it activates
and materializes the social. Appetite, i.e. desire, gives
birth to social consciousness precisely because it signals
distance, absence, emptiness, and, by extension, social dislocation. Eating and ingesting, on the other hand, equate
with proximity, presence, and social rapprochement. At the
level of the social, language, too, serves to reduce the
space between 'me' and the 'other.' Needless to say, eating
and speaking share the same motivational structure; language
is nothing more than the praxis of eating transposed to the
semiosis of speaking: both are fundamentally communicative
acts by which man appropriates and incorporates the world.

Up to now our discussion of the psychogenesis of the act
of eating has shown that through a gradual process of transition the symbolic emerges from the biological: the original space (appetite) between the desiring subject and the

object of his desire (food) projects itself into the domain
of communication and semiosis in general. The literary text
constitutes one form of this projection, as may be witnessed,
for example, in certain types of narrative situations which
are engendered by the psychodynamics of eating. The appe-
tite/food axis, often metaphorically or metonymically expressed as desire/fulfilment, comprises a basic paradigm
which is actualized in many narrative codes. Greimas, for
instance, formulates his system of *actants* on binary oppositions which implicitly signal a space, a gap to be filled,
an imbalance which serves to set the narrative in motion.[11]
Similarly, Todorov describes the structure of the *récit* as
a dialectic between disequilibrium and equilibrium, a structure which in terms of this analysis sends us back to the
appetite (disequilibrium) / satiation (equilibrium) paradigm.[12] In addition to establishing the binary principle
as a basic human mental structure, desire and fulfilment
have also come to connote sexual impulses. Writers throughout history have always linked food with sexuality: food
because of the pleasures one obtains from oral gratification;
eating because of the intimacy growing out of close and immediate contact with the world. In narrative, as in reality,
an invitation to dine corresponds to an invitation to engage in sexual intercourse: 'Inviter une femme à dîner et
glisser ses jambes sous la table, c'est déjà la posséder'
(Lange, 125). Nineteenth-century French novelists in particular fully exploited the relationships between food and
fornication in their depictions of tête-à-tête meals, and,
in the novel as in contemporary society, the co-occurrence
of the culinary and the sexual acts was made explicit in
public dining houses where the *cabinet particulier* was designed specifically for amorous diners.

In the practice of nursing the infant makes his first contacts with the world. The affects associated with early oral
behaviour - closeness, warmth, security, belonging - set the
patterns for later social relationships at the table so that
the affective norms of eating centre on codes of congeniality, solidarity, community, in brief on a whole network of
positive qualities complementing the pleasures of eating
itself. Novelists maintain these norms in their portrayal
of meal scenes to such an extent that if turns of plot demand a confrontation between characters, an eating situation
seems the ideal place to accentuate differences of opinion
largely because hostility violates the normalized codes of
table etiquette and ambience. For these same reasons the
table also serves as a natural platform for the confrontation and propagation of political ideologies.

The Freudian concept of eating as the oral basis of the ego explains why writers use food or eating situations in their depiction and development of character. The well-worn cliché 'You are what you eat' finds constant renewal in fiction where narrators almost without exception use food to describe the man; it would hardly be an exaggeration to say that of all the signs associated with the culinary in fiction food serves as one of the prevalent markers of character. It reflects individual temperament as well as collective identity, abnormal psychology as well as normal states of mind. Given the centrality of his position in nineteenth-century French society, the Bourgeois, more than any other social type, undergoes total narrative dissection and scrutiny of his eating habits, themselves derided by narrators as an inferior norm. The superior elements of the complex of eating, on the other hand, coincide in fiction with the more advanced psychological activities – spirituality, metaphysical quest, communion with the divine – which border on transcendence. At the level of the fiction, moreover, transcendence may take a mimetic form as when narrators reproduce religious ceremonies and rites in an effort to be evangelistic and didactic, or it may take an aesthetic form as when the narrator uses food imagery and symbolism to poeticize the message.

The particulars of eating comprise a secondary generative code which evolves from the first: that is, the psychological aspects of eating engender and predetermine the types of phenomena associated with the social character of food and meals. Social eating practices are usually codified in the language of everyday communication and in para-linguistic systems associated with the meal. According to the logic of this evolution a social semiosis derives from a pre-linguistic symbolic process: the social organism is simply an extension of the individual. If this mechanistic principle holds true, then we would expect to find that the social dynamics of fictional meals are highly mimetic. Indeed mimesis does predominate in fictional dining episodes as regards the surface structure of the meal (i.e. order and sequence of dishes, codes of preparation and presentation, seating protocol), but at the deep textual level the model fails because nineteenth-century French novelists assume a critical posture vis-à-vis the bourgeoisie (the creators and perpetrators of new gastro-myths) and thus attempt to undermine the meal's prevailing semantic structure by transforming a cultural sign with positive social connotations into a narrative sign with negative ideological connotations. It is by virtue of the fact that novelists endeavour to re-establish and increase

the distance between the *signifier* and the *signified* of
meals – a practice which the reader usually perceives as a
form of irony – that they turn meals into signifying entities capable of effectuating a new semantification. In
their critical capacity nineteenth-century French novelists
use the fictional meal in order to demythify the bourgeois
ideology; in their creative capacity, they use the same
sign to remythify ancient, more natural eating practices.

In terms of social psychology the table symbolizes maternal affection and physical contact with the environment.
Just as the mother serves as the infant's first introduction
to the world, so the table becomes the locus of his initiation into society. By extension the table represents the
mother-country, and eating figures as an act of identification with one's compatriots and adherence to their values.
Society maintains and perpetuates itself at the table: eating is a form of apprenticeship by which the child acquires
the customs, manners, and beliefs of his fellow countrymen.
Like an individual, a nation defines itself by its eating
habits and attitudes about food. Given this particular set
of circumstances, it is quite understandable that as a social structure the eating complex symbolizes repetition,
regularity, stability, solidarity, uniformity, in short all
of those qualities signalling social coherence. Because of
the central, even conservative, role it plays as the very
epicentre of society, the table functions in reality and
in fiction as a stabilizing force without parallel. It is
no wonder, then, that the eating complex is the most highly
codified activity in society: 'Le repas est certainement,
avant même les pratiques sexuelles, l'activité humaine la
plus sévèrement codifiée et la plus stable quant au maintien
de son code' (Lange, 41).

In fiction the table appropriates the social structure of
a nation, its geographical diversity, and even a larger
world-space:

Au commencement de l'âge d'or, la table semble un lexique
de l'univers, des territoires proches et lointains, de
l'Europe conquise et de la France intégrée dont la commune
capitale est Paris. On dirait qu'alors le mot se réfère
davantage au produit qu'au plat, qu'il ne renvoie à des
données géographiques identifiables que pour laisser le
champ libre au rêve: celui-ci leste le comestible d'hori-
zons lointains, de voyages, d'inconnu, qui contribuent à
sa séduction alimentaire: 'Et dans mes arguments, remar-
quez, messieurs, que je ne comprends même pas les pâtés

de mauviettes de Pithiviers, ceux des canards d'Amiens,
ceux des guignards de Chartres, les rouges-gorge de Metz,
les perdrix de Cacheux, les oies d'Alençon, les langues
fourrées de Constantinople, le bœuf fumé de Hambourg, ...'
(Aron, 177)

This metonymical appropriation of the world serves as the
fundamental device whereby novelists transpose the socio-
cultural phenomena of the extra-textual into fictional
structures: in nineteenth-century French novels food and
meals, more than any other semiotic entities, function as
metonyms of contemporary society and the world at large:
'Le choix des aliments, leur préparation, l'ordonnancement
des plats, les ustensiles et les manières de table sont
révélateurs de la manière dont une société est organisée,
dont elle perçoit le monde et les rapports sociaux' (Lange,
58). Focusing on the table as a metonym of nineteenth-century
French society enables us to examine the various subcodes
of that society as they manifest themselves at the table.
Obviously, I cannot analyse the entire system of codification in this book, so I have chosen to centre on how the
universals of eating are integrated with the specifics of
the bourgeois phenomenon, the dominant socio-cultural ideology of the period under consideration.
  More than any other group the bourgeoisie altered the meal
structure and signification in nineteenth-century France.
Cuisine and gastronomy epitomize the creative genius of a
group often criticized for its excessive materialism and
insensitivity. Not altogether impartial to this bourgeois
creation, novelists identified the meal specifically with
the middle class, and used fictional dining episodes with
all their ideological connotations as a weapon to counter-
attack bourgeois values. Essentially novelists borrowed
for their fictions the new meal codes which had evolved
from the bourgeoisie and which signalled their values; this
mimesis of form turns into a mockery of content by means of
an authorial irony directed at subverting the bourgeois
ideology through evocations of former eating codes which
had been superseded after the Revolution of 1789.
  I shall now indicate some of the values with which the
bourgeoisie invested the meal and which novelists later
transposed into fictional signs. First of all, the meal became a sign of equality and democracy as a result of the
Revolution; but such an idealized concept soon degenerated
into a marker of distinction and social status. Once again
the meal serves to differentiate between the various strata

of society. The new distinctions, however, enjoy no a priori
privileges based on class affiliation, but rather grow out
of the industriousness of the bourgeoisie, who controlled
the economic market. Financial prosperity, achieved, by
means of hard work, now determines social status with the
result that success is intimately related to money. A second
subcode thus derives from the first: *la bonne chère* begins
to function as an economic sign. Food and, by extension,
dining-room furnishings, tableware, and china are transformed into currency. Moreover, social mobility now depends
on the acquisition of money: the more you earn the more
mobile you become. The possibility of changing one's lot
leads to a kind of social polyvalency wherein each conquest
in fashionable society marks the parvenu's newly acquired,
often tenuous status: invariably the table coincides with
the various stages of social ascendancy. The success of the
parvenu thus becomes proportional to the reputation of the
tables at which he is invited to dine. Similarly, according
to the codes of social success the parvenu must reciprocate:
an invitation to dine in fashionable society necessitates
the same courtesy in return with the consequence that such
gastronomical exchanges parallel and reflect the flow of
economic currency.

Finally, new social and economic status entails a change
in ideology, also characteristic of the parvenu. In conformity with a coding system in which dinner parties signal
financial success, gastronomical savoir-faire acts as a
marker of more cultivated sensibilities, and the Bourgeois,
heretofore accused of insensitivity, transforms himself
from materialistic entrepreneur into refined gourmet. At
the table he displays equal ease at disserting on the virtues of a new recipe or at pronouncing on the viability of
nascent political movements. Examples of the bond between
politics and the table reach back into history, but nowhere
do they accumulate to such an extent as in nineteenth-century
French culture and literature.

Finally, I shall mention two other subcodes which emerge
from the bourgeois ideology. On the one hand, an accentua-
tion of the principle of economic exchange induces the Bourgeois to treat everything, including women, as currency:
consequently, sexual favours from courtesans and actresses
are bought with meals in fashionable dining establishments.
Eating practices in nineteenth-century France also reflect
a certain antifeminist bias, for the respectable Bourgeoise
is excluded from meals taken in restaurants because they
are frequented by notorious *mondaines*. Also, intent upon

denigrating the Bourgeois morally, novelists often associate
orgiastic feasts with capitalism, making decadence at mealtime emblematic of the degenerating sexual mores caused by
the advent of the middle class. On the other hand, the as-
cent of capital and the decline of morality were taken by
novelists to represent specifically Parisian phenomena;
from this there developed in the novel the theme of Paris-
as-Inferno. Accordingly, province came to signify paradise,
especially as regards eating practices: the spatio-moral
dichotomy existing between the capital and the countryside
extends to the domain of cookery where Parisian culinary
sophistication corresponds to artificiality and superficial-
ity as opposed to the simplicity and sincerity of pastoral
meals, which mark the simple virtues of the peasant life,
a return to natural felicity, and which also show a moral
concern for the quality of food as substance.

Types of Meal Signs

A discussion of the semiotic universe of meals would not be
complete without mentioning the types of signs treated in
this book. Basically, a description of the culinary, gastronomical, or alimentary sign would correspond to a typology
of signs in general; however, I intend to focus only on the
functions of the following signs: *informations*, *catalyses*,
indices, symptoms, signals, symbols, metaphors, metonymies,
and icons. The first three kinds of signs belong to Genette's
functional categories of narrative as developed in *Figures
III*; *informations* occur in direct narrative statements in-
tended for the purpose of conveying information explicitly;
catalyses represent inconsequential acts which communicate
narrative facts implicitly, and often cumulatively; *indices*
impart narrative information indirectly but intentionally.
In practice, I have generally grouped the three together
and use the term index for all. The remaining signs have
not been elaborated with any particular precision vis-à-vis
narrative codes; nevertheless, they have always belonged
to the repertory of fictional signs though without necessarily enjoying the consistency of fixed definitions. In
this book I use them with the following meanings: signals
refer to intentional signs precipitating instinctive or
reflex responses; symptoms, on the other hand, behave like
indexes but they are non-intentional; a symbol here denotes
a generalized sign which points to something other than itself, though I also use the term to refer to a semiotic entity which functions paradigmatically, that is, a sign with

a more or less fixed signification in the larger socio-
historical context; for metaphor, metonymy, and icon I have
retained traditional definitions and equated the first with
a transferral of sense based on analogy, substitution, or
interaction; the second with a shift in meaning resulting
from contiguity or logical extension; the third with a verbal sign that presents or imitates the properties of the
object it denotes. Needless to say, in any given meal scene
many of these signs will be present simultaneously, so in
such cases I have chosen to emphasize only the primary sign
and its referents.

My basic premise that meals are metonyms of the social
structure of nineteenth-century France leads to two method-
ological problems. First, a description of the metonymic
potentials of the meal would inevitably necessitate a description of the entire system of social organization during
the period under discussion. I have decided to eschew such
a description by focusing specifically on those aspects of
the meal which are related to the bourgeois ideology and
also by centring on 'fictionally' depicted events occurring
during the July Monarchy. Second, the postulation of an
underlying metonymic structure leaves me vulnerable to the
problematic of delineating the so-called 'middle range'
between the aesthetic and the social. Justifiably, socio-
logically-oriented critics argue for the necessity of iden-
tifying specific areas of overlap between these two domains.
I should like to contend that there already exists a theoretical semiotic entity which is situated at the point of
intersection between the social and the literary. Kristeva's
definition of the *idéologème* will adequately serve as the
critical link in the problematic of the 'middle range':
'L'Idéologème est cette fonction intertextuelle que l'on
peut lire matérialisée aux différents niveaux de la structure de chaque texte, et qui s'étend tout au long de son
trajet en lui donnant ses coordonnées historiques et sociales.'[13] The intertextual nature of the *idéologème* clearly
allows for an extratextual element which would appear as a
common seme in many texts, historical and literary.

It can now be stated that the object of this book is to
describe those socio-cultural codes which are actualized in
the meal sign and to interpret these codes in relation to
the *idéologèmes* characteristic of the Bourgeois phenomenon.
Finally, I shall seek to uncover the global meaning(s) of
fictional meal scenes in the nineteenth-century French novel,
that is, the range of representations and connotations con-
nected with a certain symbol. Therefore, I have organized

my chapters according to the primary sign-functions of meal
scenes in the work of a particular author, though that is
not to say that progression from Balzac through Flaubert
necessarily represents a positive or negative evolution
vis-à-vis the meal sign. Rather it conforms to the use of
the meal as a marker of the status quo, a signal for reform,
an aesthetic sign, or whatever the case may be. As the function of the meal changes, so does my method of analysis,
particularly in my final chapter on Flaubert wherein I subject *Madame Bovary* to a close reading because of the pervasiveness of the meal-sign in this novel, and also because
it functions primarily as an aesthetic entity.

The Criteria for the Selection of Novels

The period extending from 1830 to 1848 best fulfils the
conditions upon which to base this analysis because of the
numerous social and literary factors conspiring to produce
a new aesthetics of the novel. The July Monarchy corresponds
with the supremacy of bourgeois culture and values, the rise
of the novel of manners, which in part grew out of the bourgeois phenomenon, and, among the new generation of Romantics,
a growing consciousness of the artist's social mission. The
latter development encouraged novelists to focus on contemporary problems and to look for solutions to the bourgeois
menace by promoting new ideologies designed to safeguard
less materialistic values than those held by the bourgeoisie.
The Christian Socialist movement provided novelists with a
battery of ideas for social change, not least among them
the utopian schemes whereby the principles of brotherhood
and solidarity were modelled on communal eating practices
and propagated at the table.
  The specific literary criteria governing the selection
of novels and novelists included in this study derive prin-
cipally from the frequency of meal scenes depicted in a
particular novel as well as from the aesthetic quality and
structural significance of that depiction. Most July Monarchy novelists saturated their stories with meal episodes
and references to food and eating; however, I have chosen,
for two reasons, to analyse only the works of Balzac, Sand,
Sue, Hugo, and Flaubert: firstly, because their novels best
illustrate the quantitative and qualitative standard with
regard to meal portrayals and, secondly, because as artists
they represent varied personal and literary reactions to
the bourgeois phenomenon. The absence of so important a
novelist as Stendhal may seem conspicuous, but in so far

as fictional meal scenes are concerned it is justifiable:
dining episodes are relatively rare in his novels, probably
because the Stendhalian universe describes the solitary hero
and meals are social acts. On the other hand, popular novelists such as Soulié and Ponson du Terrail are excluded because the meal scenes in their novels lack sufficient narrative development, the meal being reported in two or three
sentences, or because meals in their novels serve primarily
as contrivances and not as aesthetically motivated signs.
My last criterion for selection concerns not the novelists
but rather the novels themselves: as the July Monarchy exemplifies the peak of bourgeois activity and influence, I have
opted for a corpus of novels whose narrative events coincide
roughly with the period extending from 1830 to 1848 and
whose plots unfold in France.

1 / BALZAC

The Meal as Metonym and Index of Social and Economic Spheres

Balzac's universe is dualistic, based on the contrast between matter and spirit, poverty and wealth, *Le fou et le
savant*.[1] Such a vision lends itself particularly well to
semiotic expression because the sign is inherently a binary
structure. Moreover, Balzac's intention to 'faire concur-
rence à l'état civil' clearly places his aesthetics in a
mimetic perspective, and this endeavour to reproduce French
society under the July Monarchy further bears witness to
the fact that fictional meals model themselves on actual
meal codes of the period. The July Monarchy corresponds to
the supremacy of bourgeois power as evidenced in the reign
of Louis-Philippe, 'le roi bourgeois,' so in his attempt to
re-create all of French society, Balzac had little choice
but to acknowledge and depict the mores of the middle class.
First on the list of priorities in the bourgeois value system is financial success: any definition of this class depends on its economic function, money being the means by
which the Bourgeois relates to and ultimately controls the
society in which he lives.[2] And, since the meal complex represents society in microcosmic form, it is quite natural
that Balzac uses fictional meal scenes as metonyms of economic spheres. Nowhere is the relation between food and
money more apparent than in *La Comédie humaine* where economic and social distinctions are established or resolved at
the table.

The primary function of meal scenes in *La Comédie humaine* is to signal differentiation. Social and economic distinctions may be revealed, for example, in the types of food served on bourgeois or aristocratic tables as opposed to those types presented in more modest settings, or, in the event of extreme poverty, in the absence of food altogether. In general, sophistication or the lack of it, as depicted in feasting scenes, indicates class affiliation and, to a large extent, degree of wealth. The meals served at the homes of rich merchants are usually the most elaborate in both culinary elements and ornate surroundings. They represent an ostentatious display of the host's financial position and often induce poverty-stricken upstarts newly arrived from the provinces to seek out luxury as an end in itself. In these scenes, food indexes the good life, especially as it manifests itself in gastronomical savoir-faire. In the novels of Balzac there is usually a parallel treatment of meal scenes in the homes of misers, since they too think of food in terms of money; however, in contrast to the wealthy capitalists, the avaricious provincials barely eat enough to subsist, and their abstinence bespeaks their propensity for economizing. For the spendthrifts in *La Comédie humaine*, elaborate dining signals financial status and success; for the miserly, refusal to spend money on food betrays greed: in both cases, food is metonymically related to economic currency.

Food and meals serve as an index of provincial avarice in *Eugénie Grandet* and *La Rabouilleuse* where their major function is to accentuate and delineate the character of the miser. In the early pages of *Eugénie Grandet*, for example, the reader learns that old Grandet rarely buys food, but rather as a landowner is in a position to require his tenant farmers to supply him with the daily necessities: 'M. Grandet n'achetait jamais ni viande ni pain. Ses fermiers lui apportaient par semaine une provision suffisante de chapons, de poulets, d'oeufs, de beurre et de blé de rente.'[3] The reader implicitly understands that such a steady supply of mundane victuals allows for little culinary variety: Grandet not only accepts the fruits of other men's labour – a mark of the capitalist – he also eats merely to live. Within the framework of the narrative this reference to daily provisions acts as a sign of Grandet's parsimony.

Perhaps not so unusual in the provinces, but nevertheless clearly in keeping with the theme of miserliness, is Grandet's practice of having the maid do all the baking and cooking.

These arrangements allow him to economize, usually at the expense of others. In addition to receiving goods from his tenant farmers for his own use, he sells the surplus food for a profit: 'M. Grandet s'était arrangé avec les maraîchers, ses locataires, pour qu'ils le fournissent de légumes. Quant aux fruits, il en récoltait une telle quantité qu'il en faisait vendre une grande partie au marché' (*EG* 487). Grandet also economizes by never inviting guests to dinner: as far as he is concerned, dinner parties are an added expense, a luxury which he allows neither himself nor his family. Since offering dinners proves to a certain extent one's gregariousness, it goes without saying that Grandet's reputation suffers. Another means of economizing consists of rationing food; hence it becomes part of the old man's daily ritual to oversee the distribution of goods in his house: 'Depuis longtemps l'avare distribuait dès le matin le pain et les denrées nécessaires à la consommation journalière' (*EG* 494). As a result of constant exposure to Grandet's excessive behaviour, both Eugénie and Mme Grandet become passive in their eating habits, losing their character as it were as they lose their appetite.

Miserliness not only contributes to family discord, it violates the codes of socialization as well. The offering of food and lodging has always been a symbol of Western congeniality and hospitality. As far back as the Middle Ages the bonds and obligations of the host toward the guest were operative. According to the code of ethics expounded by Chrétien de Troyes in many of his romances, for example, it was proper for the host to suspend all his normal rights over his castle and to transfer them to his guest. Thus the honour of the host and the safety of the guest were assured at all times. For the most part this code was inviolable, and the tradition of hospitality continued in modified form throughout French history. In the nineteenth century, common courtesy dictated that the host make special concessions to his guests, if only the offering of a meal. Consequently, when Charles Grandet, the miser's nephew, pays his uncle a visit, the reader expects to find the old man conforming at least partially to this tradition. The particular circumstances would demand that Grandet offer Charles a bite to eat after his long journey; Eugénie reminds her father of this simple courtesy, but he refuses because he recognizes in Charles a young Parisian dandy accustomed to overindulgence in luxury and capable of costing him a fortune in food. Grandet subsequently outlines for his nephew the daily eating routine in his home: 'Ici, nous déjeunons à huit heures. A midi nous mangeons un fruit, un rien de pain sur le pouce, et nous buvons un verre de vin blanc; puis nous dînons, comme les Parisiens, à cinq heures. Voilà l'ordre' (*EG* 521).

Everyone in the Grandet household, with the exception of the old man, views the arrival of Charles as a special occasion. To them he represents the very existence they have been denied; even the niggardly maid, Nanon, who normally conforms to Grandet's exigencies by maintaining what the author calls a 'miser's cuisine,' suggests that Grandet serve a piece of meat from the butcher's, but the old man replies that chicken bouillon will be sufficient. Forced into offering something special, he thinks of the most frugal dish, the one most capable of rendering the most for the least. This abuse of the principle of nourishment takes on absurd proportions when, on second thought, he suggests that Nanon obtain a crow from one of his tenant farmers: 'Mais je vais dire à Cornoiller de me tuer des corbeaux. Ce gibier-là donne le meilleur bouillon de la terre' (*EG* 532). In addition to the obvious economic saving, the psycho-symbolic implications of his demand are revealing: when Nanon reminds him that crows live off dead animals, he enters into a veritable tirade using the scavenger as an analogy for all of mankind: ' - Tu es bête, Nanon! ils mangent, comme tout le monde, ce qu'ils trouvent. Est-ce que nous ne vivons pas pas des morts? Qu'est-ce donc que les successions?' (*EG* 532). According to the logic of this example, money has become food, a source of nourishment; but this entire concept stands in opposition to natural nourishment, or food as sustenance for life, since the crow represents the embodiment of the anti-food and thus reveals symbolically Grandet's obsession with necrophagy.

Celebrations, feasts, and banquets form an integral part of national eating habits. Normally they range from the ritualized patterns associated with holidays, birthdays, and weddings to the more informal structure of meals on special occasions. In the Grandet home, New Year's Day provides the apparent motivation for celebrating with an elaborate breakfast consisting of a *pâté de fois gras truffé*. In reality, however, Grandet is jubilant not because it is New Year's Day but because he has just used all his gold in a financial speculation which is sure to succeed. In miserly fashion Grandet transfers the normal symbolic celebration from the socio-culinary aspects to the purely financial ones; he pays no heed to conviviality and the holiday spirit but is instead interested only in Eugénie's financial position.

As the family sits down to eat, Grandet joyously asks Eugénie to show him her gold because 'Ça nous aidera tous à digérer' (*EG*, 603), and, since their neighbours, the des Grassins, supplied them with the food for this meal, Grandet encourages everyone to eat heartily: 'Manges-en donc, ma femme! Ça nourrit au moins pour deux jours' (*EG*, 603). The importance of this scene lies in the metonymical relationship between food and money. Eagerly anticipating Eugénie's gold, Grandet eats gaily and profusely; by contrast, Eugénie and Mme Grandet cannot eat at all because they know that Eugénie has given her gold to Charles. In a symbolic transformation of money into food, Grandet orders Nanon to clear the table so that Eugénie can spread out her gold coins for her father's eyes to devour. Grandet's monomania thus reveals itself in gastronomical terms; the character is transformed into what he eats. The essence of this good-money metonym becomes even more apparent in terms of Grandet's digression on the crow as a source of nourishment; the crow lives off death, therefore we all live off death: 'To be human is to be eaten, to be sacrificed ... This world as sacrifice; this world as food; to be is to eat and to be eaten.'[4]

Transgression of the miser's code results in food deprivation for Eugénie and has alimentary repercussions on the entire family. As punishment for giving away her gold Eugénie is forced to live on a diet of bread and water, and the incident so disrupts normal eating practices that Mme Grandet becomes ill and refuses to eat at all. Given the stabilizing function of the table in society, it is not surprising that the break in family relations is signalled by the dispersal of its members at mealtime. Grandet's action is a symbolic devouring of his own flesh and blood, and, simultaneously, an inversion of the celebratory social codes which normally operate on New Year's Day; thus, for the first time in his life, the old man eats alone.

One ostensible contradiction to the motif of the 'miser's kitchen' is the dinner which Grandet calls a 'repas de condoléance.' In effect this kind of dinner belongs to the broader category of celebration meals in so far as it depicts the ritual custom of serving a meal following a death in the family. Superficially, at least, Grandet seems to be paying tribute to his deceased brother, but in fact his real motive is not so disinterested. When, for instance, the guard on his estate arrives with a hare, some partridges, and several fish, Grandet announces to everyone's surprise that he will provide a repast. Mme Grandet interprets his unusual behaviour in gastronomical terms, as a deviation in the family's

normal eating routine: 'Décidément, il se passe ici quelque chose d'extraordinaire, dit Madame Grandet. Voici la
troisième fois que, depuis notre mariage, ton père donne
à dîner' (*EG* 560). Indeed the dinner serves as another example of the inversion of eating practices and customs, for
the entire meal is actually a ruse on the part of Grandet
to enlist the services of his guests in settling his brother's
estate.

In *La Rabouilleuse* the reader encounters another provincial miser who rations food. The narrator first presents
the niggardly character of Hochon by alluding to his distribution of food in his home: 'Grand, sec, maigre, à teint
jaune, parlant peu, lisant peu, ne se fatiguant point, ob-
servateur des formes comme un Oriental, il maintenait au
logis un régime d'une grande sobriété, mesurant le boire et
le manger à sa famille...'[5] The association between food
and character becomes manifest in the very physical description of the old man; for want of an adequate diet, he is
thin and jaundiced, the classic anal-recessive type whose
vice exists at the expense of his body. Like Grandet's wife
and daughter, the Hochon family also suffers the privations
inflicted by the miserly patriarch. When Hochon's sister,
Mme Bridau, and her son Joseph arrive in Issoudin to request
their part in Mme Bridau's paternal inheritance, the old
man offers them a dinner, a gesture apparently motivated
by the prospects of a warm reunion but which in reality has
economic ramifications: Hochon wants to inform Mme Bridau
and her son how to go about getting their rightful inheritance from another relative.

Unlike Grandet's dinner for his nephew, the welcoming meal
in *La Rabouilleuse* contains many culinary references whose
purpose it is to accentuate the theme of avarice; moreover,
the elaborate description of the Hochan meal serves in part
to delineate the contrast between provincial and Parisian
cuisine, hence to highlight the economic infrastructure as
it becomes apparent in the gastronomical sign. From time to
time the narrator permits the reader to see the reactions
of Joseph as he ingests his first meal at a miser's table:
'Il fut alors saisi de cette brusque transition du poétique
Paris à la muette et sèche province. Mais quand, en descen-
dant, il aperçut monsieur Hochon coupant lui-même pour chacun des tranches de pain, il comprit, pour la première fois
de sa vie, Harpagon de Molière' (*La Rabouilleuse*, 1001).

It might be appropriate to examine the Hochon meal in detail since of all the provincial dinners depicted in Balzac's
novels this one is the most developed in terms of its culinary

elaborations. Although the quantity of dishes evoked tends
to obscure their gastonomical poverty, this meal accurately
represents provincial fare and eating practices of the
period:

> Après une soupe dont le bouillon clair annonçait qu'on
> tenait plus à la quantité qu'à la qualité, on servit un
> bouilli triomphalement entouré de persil. Les légumes,
> mis à part dans un plat, comptaient dans l'ordonnance du
> repas. Ce bouilli trônait au milieu, accompagné de trois
> autres plats: des œufs sur de l'oseille placés en face
> des légumes; puis une salade tout accomodée à l'huile de
> noix en face de petits pots de crème où la vanille était
> remplacée par de l'avoine brûlée, et qui resemble à la
> vanille comme le café de chicorée ressemble au moka. Du
> beurre et des radis dans deux plateaux aux deux extrémités,
> des radis noirs et des cornichons complétaient ce service,
> qui eut l'approbation de madame Hochon.
>
> (*La Rabouilleuse*, 1002)

Evidently, the meal seems plentiful enough, but upon close
inspection the reader ascertains that such items as *bouillon*,
persil, *œufs*, and *radis* in abundance hardly signal *grande
cuisine*. Indeed the narrator's irony becomes apparent in
his portrayal of the adulterated or altered dishes such as
the inclusion of vegetables as part of the main course and
the *pots de crème* made with a vanilla substitute: the meal
is all form and no substance.

This dinner is quite characteristic of provincial gastronomy with one exception: namely, the arrangement of the
table service. The art of table setting, of careful and
symmetrical arrangements of crystal, china, and silverware,
which so typifies Parisian sophistication is rare in the
Provinces. Hochon denigrates the extravagance lavished upon
his guests and, as a compensatory gesture to all of this
pomp, he carves the meat '... en tranches semblables à des
semelles d'escarpins ...' (*La Rabouilleuse*, 1002). In spite
of his parsimony his welcoming dinner assumes banquet proportions when compared with the Grandet meals. During the
second service, for example, the guests enjoy a hearty succession of dishes: '... le bouilli fut remplacé par trois
pigeons ...' and 'Le vin du cru fut du vin de 1811' (*La
Rabouilleuse*, 1002). The dessert course, moreover, forms
an appropriate finale to the repertory of dishes which
precede; though it is by no means emblematic of classical
cuisine, the cheese offered to the guests is renowned as

a regional speciality and it is served in regal fashion:

> La servante apporta pour dessert le fameux fromage mou
> de la Touraine et du Berry, fait avec du lait de chèvre
> et qui reproduit si bien en nielles les desseins des
> feuilles de vignes sur lesquelles on le sert, qu'il aurait
> dû faire inventer la gravure en Touraine. De chaque côté
> de ces petits fromages, Gritte mit avec une sorte de
> cérémonie des noix et des biscuits inamovibles.
> (*La Rabouilleuse*, 1003)

After dessert, Madame Hochon decides to offer a cordial in
the salon: as she serves Joseph, she unwittingly summarizes
the ethic of the 'miser's kitchen': 'Eh! bien, mon pauvre
garçon, ce dîner ne te donnera pas d'indigestion; mais j'ai
bien de la peine à te l'obtenir. Tu feras carême ici, tu ne
mangeras que ce qu'il faut pour vivre, et voilà tout. Ainsi
prends la table en patience ...' (*La Rabouilleuse*, 1004).

Balzac's eating scenes in the dining rooms of fashionable
Parisians are situated at the opposite extreme from those
scenes delineated in the homes of provincial misers. Almost
without exception the former reflect the high degree of
sophistication and stylization which so characterizes elegant
cuisine. Whereas the provincial families discussed in this
chapter were content to eat to live, the Parisians, in conformity with their reputation as *bons vivants*, prefer to
live to eat. In so far as meals are concerned, the novels
included in this discussion point out not only the spatial
dichotomy between Paris and the provinces but also the economic oppositions implicit in each region. Balzac generally
associates provincial meals with avariciousness and Parisian
repasts with prodigality: in both cases food and eating become metonyms of money and status.
   The banquet described in *La Peau de chagrin* is the best
example of a typical Balzacian depiction of an opulent
Parisian meal. It differs from provincial meals in two ways:
on the one hand, it exemplifies Parisian cuisine, that is,
it represents the epitome of gastronomy, and, on the other
hand, it emphasizes the importance of entertaining others,
in which case the meal becomes a marker of socialization.
Furthermore, this particular banquet is unique to the extent that it portrays an entirely new kind of meal situation
in the nineteenth-century French novel - the orgy. Under
these circumstances the table acquires a double significance:
it signals both the socio-economic elements of the meal and

its moral connotations. The banquet takes place at the home
of the wealthy Parisian capitalist, M. Taillefer, and reveals
many interesting aspects of prodigality while concomitantly
realizing the desire of the young hero, Raphaël de Valentin,
to be totally immersed in pleasure and luxury. Unlike his
rather cursory descriptions of provincial meals, Balzac's
presentation of the Taillefer banquet consists of elaborate
culinary details and practices; he simultaneously evokes
the profuse ingredients of the meal and also the sumptuous
décor in which it is served, thus creating a sort of semiotic redundancy which contributes to the effect of saturation
and affluence he intends to produce.

The narrative unfolding of the meal itself constitutes
one of the most meticulously delineated banquet scenes in
La Comédie humaine. Balzac divides the scene into several
parts, each treated in minute detail in order to accentuate
the total impact of the message on the reader: taken in
its global capacity, the meal complex serves as a sign of
the economic, moral, and gastronomical aspects of supping
in the capital which mark social differentiation. The sequence of scenes focusing on the table corresponds to the
first stage in the unfolding of the banquet proper and it
indicates Taillefer's economic status by centring on the
brilliant effects produced by the crystal, the silverware,
and the table setting, all of which connote wealth and
prestige:

D'abord et par un regard plus rapide que la parole, chaque
convive paya son tribut d'admiration au somptueux coup
d'œil qu'offrait une longue table, blanche comme une
couche de neige fraîchement tombée, et sur laquelle
s'élèvaient symétriquement les couverts couronnés de
petits pains blonds. Les cristaux répétaient les couleurs
de l'iris dans leurs reflets étoilés, les bougies traçaient
des feux croisés à l'infini, les mets placés sous des
dômes d'argent aiguisaient l'appétit et la curiosité.[6]

This classic example of culinary stylization contrasts with
descriptions of provincial tables where utensils and china
have a utilitarian purpose, not an aesthetic motivation.
In this scene the table is artistically transformed into a
winter landscape and the focus is shifted from eating as an
end to eating as a sign: the exquisite table with its sparkling 'cristaux' and its 'dômes d'argent' reflects the chill
of currency as opposed to the affect of warmth which is
usually evoked at mealtime.

The second stage in the presentation of this banquet entails a description of the culinary delights of the meal. Conforming to the chronology of the meal itself, and not the duration of the entire meal complex, this part corresponds to the first course. During the first service the types of food and drink again mark Taillefer's wealth and status:

> Puis le premier service apparut dans toute sa gloire, il aurait fait honneur à feu Cambacérès, et Brillat-Savarin l'eût célébré. Les vins de Bordeaux et de Bourgogne, blancs et rouges, furent servis avec une profusion royale. Cette première partie du festin était comparable, en tout point, à l'exposition d'une tragédie classique.
>
> (PC, 51)

It is interesting to note here that, except for the presence on the table of Bordeaux and Burgundy wines, the narrative descriptive process relies on a reference to an intertextual culinary context; that is, the verbal status of the meal sign is put into relief in order to give the meal an aura of majesty. Every amateur of French cuisine knows that the names Cambacérès and Brillat-Savarin connote superlative dining just as the comparison of the meal to a classical tragedy reflects the ultimate theatrical experience. All signs, verbal and gastronomical, coalesce in this re-presentation of *la grande cuisine* and crystallize around the word 'gloire.'

With the advent of the second course the wine has made its impact and the entire atmosphere becomes animated and unrestrained: 'Le second service trouva donc les esprits tout à fait échauffés. Chacun mangea en parlant, parla en mangeant, but sans prendre garde à l'affluence des liquides, tant ils étaient lampants et parfumés, tant l'exemple fut contagieux' (PC, 51-2). The reader begins to sense at this point the imminence of the orgy which will follow, for in this scene the narrator abandons all reference to classical restraint and perfection by drawing attention to the consumption and circulation of exotic wines:

> Taillefer se piqua d'animer ses convives, et fit avancer les terribles vins du Rhône, le chaud Tokay, le vieux Rousillon capitaux. Déchaînés comme les chevaux d'une malle-poste qui part d'un relais, ces hommes fouettés par les piquantes flammèches du vin de Champagne ...
>
> (PC, 51-2)

The remainder of the meal is described in terms similar to those used for the depiction of the second course; that is, the narrator presents the sequence of events and dishes which follow in an enumerative, and often hyperbolic, context. This description, then, attests to the fact that Balzac's fictional meals exhibit mimesis of both form and content in relation to actual meals served in bourgeois homes in nineteenth-century France. The formal similarities become evident in the temporal sequence of the fictional meal which models itself on conventional practices: following the description of the first and second courses, the narrator concludes the scene with an evocation of the dessert course. Significantly, this final course contains two descriptive contexts which overlap and which, from the semantic viewpoint, signal the same content: namely, the affluence of the host. The first description reveals opulence by means of focus on the paraphernalia associated with the meal:

> Le dessert se trouva servi comme par enchantement. La table fut couverte d'un vaste surtout en bronze doré, sorti des ateliers de Thomire ... Les couleurs de ces tableaux gastronomiques étaient rehaussées par l'éclat de la porcelaine, par les découpures des vases ... L'argent, le nacre, l'or, les cristaux furent de nouveau prodigués sous de nouvelles formes ...
>
> (*PC*, 61)

The second sequence also attests to wealth by means of an enumeration of succulent fruits served in magnificent vessels:

> De hautes figures douées par un célèbre artiste des formes convenues en Europe pour la beauté idéale, soutenaient et portaient des buissons de fraises, des ananas, des dattes fraîches, des raisins jaunes, de blondes pêches, des oranges arrivées de Sébutal par un paquebot, des grenades, des fruits de la Chine, enfin toutes les surprises du luxe, les miracles du petit-four, les délicatesses les plus friandes, les friandises les plus séductrices.
>
> (*PC*, 61)

This is a highly sensual scene to be sure, with its vast array of colours and fragrant odours, a description which is designed to signal wealth and culinary plenitude by virtue of the fact that money permits an appropriation of the world, here metonymically represented by the exotic fruits which adorn the Taillefer table and which transform it into an Earthly Paradise. The narrator has taken special care to depict this elegant Parisian feast with its planned division into courses, its abundant dishes, its strict regimentation and service in order to show the reader the extent to which luxury tempts Rapahël de Valentin, for he, like Eve, is seduced by the fruits of worldly knowledge.

In conformity with Balzac's tendency to make food a metonym of money in *La Comédie humaine*, meal situations and allusions to food are often used as character markers for potential *arrivistes* or as indices of poverty for young provincials. Although Rastignac easily represents the classic stereotype of this phenomenon, he is one among many Balzacian heroes who often wander the streets of the capital wondering where their next meal will come from. In his depiction of the hero before he challenges the capital, Balzac frequently uses the character's eating habits as a sign of his indigence. Raphaël de Valentin, the protagonist of *La Peau de chagrin*, exemplifies this sort of gastronomical penury: 'J'ai vécu près de trois ans ainsi, répondit Raphaël avec une sorte de fierté. Comptons? reprit-il. Trois sous de pain, deux sous de lait, trois sous de charcuterie m'empêchaient de mourir de faim et tenaient mon esprit dans un état de lucidité singulière' (*PC*, 88). Raphaël was able to forbear with the help of a woman who lodged him, studying assiduously until he met Foedora, the courtesan who led him into a life of dissipation by arousing his desire for luxury. Her insidious charms begin to affect him when she and Raphaël dine together for the first time, giving him his first taste of the good life: following the meal he breaks the ascetic pattern of his existence and seeks to maintain a façade of luxury even at the expense of his health. Significantly, the change in his character is revealed by a change in his eating habits:

Je ressentis alors mes souffrances premières, mais moins aïgues: je m'étais familiarisé sans doute avec leurs terribles crises. Souvent les gâteaux et le thé, si parcimonieusement offerts dans les salons, étaient ma seule nourriture. Quelquefois, les somptueux dîners de la comtesse me soutenaient pendant deux jours.

(*PC*, 126)

Similarly, in *La Rabouilleuse*, Balzac makes explicit the poverty of the Bridau family by describing their meagre

dining facilities: 'La salle à manger, tendue d'un petit
papier jaune à fleurs vertes, et dont le carreau rouge ne
fut pas frotté, n'eut que le strict nécessaire: une table,
deux buffets, six chaises, le tout provenant de l'appartement quitté' (*La Rabouilleuse*, 861). Under the circumstances,
the only course of action open to Philippe, the prodigal son
of the family, is to seek a fortune by gambling; consequently,
when he has a run of luck he overcompensates for the subsistence meals provided by his mother by squandering his money
on food and drink:

> Il sentit en lui-même l'impossibilité de vivre autrement
> qu'il n'avait vécu depuis un an. Le luxe qui régnait chez
> Mariette, les dîners et les soupers, la soirée dans les
> coulisses ... cette vie, qui ne se trouve d'ailleurs qu'à
> Paris, et qui offre chaque jour quelque chose de neuf,
> était devenue plus qu'une habitude pour Philippe ...
> (*La Rabouilleuse*, 894)

Eugène de Rastignac epitomizes the young *Bildungsroman*
hero whose aversion for poverty induces him to seek success
at all costs. For Rastignac especially, the table of the
Maison Vauquer serves to mark the contrast between the elegant Parisian dining rooms and the penurious conditions of
the boardinghouse. He situates himself somewhere between
the two worlds, with the *Maison Vauquer* acting as a constant
reminder of the fate of those who fail in their attempt to
gain admittance to *le beau monde*, for they are condemned
to a seemingly endless diet of typical boardinghouse fare.
In *Le Père Goriot*, Balzac develops the opposition between
wealth and poverty in two meal scenes, one at the home of
Mme de Beauséant, the other at the *pension Vauquer*. The
narrator presents these two meal scenes contiguously in
order to accentuate the polarization of economic spheres.
When, for example, Rastignac returns to the boardinghouse
after a visit with Mme de Beauséant, the contrast between
the elegance of the Beauséant world and the squalor of the
pension Vauquer shock him considerably, making its mark in
gastro-culinary terms:

> Arrivé rue Neuve-Sainte-Geneviève, il monta rapidement
> chez lui, descendit pour donner deux francs au cocher,
> et vint dans cette salle à manger nauséabonde où il aper-
> çut, comme des animaux à un râtelier, les dix-huit convives
> en train de se repaître. Le spectacle de ces misères et
> l'aspect de cette salle lui furent horribles. La transition

était trop brusque, le contraste trop complet, pour ne pas
développer outre mesure chez lui le sentiment de l'ambition.[7]

The narrator portrays Rastignac's disgust using two sensory
impressions, feeling and seeing. The pejorative adjective
'nauséabonde' conveys Rastignac's original reaction to the
impecunious world of the boarders and, simultaneously, the
pensionnaires are symbolically transformed into animals as
may be witnessed by the simile 'comme des animaux à un
râtelier' and the use of the verb *se repaître*, which activates the entire field of associations. Thus it is only
when Rastignac returns to the poverty of his surroundings
and the horror of his meal that he really notices the distinction between the two ways of life and becomes determined
to attain success at any price. It is interesting to note
that he does not flee the boardinghouse existence or desire
the worldly sphere because they have inherent qualities
which either repel or attract him, but rather reacts to
material symbols of these two domains, food and dining
being among the most apparent. Because of their social connotations, certain kinds of food serve as signs of differentiation and, for Rastignac, success depends on distinguishing himself; he well understands that food in a materialistic society becomes an extension of currency. Rastignac
decodes all signs - culinary, gastronomical, vestimentary -
using an economic grid.

The dinner at the home of Mme de Beauséant forms the
structural counterpart to the meals taken at the *Maison
Vauquer*. The importance of the meal itself, the service,
and the ambience in which it unfolds are closely related
to the economic themes of the novel, with the table in this
case becoming the primary metonym of money. In only a few
pages the reader makes the journey with Rastignac from the
world of indigence to the realm of opulence and, as may be
expected, it is the Beauséant meal which will induce Rastignac to seek out material success for its own sake. Consequently, the Beauséant dinner figures as the ultimate example of Rastignac's temptation and seduction by the Parisian gentry. In his depiction of the meal the narrator makes
frequent intrusions into Rastignac's thoughts in order to
keep the reader abreast of the neophyte's interpretation
and impression of the surrounding splendour. It might be
appropriate to mention that this meal elucidates a very
important element in the formation of the *Bildungsroman*
hero; for the young man endeavouring to adapt himself to
fashionable society, a first *dîner en ville* signifies that

his initiation has begun: 'Jamais semblable spectacle n'avait frappé les yeux d'Eugène, qui dînait pour la première fois dans une de ces maisons où les grandeurs sociales sont héréditaires' (PG, 947). Having first established the glorious historical background and placed the meal in the tradition of epicurean excellence, the narrator then shows the effects of the feast on Rastignac: 'Eugène n'avait encore assisté qu'à des bals. L'aplomb qui le distingua plus tard si éminément, et qu'il commençait à prendre, l'empêcha de s'ébahir niaisement. Mais en voyant cette argenterie sculptée, et les mille recherches d'une table somptueuse, en admirant pour la première fois un service fait sans bruit, il était difficile à un homme d'ardente imagination de ne pas préférer cette vie constamment élégante à la vie de privations qu'il voulait embrasser le matin' (PG, 947-8). Rastignac is overwhelmed with surface elegance, enamoured only of the sign: he fails to notice the substance, the food itself. Significantly in this respect, the narrator does not mention any of the dishes served at the Beauséant table: like the 'argenterie sculptée' and the 'mille recherches d'une table somptueuse,' food is assumed to be noticeable only as a marker of wealth and distinction, the least important element of the dining situation as far as Rastignac is concerned. Rastignac completes the first stage of his initiation into fashionable society at this point; he subsequently decided to leave the *Maison Vauquer* and to improve his material condition. For the *arriviste* in *La Comédie humaine*, desire clearly expresses itself in the form of excessive appetite, the need to indulge oneself in luxury and to appropriate the bounteous delicacies offered by the capital.

The Effects of Food on the Human Personality

If the maxim 'You are what you eat' encourages narrators to depict character in terms of food and appetite, then it also allows them to record changes in temperament and behaviour caused by the ingestion of certain kinds of foods or by the ambience created for festive dining situations. Perhaps the most obvious way in which meals affect personality is by means of the congenial atmosphere they provide during commensal dining: 'Lunching together, dining, banqueting, supping, feasting, the family meal ... these and scores of other examples will come to mind as instances in which that which is absorbed by the stomach is probably much less important for the well-being of the individual than that which the process of eating and eating together accomplishes psychologically.'[8] Examples of this serenity syndrome may be found in nearly all descriptions of meals in nineteenth-century French novels, - and in dining descriptions in other literatures as well; such an atmosphere is expected at mealtime, where it fosters relaxation, communication, and trust. Because of the positive affects associated with commensality, however, food and congeniality may also be used to manipulate others. The misuse of conviviality thus becomes a type of coercion, as we have already witnessed with regard to certain meals served by misers; in its most benign form, food may inspire young Balzacian heroes to seek success for its own sake. An egregious violation of trust invested in others at mealtime occurs in *L'Auberge rouge* where the narrator of the story relates the events of a dinner shared by two French soldiers and a German industralist at a renowned inn on the Rhine. During the unfolding of the meal the Frenchmen encourage the German to imbibe large draughts of wine so that he will reveal his financial status. The amiable atmosphere created by the famous vintages and the exquisite cuisine cause the German to become overly loquacious, and the soldiers, tempted by the enormous amount of money in the German's wallet, murder him during an after-dinner stroll. The meal, usually a means for sustaining life and friendship, in this instance has become an agent of death and dishonour.

Balzac also explores the relation between food and the psyche by showing the potential of special diets to modify behaviour. In *La Physiologie du mariage* he does so with a comic intent. The second part of *La Physiologie du mariage* is entitled 'Des Moyens de Défense à l'intérieur et à l'extérieur' or the means by which a husband can safeguard the virtue of his wife. The purpose of the diet prescribed by the narrator is to master and dominate the female, in the belief that physical impositions will affect moral conduct. Ultimately, the narrator maintains, the husband can attenuate his wife's sexual desires by manipulating her food intake; in the twelfth *Méditation*, entitled 'Hygiène du Mariage,' he states: 'Il s'agit de la réaction produite sur le moral par les vicissitudes physiques et par les savantes dégradations d'une diète habilement dirigée.'[9]

The narrator opens his case in favour of debilitating diets by alluding to the method which the English novelist Sterne had devised in order to reduce the effectiveness of the bachelor. The very type of food ingested reduces desire: 'Croyez-vous sérieusement qu'un célibataire soumis au régime

de l'herbe *hanea*, des concombres, du pourpier et des appli-
cations de sangsues aux oreilles, recommandé par Sterne,
serait bien propre à battre en brèche l'honneur de votre
femme?' (*PM*, 713-14). According to the logic of this exposition, food operates primarily on an individual's disposi-
tion; it has both comforting and discomforting virtualities:

> Napoléon a-t-il été en proie ou non aux horribles souf-
> frances d'une dysurie pendant la campagne de Russie? ...
> Voilà une de ces questions dont la solution a pesé sur
> le globe entier. N'est-il pas certain que des réfrigérants,
> des douches, des bains, etc., produisent de grands change-
> ments dans les affections plus ou moins aigües du cerveau?
>
> (*PM*, 714)

Just as atmospheric changes can alter our thoughts, says the
narrator, so may we impose our will on others by changing
their very organism. This insidious invasion of the female's
will aims at one goal - thwarting desire: '... mais nous es-
sayerons de développer un système hygiénique formidable, au
moyen duquel vous pourrez *éteindre le feu* quand il aura pris
à la cheminée' (*PM*, 715; italics mine). Having stated the
purpose, the narrator turns to the means needed to accomplish
this strategy:

> Jean-Jacques par l'organe enchanteur de Julie, ne pourvera-
> t-il pas à votre femme qu'elle aura une grâce infinie à ne
> pas déshonorer son estomac délicat et sa bouche divine,
> en faisant du chyle avec d'ignobles pièces de bœuf et
> d'énormes éclanches de mouton? Est-il rien au monde de
> plus pur que ces intéressants légumes, toujours frais et
> inodorés, ces fruits colorés, ce café, ce chocolat par-
> fumé, ces oranges, pommes d'or d'Atlante, les dattes de
> l'Arabie, les biscottes de Bruxelles ...
>
> (*PM*, 716)

The foods enumerated here connote purity and simplicity;[10]
there is an obvious eschewal of all meats, for it is well
known that carnivores are aggressive and passionate. 'You are
what you eat' is here actualized in order to reflect the belief that pure foods will produce pure beings. In addition
to this careful regimen, the husband must take advantage of
female vanity by inducing his wife to maintain a trim figure
by lowering her caloric intake, and, so as not to excite her
imagination, he must also serve her diluted wine. Such a
diet, if properly imposed, will inevitably lead to listlessness

and insipidity, the ultimate result of which is to decrease the female's level of energy. For this reason, it is important that considerable activity accompany the diet: 'Quelle admirable manoeuvre que de faire danser une femme et de ne la nourrir que de viandes blanches!' (*PC*, 719).

In *La Peau de chagrin* the narrator also depicts the effects of diet on the personality of the individual. After having procured the *peau de chagrin*, a metonym of his excessive appetite and desire, Raphaël must restrict himself to a regular, even flat, diet so as not to wish for those palatable specialities which might eventually cause his demise: 'Le menu est dressé pour l'année entière, jour par jour. Monsieur le marquis n'a rien à souhaiter' (*PC*, 168). In spite of attempting to lead a desireless life, Raphaël shows signs of physical disintegration and summons a group of specialists to diagnose his problem. One of the consulting physicians, a gastrologist, affirms that the stomach is the origin of all diseases, even those related to the mind:

> Enfin monsieur Bianchon a constamment observé les digestions de son malade, et nous a dit qu'elles étaient difficiles, laborieuses. A proprement parler, il n'existe plus d'estomac; l'homme a disparu. L'intellect est atrophié parce que l'homme ne digère plus. L'altération progressive de l'epigastre, centre de la vie, a vicié tout le système. De là partent des irradiations constantes et flagrantes, le désordre a gagné le cerveau par le plexus nerveux, d'où l'irritation excessive de cet organe. Il y a monomanie.
>
> (*PC*, 214)

This passage clearly aligns the man with his stomach, making all the activities of life analogues of the digestive process: most important, the very existence and pretensions of the science of gastrology attest to the fact that intellection and digestion belong to the same ontological structure wherein eating figures as a form of knowledge. It reflects *le savoir* in so far as man must learn to adapt himself to the world by avoiding excessive indulgence; it represents *le connaître* because, by the act of eating, man ingests the world-food and thus partakes of the flesh of the gods, '... les aliments, sources de vie et de plaisir, portes ouvertes sur l'intimité du monde, sont les moyens les plus naturels pour accéder au divin caché dans la structure des choses ...'[11] Knowing eliminates, or rather transcends, desiring.

La Peau de chagrin is also the best example of sexual, moral, and metaphysical potentialities of food and banqueting in *La Comédie humaine* since the occult motifs of the

novel are often expressed in reference to gastronomy or alimentary images. Raphaël de Valentin, like many other young
Balzacian heroes, has a passion for wealth and luxury along
with the desire to achieve them at any price, but Raphaël
does not choose to advance through worldly circles by learning the methods of *arrivisme*; he does so by means of a tal-
isman which grants him his every wish. At the very outset
of the novel the narrator establishes the desire-appetite
paradigm which will be operative throughout the story. In
a curiosity shop Raphaël discovers an amulet whose properties are outlined to him by the proprietor who explains
that the world is divided between *le vouloir* which consumes,
and *le pouvoir*, which destroys. Significantly, he says, the
peau de chagrin united these two concepts, but as far as he
is concerned the only peace of mind to be found resides in
the concept of *le savoir*, that is, in the perfectly ingested
world-experience which in its digestive phase enables man
to assimilate good and to reject evil. Man's problems come
from his inclination toward excessiveness or gluttony. In
this particular scene Balzac uses the metaphor of nourishment, which becomes a kind of spiritual and carnal leitmotif
throughout the novel; for the old man, study and thought
represent the most salubrious forms of nourishment, but for
Raphaël this ideal does not suffice to satiate his hunger:
'J'avais résolu ma vie par l'étude et par la pensée; mais
elles ne m'ont même pas nourri ...' (*PC*, 41). Craving corporeal pleasures, Raphaël seeks out the voluptousness and
abandonment of the good life: as is frequently the case in
Balzac's novels, desire manifests itself as appetite:

> Je veux un dîner royalement splendide, quelque bacchanale
> digne du siècle où tout s'est dit-on, perfectionné! Que
> mes convives soient jeunes, spirituels et sans préjugés,
> joyeux jusqu'à la folie! Que les vins se succèdent tou-
> jours plus incisifs, plus pétillants, et soient de force
> à nous enivrer pour trois jours. Que cette nuit soit
> parée de femmes ardentes!
>
> (*PC*, 42)

Raphaël's first wish, uniting as it does the gastronomical
and the sexual, anticipates the orgy scene earlier discussed
and betrays that excess of *vouloir* which finds transcendence
through food, wine, and carnal pleasure. In his total rejection of *savoir* in favour of *vouloir*, Raphaël ultimately
seeks that symbolic destruction to be found in oblivion: his
overexuberance translates as voraciousness, an incompatibility with life which will force him to gorge himself to death.

The Taillefer banquet, which has already been analysed
from the culinary viewpoint, serves as a prelude to the orgy
in which Raphaël's excessive desire is realized for the
first time. The reader may remember that the narrator com-
pares the Taillefer meal to a classical tragedy, and this
metaphor is sustained throughout the description; thus during
the second act of the meal the emphasis shifts from food to
drink: 'Le seconde acte devint quelque peu bavard. Chaque
convive avait bu raisonablement en changeant de crus suivant
ses caprices, en sorte qu'au moment où l'on emporta les
restes de ce magnifique service, de tempétueuses discussions
s'étaient établies' (*PC*, 51). The conversations, given an
impetus by excessive imbibing, illustrate the potential of
wine for destroying inhibitions and ultimately point to the
final degeneration symbolized by the orgy. The author clearly
depicts the first signs of inebriation by showing the physical reactions of the guests to the liquid enchantress: '...
quelques front pâles rougissaient, plusieurs nez commençaient à s'empourprer, les visages s'allumaient, les yeux
pétillaient' (*PC*, 51). Once again food assumes a metonymic
function, for clearly the verbal sequence ('rougissaient,'
'commençaient à s'empourprer,' 's'allumaient,' 'pétillaient')
signals the fact that the guests are transformed into what
they ingest. Consequently, in the subsequent description
of the banquet the bacchanalian activites of the feast
begin to prevail as the guests find themselves on the
threshold of inebriation. The degeneration into stupor reveals, moreover, that normal social behaviour is abandoned
in libidinal impulses. The description of this twilight
stage of consciousness enables the narrator to bridge the
gap between food and drink as means to satisfaction, and
food and drink as agents of licentious pleasure. In the end
the magical and dionysian properties of wine prevail with
the effect that the harmonious balance between ingesting
and imbibing degenerates into a paroxysm of increased intensity: 'L'orgie seule déploya sa grande voix, sa voix
composée de cent clameurs confuses qui froississent comme
les crescendos de Rossini' (*PC*, 52).

The dessert course, with its elaborate description of
fruits and wines, exemplifies not only the luxury motif but
also the capacity of *la bonne chère* to seduce the senses
into more pleasure. Food, then, becomes an extension of
sexuality. The narrator explicitly states the alliance between the gastronomical and the sexual in his enumeration
of the various fruits, their perfumes, and their colours.
All of these properties, he claims, comprise 'les délicates-
ses les plus friandes, les friandises les plus séductrices'

(*PC*, 61). During this course the narrator makes the transition from the animated gastronomical context to the inevit-
able sexual frenzy which follows. Initiated in the highly
sensual allusions to exotic fruits, the description develops
through the equally suggestive inducements of the wines:
'Les vins de dessert apportaient leurs parfums et leurs
flammes, filtres puissants, vapeurs enchanteresses qui en-
gendrent une espèce de mirage intellectuel et dont les liens
puissants enchaînaient les pieds, alourdissent les mains'
(*PC*, 61). Wine loses its gustatory significance in this
passage and assumes its magical personality, its ability to
transform the state of mind of the imbiber. Its intoxicating
properties so prevail that they facilitate the total annihi-
lation of social and moral inhibitions. The narrator signals
the transgression of quotidian morality by alluding to an
unbridled orality, the word and the world gone awry, and by
evolving, through the symbol of the crystal glasses which
'volèrent en éclats,' the breaking of conventional codes of
behaviour.

Although the meal proper ceases with the migration of the
gentlement into the salon, the meal context continues with
the arrival of the courtesans who serve the men coffee and
a tantalizing punch. In this last stage of the meal the
narrator focuses his attention on two women, a brunette and
a blond, who symbolize the two poles of female sexuality
and charm. Thematically, the women interest the reader from
two points of view: first, they represent the theme of carnal nourishment in so far as they devour money, life, and
pleasure, a theme aptly articulated by Euphrasie, one of
the courtesans: 'Donnez-moi des millions, je les mangerai
... Vivre pour plaire et régner, tel est l'arrêt que pro-
nonce chaque battement de mon cœur' (*PC*, 69); second,
their egoism reveals itself as an absence of charity which
in gastronomical terms is expressed as a reluctance to
nourish others and a propensity for self-indulgence: 'J'ai
été quitte [sic] pour un héritage, moi! dit-elle en prenant
une pose qui fit ressortir toutes ses séductions. Et cependant j'avais passé les nuits et les jours à travailler pour
nourrir mon enfant. Je ne veux plus être la dupe d'aucun
sourire ...' (*PC*, 69). Ironically this indulgence in pleasure and luxury does not occur without a nostalgic return
to the simple family meals of the past '... où tout respirait
un charme indéfinissable, où les mets étaient simples comme
les cœurs' (*PC*, 161).

The final phase of the meal complex occurs when the courtesans serve the men punch; it represents the definitive
descent into Hell. At this point the guests allow themselves

to be lured into a state of ecstasy, completely surrendering
to unbridled desires and sexual excesses which are here symbolized by the diabolical coalescence of potion and portent:

> Contempler en ce moment les salons, c'était avoir une vue
> anticipée du Pandémonium de Milton. Les flammes bleues du
> punch coloraient d'une teinte infernale les visages de ceux
> qui pourraient boire encore ... L'atmosphère était chaude
> de vin, de plaisirs et de paroles. L'ivresse, l'amour, le
> délire, l'oubli du monde étaient dans les cœurs ...
>
> (*PC*, 71)

Balzac brings the reader to the precipice but forces him to
leap in imagination only; instead of describing the orgy, he
evokes it indirectly by having Raphaël deliver an 'orgie de
paroles.' Just as food and drink loosen the bridle of restraint
and precipitate the guests into debauchery, so they also serve
to increase Raphaël's desire to confess. Here again the dionysian potentials of wine to alter states of consciousness are
evident; Raphaël imbibes just enough wine to transcend banal
drunkenness and enter into a veritable poetic trance:

> ' - Je ne sais en vérité s'il ne faut pas attribuer aux
> fumées du vin et du punch l'espèce de lucidité qui me
> permet d'embrasser en cet instant toute ma vie comme un
> même tableau ...' (*PC*, 74)

During his recital, Raphaël unwittingly formulates the psychodynamics of the orgy as he relates the advice given to
him earlier by Rastignac when the latter heard him express
a wish to die:

> Plonge-toi dans une dissolution profonde, ta passion ou
> toi, vous y périrez. L'intempérance, mon cher! est la
> reine de toutes les morts ... Les orgies nous prodiguent
> tous les plaisirs physiques, n'est-ce pas l'opium en
> petite monnaie? En nous forçant de boire à outrance, la
> débauche porte de mortels défis au vin.
>
> (*PC*, 146)

But Rastignac offers him an alternative which amounts to
little more than a hedonistic view of life which seeks
pleasure in forgetfulness and which translates into gastronomical terms as a kind of excessive gourmandise: henceforth Raphaël's life will correspond to a slow and insidious
suicide.[12]

*The Meal as Mimesis: Food and Its Relation to Culture,
History, and Politics in 'La Comédie humaine'*

In concluding this discussion of meals in the novels of
Balzac a glimpse at the historical, political, and cultural
elements of dining episodes might be helpful for an understanding of his total meal thematic. A large part of Balzac's
realism depends on actual allusions and references to the
events of his times. In so far as these events relate to
dining situations, they consist of para-culinary phenomena
such as eating customs, regional differences in cuisine,
and a general interest in the art of gastronomy, all of
which reflect cultural specificity and thus figure as a
mimesis of nineteenth-century French cultural practices.
The reader often detects a certain chauvinism in Balzac's
narrators with regard to culinary and cultural superiority;
in *La Physiologie du mariage*, for example, cooking reaches
its apotheosis during the Restoration period: 'Notre civilisation actuelle a prouvé que le goût était une science, et
qu'il n'appartenait qu'à certains êtres privilégiés de
savoir boire et manger' (*PM*, 648). Many such axiomatic
statements appear throughout *La Comédie humaine* in the form
of gratuitous narrative digressions on food, cooking, and
culture.
    In spite of the intimate relation between meals and money
in *Eugénie Grandet* and *La Rabouilleuse*, references to cooking and gastronomy also serve to depict provincial life in
nineteenth-century France. It would certainly be a mistake
to assume from the outset that because meals are provincial
in nature they are consequently inferior to Parisian cuisine,
or that all provincials are misers like Grandet and Hochon.
In *La Rabouilleuse*, for instance, Flore Brazier, a maid in
the Rouget household, takes her part as cook very seriously:
'Depuis six mois elle étudiait, sans en avoir l'air, les
procédés culinaires qui faisaient de Fanchette un Cordon
Bleu digne de servir un médecin' (*La Rabouilleuse*, 976).
Flore's initial efforts indeed reveal the great esteem in
which cooking was held in provincial France. The subject of
food and cooking in the Rouget home also induces the narrator to include a digression on gastronomy in general; in
such passages the function of the digression is usually
superfluous since the sign-value of the meal as a literary
entity has been completely abandoned so that the narrator
may immerse himself entirely in the joys of elaborating on
fastidious fare or various eating practices. He first pre-
occupies himself with a depiction of different types of

epicures: 'En fait de gourmandise, on peut mettre les méde-
cins au même rang que les évêques' (*La Rabouilleuse*, 976).
The intention here is ironical, for obviously the narrator
profits from the notoriety of those amphitryons who should
show the most temperance but who in fact have shown the
least throughout history.

   If the art of cooking has become an end in itself in Paris,
this is not necessarily the case in the provinces where
cooking is often a means of fending off boredom: 'En province,
le défaut d'occupation et la monotonie de la vie attirent
l'activité de l'esprit sur la cuisine' (*La Rabouilleuse*,
976). Henceforth, the narrator subjects the differences between Parisian and provincial cuisine to careful scrutiny
with the result that, in these digressions at least, food
and meals are transformed into geographical metonyms:

> On ne dîne pas aussi luxueusement en province qu'à Paris,
> mais on y dîne mieux; les plats y sont médités, étudiés.
> Au fond des provinces, il existe des Carêmes en jupon,
> génies ignorés, qui savent rendre un simple plat de
> haricots digne d'un hochement de tête par lequel Rossini
> accueille une chose parfaitement réussie.
>
> (*La Rabouilleuse*, 976)

Cooking occupies such an important place in provincial life
that even the men take pride in culinary innovations and
the invention of recipes:

> En prenant ses degrés à Paris, le docteur [Rouget's father]
> y avait suivi les cours de chimie de Rouelle, et il lui
> en était resté des notions qui tournèrent au profit de la
> chimie culinaire. Il est célèbre à Issoudin par plusieurs
> améliorations peu connues en dehors du Berry. Il a décou-
> vert que l'omelette était beaucoup plus délicate quand
> on ne battait pas le blanc et le jaune des œufs ensemble
> avec la brutalité que les cuisinières mettent à cette
> opération. On devait, selon lui, faire arriver le blanc
> à l'état de mousse, y introduire par degrés le jaune, et
> ne pas se servir d'une poêle, mais d'un cagnard en proce-
> laine ou de faïence.
>
> (*La Rabouilleuse*, 976)

In essence the ideal application of science to the art of
cooking so characteristic of nineteenth-century France becomes apparent in this passage which practically assumes
the character of a recipe. Not one detail is left to the

imagination; even the proper cooking utensils are indicated
and form an integral part of the recipe itself. In fact,
the narrator embarks on a history and description of the
cagnard, leaving the story aside as it were in order to indulge himself in the culinary digression:

> Le cagnard est une espèce de plat épais qui a quatre pieds,
> afin que, mis sur le fourneau, l'air, en circulant, em-
> pêche le feu de le faire éclater. En Touraine, le cagnard
> s'appelle un cauquemarre. Rabelais, je crois, parle de ce
> *cauquemarre* à cuire les cocquesigrues, ce qui démontre
> la haute antiquité de cet ustensile.
>
> (*La Rabouilleuse*, 977)

Many of Balzac's digressions on food, gastronomy, and eating practices occur in a Parisian context, undoubtedly because the culinary arts received their most eloquent expression in the dining rooms and the restaurants of the capital.
The meal scene in *L'Auberge rouge*, for example, differs in
many respects from the provincial repasts in *Eugénie Grandet*
and *La Rabouilleuse*. Firstly, this meal occurs at the home
of a wealthy banker and consists of a society of close
friends and associates, all of whom are accustomed to a life
of luxury and pleasure. Secondly, the primary purpose of
this meal is to assemble old and new acquaintances in a
congenial atmosphere solely in order to indulge in and appreciate the pleasures of the kitchen. Finally, rather than
emphasize the culinary elements of the banquet, the narrator alludes to the ambience in which the meal is consumed
so as to accentuate the virtues of supping in good company.
That the description of the meal surpasses the normal boundaries of storytelling and assumes the character of a universal gastronomical ethic may be witnessed in the narrator's tableau-like portrayal of the felicities of dining:

> Le dos appuyé sur sa chaise, le poignet légèrement soutenu
> par le bord de la table, chaque convive jouait indolemment
> avec la lame dorée de son couteau. Quand un dîner arrive à
> ce moment de déclin, certaines gens tourmentent le pépin
> d'une poire; d'autres roulent une mie de pain entre le pouce
> et l'index; les amoureux tracent des lettres informes avec
> les débris des fruits; les avares comptent leurs noyaux et
> les rangent sur leur assiette comme un dramaturge dispose
> ses comparses au fond d'un théâtre. C'est de petites féli-
> cités gastronomiques dont n'a pas tenu compte dans son
> livre Brillat-Savarin, auteur si complet d'ailleurs.[13]

Moreover, having complemented the observations of Brillat-
Savarin with some of his own, the narrator cannot avoid the
temptation to abandon himself totally in gastronomical ful-
gurations and aphorisms:

> Nous ne connaissons point d'homme qui se soit encore at-
> tristé pendant la digestion d'un bon dîner. Nous aimons
> alors rester dans je ne sais quel calme, espèce de juste
> milieu entre la rêverie du penseur et la satisfaction des
> animaux ruminants, qu'il faudrait appeler la mélancolie
> matérielle de la gastronomie.
>
> (AR, 956)

Then, shifting to a new perspective, the narrator paints
the effects of the food on the faces of the guests:

> Chercheurs de tableaux, j'admirais ces visages égayés par
> un sourire, éclairées par les bougies, et que la bonne
> chère avait empourprés; leurs expressions diverses produis-
> aient de piquants effets à travers les candélabres, les
> corbeilles en porcelaine, les fruits et les cristaux.
>
> (AR, 957)

This scene captures the aesthetic harmony attained when an
exquisite repast and luxurious surroundings are combined.
The narrator does not overpower the reader with the dazzling
but superficial effects of china, crystal, and flamboyant
foods. In this case the meal is evoked for its own sake,
and the entire scene figures as a sensual yet measured blend
of mood, décor, and fare.

In *Le Père Goriot*, on the other hand, the narrator digres-
ses from time to time on the history of French cuisine. During the Beauséant meal, he intrudes in order to revive the
eating customs of the past: 'La mode venait de supprimer les
soupers qui terminaient autrefois les bals de l'Empire, où
les militaires avaient besoin de prendre des forces pour se
préparer à tous les combats qui les attendaient au dedans
comme au dehors' (PG, 947). In a similar scene the narrator
gives the reader a chronological perspective of the luxury
and pleasure which characterize meals during the Restoration
period; needless to say, he places the Beauséant meal in
this tradition of opulence and gastronomical excellence.
Next, he summarizes the repertory of banquets given during
the Napoleonic era when it was customary to follow the great
balls with equally elaborate meals. But as political institutions change, so do eating habits: during the Restoration

the protocol was modified so that only the dance remained, clearly a mark of degenerating eating practices caused by the advent of the bourgeoisie.

The narrator in *Les Deux Rêves* also uses an historical perspective when he has the guests at the Saint-James table converse about renowned dinners of the past. This digression reveals the function of the meal-as-mirror-of-the-meal: 'En ce moment, madame de Saint-James nous avait mis, je ne sais par quel hasard de conversation, sur le chapitre des merveilleux soupers du comte de Cagliostro, que donnait le cardinal de Rohan.'[14] This digression places such meal scenes in an extra-temporal dimension: the narrator here makes the organically unified time of this succession of banquets coextensive with the chronological time-sequence of the narrative; in other words, the culinary tradition has a history and a continuity of its own. Such meals enjoy all the characteristics of rituals – with the passing of time they are mythologized in the national memory.

Many of the practices associated with the meal tend to pervade the customs of all Frenchmen, not just those of the upper classes. Political discussions at the table form an integral part of French conversational habits and they figure in numerous Balzacian eating episodes. The feasters at the Taillefer table in *La Peau de chagrin* engage in a vigorous and heated dialogue on the virtues and the vices of nineteenth-century France; in this particular debate the table serves as a metonym of social progress. Food and civilization become synonymous:

> – Monstre! dit Emile en interrompant le misanthrope, comment peux-tu médire de la civilisation en présence de vins, de mets si délicieux, et à table jusqu'au menton? Mordre ce chevreuil aux pieds et aux cornes dorées, mais ne mords pas ta mère.
>
> (*PC*, 58)

In *La Rabouilleuse* the annual banquets in honour of Napoleon's coronation show the fundamental practice of linking food with political events. Issoudin, the locale of the events of the narrative, is a highly conservative village consisting of families who take pride in their respectability. In order to undermine the bourgeois ethic Maxence Gilet, a former soldier in Napoleon's army and a rogue at heart, has formed the *Ordre de la désœuvrance*, which consists of young and rebellious spirits who carry on their mischievous deeds after midnight, then assemble at the inn of *La Cognette* at three o'clock in the morning to celebrate their triumphs over a hearty meal and a heady brew. This practice of carousing and feasting places these episodes in the picaresque tradition which frequently delineates the spirit of revelry at the table so often associated with pranks or crimes. The young people of Issoudin respect Max because he has liberated himself from the constraints of society and family under which they have been forced to live; the break with traditional codes of conduct is here signalled by the radical change in eating routine, the nocturnal festival connoting asocial and anti-bourgeois sentiment.

As regards contemporary cultural fads, elements of conversation at the table also illustrate non-political customs and national practices. In *Le Père Goriot*, for instance, the narrator describes the Parisian's interest in verbal witticisms and popular language games. One of the meals at the *pension Vauquer* begins with such a game: the practice of suffixing 'rama' to all utterances at the table reveals not only the cleverness of those who play the game well, but also the dullness of those who are not aware of the latest fads. When madame Vauquer serves the soup, the boarders react by calling it a 'soupe-au-rama.' In an obvious misinterpretation she corrects the others by assuring them that it is indeed a 'soupe aux choux.' At this stage the game remains benign, but when the morning fog is described as a 'Goriorama' because it is so thick, the boarders deride the old man twice over precisely because he fails to get the joke. Language, like food, works at the expense of those who are unaware of its subtleties, and the table thus becomes the locus of exclusion, both social and intellectual.

In Western culture writers have always associated food with sex, but in nineteenth-century France in particular novelists exploit the similarities between sensual and sexual pleasures, perhaps because they were made explicit in the society at large. So pervasive is the tendency to ally the gastronomical with the sexual in contemporary novels that it could well become the subject of a separate enquiry. For this reason it might be prudent to concentrate on one aspect of this phenomenon in Balzac: namely, the relationship between food and sexuality, the latter being understood in this context as the sexual differences and discriminations pertaining to males and females living in nineteenth-century France. In *La Physiologie du mariage* especially, the proximity between food and sexuality becomes the subject of many of the meditations appearing throughout the book. In the fourth meditation, entitled *De la femme vertueuse*, the narrator examines the dangers facing a husband as regards the

chastity of his wife. From the pseudo-scientific viewpoint
adopted by the narrator, sex is portrayed as a physiological
need which cannot be denied, so, naturally, men must understand the needs of the female in order to channel them. In
developing this idea the narrator uses a series of interre-
lated axioms and theorems which fundamentally relegate the
sexual urge to the biological level by comparing it to the
appetite, an old but effective metaphor to be sure.

The first theorem occurs in the form of a simile: 'L'amour
physique est un besoin semblable à la faim, à cela près que
l'homme mange toujours, et qu'en amour son appétit n'est pas
aussi soutenu ni aussi régulier qu'en fait de table' (PM,
631). In effect, both physical love and hunger belong to
the semic category of lexical items associated with the appetite. Using the idea of hunger as the focus of the metaphor, Balzac expands it in terms of the relationship of elements which constitute this polarity. Hence the entire imagistic system depends on an extended metaphor exploiting the
similarities between food and sex; difference occurs only
with respect to the intensity of the appetite, hunger being
the more demanding. The following axioms also derive from
the theorem, where the basis for relationship is the similar
tenor of the metaphor, notably the lexical items borrowed
from culinary and gastronomical terminology: 'Un morceau de
pain bis et une crûchée d'eau font raison de la faim de tous
les hommes; mais notre civilisation a créé la gastronomie'
(PM, 631). The sudden shift in emphasis from basic nourishment to refined over-indulgence is quite significant: the
reader easily detects the irony and laconicism in the second
part of the axiom which places food and appetite in the domain of culinary stylization. The word *gastronomie* does not
connote the idea of nourishment only, or eating to live;
rather it suggests an entire way of life, an art, an apotheosis of the gustatory act, living to eat.[15] In the second
axiom, Balzac returns to the alliance between food and sex:
'L'amour a son morceau de pain, mais il a aussi cet art
d'aimer, que nous appelons la coquetterie, mot charmant qui
n'existe qu'en France, où cette science est née' (PM, 631).
Once again food is the metaphorical term of the analogy
morceau de pain:gastronomie::amour::coquetterie, and, just
as in the first axiom, the original circumstances have been
altered in order to effect the transformation from the
physiological to the psychological. Perhaps even more interesting in this axiom is the allusion to a national
social phenomenon: the science of coquetry like that of
gastronomy reached one of its highest points of refinement
in nineteenth-century France.

If the above postulates establish the relation between
hunger and sex both on a primitive and an advanced social
level, the resulting means to satiation also have certain
similarities. Balzac reiterates an essential truth of human
nature using a well-worn metaphorical cliché: man's hunger
must be sated, but there exists a variety of ways in which
satiation may be accomplished. A steady diet, for example,
might suffice to maintain life but it hardly makes it interesting; just as man feels the need to vary his diet, so he
must also experience the urge to change sexual partners:

> Eh! bien, n'y a-t-il pas de quoi fair frémir tous les
> maris s'ils viennent à penser que l'homme est tellement
> possédé du besoin inné de changer de mets, qu'en quelque
> pays sauvage où les voyageurs aient abordé, ils ont trouvé
> des boissons spiritueuses et des râgouts?
>
> (PM, 631)

New foods offer intense pleasures, as do new lovers. However,
love's yearnings are more violent than hunger's pangs:

> Mais la faim n'est pas si violente que l'amour; mais les
> caprices de l'âme sont bien plus nombreux, plus agaçants,
> plus recherchés dans leur furie que les caprices de la
> gastronomie ...
>
> (PM, 631)

Since this entire metaphorical network has been developed in
order to inform the unwary husband of the possible transgres-
sions of his wife, Balzac terminates with an appropriate allusion to the most fearsome beast the husband might encounter
- the bachelor: '... mais tout ce que les poètes et les
événements nous ont révélé de l'amour humaine arme nos celi-
bataires d'une puissance terrible: ils sont les lions de
l'Evangile cherchant des proies à dévorer' (PM, 631).
   Food and sex in this series of axioms relate to contemporary mores and they constitute a social phenomenon which
has obviously evolved from a biological need. From the
psycho-cultural viewpoint, Balzac's metaphors are indicative
of the thought patterns of a society which associates two
biologically different functions using identical linguistic
components. The sexual urge and the gastronomical need are
both called appetites, and both undergo a similar semiosis
which may be represented as follows - food:gastronomy::
sexual love:coquetry. Both instances show a definite evolution from the *cru* to the *cuit*, that is, from the raw material

necessary for the maintenance of life to the finished
product of which only a small part remains vital as sustenance, the rest constituting a form of stylized luxury. It
seems, then, that a society which permits sophistication
and symbolization of one biological function to develop will
also encourage other functional elements to do so accordingly:
thus a gastronomically sophisticated society is also a sex-
ually sophisticated society. A process of artistic codification occurs wherein stylized eating customs - the art of
cookery - coincide with refined sexual behaviour - the art
of loving. In both cases the emphasis shifts from performance to technique, from the end to the means, from the substance to the sign.

In assessing the role of meal scenes in Balzac's novels, one
may deduce that the gastronomical sign reveals more about
the sociology of Balzac's narrative universe than about food.
In general, meals occupy that part of the author's thematic
which associates food with various social spheres, for indeed Balzac creates a meal semiosis consisting of a network
of gastronomical myths whose function is to depict the existence of fundamentally hostile groups in confrontation in
La Comédie humaine. For Balzacian heroes in particular, the
meal is situated at the frontier of social differentiation:
if he is a young upstart like Rastignac, an invitation to
dine with the fashionable set is a prelude to success; if
he is a miser like Grandet, an elaborate meal for even the
most distinguished guest is unthinkable.
      For the most part, meals in *La Comédie humaine* centre on
the theme of the table-as-exclusion, a kind of negative reversal of the social and psychological motivations which
make people dine together. The socialization process evoked
in Balzac's novels does not generally entail gracious out-
pourings of warmth among the participants, as in the novels
of Sand, for instance, nor does it produce a reassuring
state of mind free of anxiety and conflict for the diners;
rather it betrays a latent hostility. 'Insiders' and 'outsiders' sometimes break bread together, but the communal
function of their act is nullified because they frequently
belong to different social spheres: consequently, the meal
complex serves to reinforce their differences and thus signals a perpetual hiatus, a resistance to social fusion. In
the novels of Sand, Sue, and Hugo, as we shall see, the
distance between social spheres is overcome by means of the
principle of commensality, which these novelists often bor-
row from Christian socialist doctrines of the period. To

this extent, the reader can well observe a kind of social
and moral progression in their meal episodes as opposed to
the more static view taken by Balzac of reproducing rather
than improving society. From the ideological perspective,
then, Balzac's gastro-alimentary sign may be described as
neutral in contrast with those of Sand, Sue, and Hugo, whose
discourse is saturated with socialist ideology, and with
those of Flaubert, whose doctrine of *l'art pour l'art*, and
whose alimentary discourse, purports to be anti-ideological.
There also exists in *La Comédie humaine* a socio-economic
hierarchy of meals which illustrates the struggles the young
arriviste must endure if he wishes to gain acceptance in
upper social echelons. Usually, then, Balzac's meal scenes
belong to a larger network of signs and images which exploit
the theme of life as a battle: clearly, the war may be fought
on economic, social, sexual, or gastronomical grounds.

Finally, from the structural perspective, meals seem to
have an antithetical motivation, since they are often a
means to bring people together for purposes of confrontation.
Balzac's tables exemplify heterogeneous grouping: ultimately,
his diners sup at a divided table. Within the structure of
the particular novels described in this book, and even of
La Comédie humaine in general, this division takes the form
of meals that contrast with one another and serves to accentuate the Balzacian principle of dualism, especially as it
occurs in relation to the wealth/poverty axis. In any event
the contrasting pattern established in the dining scenes,
that is, the constant juxtaposition of elaborate meals with
modest repasts, indicates a division in the mythical society
of *La Comédie humaine*, and in so far as Balzac is an early
practitioner and forerunner of literary realism, it characterizes and satirizes the vices of contemporary materialism.

2 / SAND

The Meal as Symbol of Ethical Distance between the Classes: Gastro-alimentary Antitheses in the Novels of George Sand

In considering the role of the meal in George Sand's novels the reader might well expect to find a variety of uses for dining situations, corresponding to the variety of her vision. Sand's novels are generally classified according to three distinct periods: the personal or idealistic novels, the social or humanitarian novels, and the rustic or pastoral novels. In theory, the meals portrayed under each of these categories would be quite different in form and content; in fact, they are not. A striking similarity exists at all levels, especially as regards the semiotic structure of her fictional meals. This unified meal structure, which in Sand's case might better be termed an ethic, is all the more remarkable because of the dissimilarities between social groups present in her meal scenes, which depict aristocratic, bourgeois, and peasant tables. Nevertheless, in spite of these descriptions of different social registers, there emerges a unity of vision and purpose which ultimately reveals Sand's desire to bring about a rapprochement between the classes. All meals, then, share an implicit socio-economic infrastructure which draws them into the socialist sphere of thought; all have an underlying ideological significance which attests to Sand's deep concern for *le Peuple*.

In essence, Sand's meal scenes present the other side of the Balzacian universe: whereas Balzac glorifies prodigal Parisian meals and chastises avaricious provincial dinners, Sand sings a hymn of praise to the peasants, enthusiastically

lauding their virtue, simplicity, and pastoral meals. Moreover, in Sand's view there exists an intrinsic relation between the natural generosity and hospitality of the peasant
and the concept of brotherhood at the table. Unlike Balzac,
who emphasizes the importance of the meal as a differentiating factor, Sand attempts to destroy social barriers by
using the table as a symbol of social assimilation as well
as the chosen locus for the desired rapprochement. Perhaps
it is because they lie at the base of the social pyramid
that rural folk open their hearts and tables to everyone.
In any event, it comes as no surprise to find peasants in
Sand's novels inviting aristocrats to partake of a meal
with them in their humble surroundings, but it must have
shocked the nineteenth-century reader to discover one of
Sand's noblemen extending a dinner invitation to a worker
or peasant.

By shifting conventional narrative perspectives, that is
by de-emphasizing the elegant aristocratic or bourgeois
meal in favour of the rural repast, Sand is able to depict
the plight of the peasant living in a materialistic society;
at the same time, by accentuating the generous simplicity
of the peasant in his gastronomical and culinary practices,
she lays the foundation of her socialist ideology. Peasants
and workers often dine in groups in Sand's novels, and they
almost always invite visitors to share their meal. Furthermore, by means of this concept of generosity, Sand constructs
the framework for the utopian ideal of communal banqueting:
ultimately her meal scenes evolve toward the most fraternal
feast of all - the Heavenly Banquet. The practice of dining
together, rich with poor, old with young, good with bad,
thus becomes the supreme manifestation of Sand's Christian
Socialism. Food, in its socializing and equalizing function,
becomes a symbol of emancipation and equality, not a marker
of social distinction as in Balzac's novels. Moreover, while
serving as a means of eradicating social differences, food
also becomes an end in itself in Sand's novels, for it is
the backbone of the peasant's existence: the ploughman
rarely evaluates his life on the basis of currency as do
Balzac's characters; rather his worth derives from his ability to provide a living for his family, to put food on the
table. For this reason food is considered to be a useful
and practical substance; the reader rarely experiences
prodigal feasts in Sand's novels, since her peasants are
motivated to eat by hunger alone. Accordingly, her characters have very definite attitudes about food, which have
little to do with elaborate tableware, exotic dishes, and

elegant dress. They react to food by commenting on its taste
or the manner of its preparation, thus attenuating its
semiotic status and accentuating its phenomenological character.

For George Sand the table functions primarily as a symbol
of equality. Although it is not stated in such explicit
terms as in Balzac's novels, Sand's meal scenes also have
an underlying socio-economic significance which betrays her
strong anti-bourgeois sentiments. Much influenced by socialist thinkers such as Leroux, Lammenais, and Saint-Simon,
Sand felt compelled to cry out for social reform. Leroux,
especially, induced her to investigate this reform according
to a mystico-religious doctrine which, it was hoped, would
lead to the salvation of the people, who were being degraded
and exploited by an advancing capitalism. The first step in
the restoration of human dignity must occur in some form of
rapprochement between the social classes. Conveniently, one
of the obvious prototypes for the desired unification was
the agape feasts of the early Christians: sitting at the
same table and breaking bread together have, historically
speaking, been fundamental symbols of universal brotherhood.
These kinds of fraternal gestures, then, are at the base of
the doctrines of the socialist theorists.
    In order to make the reader aware of the social inequities
in nineteenth-century France, Sand develops a number of contrasts related to the eating practices and customs of the
groups in confrontation. In other words, her ideological
message is transmitted by means of culinary, gastronomical,
and alimentary symbols. Essentially, the symbols associated
with the bourgeoisie (and occasionally with the aristocracy)
and their eating mores carry negative connotations, while
the symbols indicating peasant customs invariably carry
positive ones. This process of gastro-culinary symbolization
remains coherent in Sand's total opus, where it functions
on the one hand to denigrate capitalism and the entire bourgeois ideology, and, on the other, to valorize peasant simplicity and integrity. References to food and eating in
Sand's novels have a propagandistic rationale; they persuade
the reader to sympathize with the peasant and thereby to
accept, and even adopt, his ethic.
    Sand does not often rely on explicit social and economic
contrasts between the classes in making her point; rather
she prefers to let peasant virtues speak for themselves,
either directly as in dialogues between her characters or
indirectly by means of narrative signs which exploit those

symbolic values of food associated with Christianity. Occasionally, however, she makes an overt statement about the
plight of the peasant. In *La Mare au Diable*, for example,
the narrator speaks of the peasant's need to lose himself
in drink: alluding to a Holbein entitled *Le Laboureur et la
Mort*, the narrator uses alcohol as a symbol of forgetfulness and evasion from the rude conditions which the labourer
must endure: 'Les buveurs d'Holbein remplissent leurs coupes
avec une sorte de fureur pour écarter l'idée de la mort ...'[1]
Moreover, to arouse the reader's compassion for the peasant,
Sand uses certain types of food to symbolize poverty: 'Sans
doute il est lugubre de consumer ses forces et ses jours
à fendre le sein de cette terre jalouse, qui se fait ar-
racher les trésors de sa fécondité, lorsq'un morceau de
pain le plus noir et le plus grossier est, à la fin de la
journée, l'unique récompense et l'unique profit attachés
à un si dur labeur' (*MD*, 13). In this instance *pain noir*
symbolizes both the indigence of the peasant and the inequity
of a social system which reduces a man to such an ignominous
state – an obvious irony since bread is ubiquitously considered the fundamental element of the peasant diet. An important theme in Sand's gastro-thematics grows out of this
reference to *pain noir*: namely, the relation between food
and work. Strenuous activity stimulates the appetite, so
workers require enormous quantities of food to subsist. Yet
these same workers fall victim to an economic indignity because they do not always reap the benefits of their labour.
Sand does not hesitate to make the inequality between owner
and producer evident; the latter, though virtually surrounded
by *les nourritures terrestres*, rarely gets the chance to
enjoy them: 'Ces richesses qui couvrent le sol, ces moissons,
ces fruits, ces bestiaux orgueilleux qui s'engraissent dans
les longues herbes, sont la propriété de quelques-uns et les
instruments de la fatigue et de l'esclavage' (*MD*, 13). The
peasant ever remains an exile in the earthly garden in which
he labours while the capitalist enjoys the country life and
collects the fruits from the garden which the peasant has
cultivated: 'L'homme de loisir vient chercher un peu d'air
et de santé dans le séjour de la campagne, puis il retourne
dépenser dans les grandes villes le fruit du travail de ses
vassaux' (*MD*, 14).

In another eating episode, which may be read in contrast
to the average meal scenes in her novels and in conformity
with Balzac's meal thematic, Sand transports the reader from
the centre to the perimeter of her peasant ideal; that is,
she introduces him to the sphere of the bourgeoisie, a social

class which utlizes food as a sign of wealth and prosperity.
In *La Mare au diable* the widower Germain's father-in-law
has told him to seek out a new wife to care for his child,
and accordingly has made arrangements for Germain to meet
the daughter of a friend, Père Léonard. When Germain arrives
at the Léonard home he finds other pretenders to Mlle
Léonard's hand gathered at the family table, which is replete
with food and wine, an obvious display designed to attract
suitors: 'Les trois prétendants étaient assis, à une table
chargée de vins et de viandes, qui étaient là en permanance
pour eux toute la matinée du dimanche; car le père Léonard
aimait à faire montrer de sa richesse, et la veuve n'était
pas fâchée non plus d'étaler sa belle vaisselle, et de tenir
table comme une rentière' (*MD*, 97). As in many depictions
of bourgeois and aristocratic meals in Sand's novels, this
one signals the prostitution of nature's bounty, for food
has lost its significance as substance only to acquire a
metonymic status as currency.[2]

The use of food as a metonym of money also occurs in *Le
Meunier d'Angibault* where Sand chooses to portray the bourgeoisie in terms of the social importance it attributes to
eating: 'Aucune idée sociale, aucun sentiment de progrès ne
les soutient. La digestion devient l'affaire de leur vie
...'[3] This relation between food and digestion is reminiscent
of M. Grandet's 'you are what you eat,' and in the novels
of Sand and Balzac appetite symbolizes the cupidity of the
Bourgeois, his endeavour to acquire, even hoard, the very
products of nature and transform them into currency. The
word *digestion* in this context suggests both material and
alimentary assimilation; just as the Bourgeois tends to
amass money so is he also inclined to intemperance in food
and drink, a vice which makes him susceptible to a form of
physical decadence: 'Mais il suffisait de voir ses yeux un
peu bridés, son vaste abdomen, son nez luisant, et le trem-
blement nerveux que l'habitude du coup du matin (c'est-à-
dire les deux bouteilles de vin blanc à jeun en guise de
café), donnait à sa main robuste, pour présager l'époque
prochaine où cet homme si dispos, si matinal, si prévoyant
et si impitoyable en affaires, perdrait la santé, la mémoire,
le jugement et jusqu'à la dureté de son âme, pour devenir
un ivrogne épuisé ...' (*MA*, 78).

It should be evident that Sand frequently uses gastronomical attitudes and preoccupations to symbolize the vices
of the Bourgeois, yet she maintains this particular gastro-
culinary symbolism in positive form when discussing the
characteristics of the peasant. In Sand's novels peasants

are naturally virtuous, and the peasant woman in particular
is idealized because of her knowledge of good nourishment,
her simple manner of preparing foods, her modest appetite,
and her capacity for understanding the alimentary needs of
others. Perhaps the finest expression of the ideal peasant
woman occurs in *La Mare au diable* where la petite Marie embodies the principle that a *paysanne* is above all a good
mother and a good cook, not a *gourmande*. Germain, the widowed
hero of the novel, carefully observes Marie's actions and
attitudes to determine whether she would make a good mother
for his child; most frequently his attention focuses on her
gastronomical and culinary savoir-faire. The peasant woman
is ever cognizant of and attentive to the needs of others;
she is especially aware of proper nourishment for children.
When Germain's son completes a hearty meal, Marie reveals
her perception of the 'eat to work' ethic as she reiterates
a rural truism: 'Tenez, voyez comme il s'y prend! Oh! ce
sera aussi un rude laboureur!' (*MD*, 71). Unlike the Bourgeois, who often indulges himself to excess for the sheer
delight of supping, Marie eats only when she is hungry; on
one occasion, for example, Germain offers to buy her a meal,
but she refuses, saying: '-Oh! je n'avais pas faim, j'avais
trop de peine! et je vous jure qu'à présent encore je ne
sens aucune envie de manger' (*MD*, 56). Then, on another occasion, references to the eating habits of the *paysanne* as
contrasted to those of the *paysan* are used to reveal the
peasant woman's gastronomical ethic, and, by extension, her
fundamental generosity. Germain again wishes to provide her
with a hearty repast, but she replies: 'Je ne suis pas ha-
bituée, comme vous, à faire quatre repas, et j'ai été tant
de fois me coucher sans souper, qu'une fois de plus ne
m'étonne guère' (*MD*, 67). Finally, Marie's culinary dexter-
ity becomes manifest, to Germain's pleasure, when en route
to a distant village they find themselves in a remote area
of the forest at dinner time. The ensuing conversation illustrates the peasant woman's culinary ingenuity and her
ability to cope with a difficult situation on the spur of
the moment:

> - Vous avez six perdrix et un lièvre! Je pense qu'il ne
> vous faut pas tout cela pour vous rassasier?
> - Mais faire cuire cela ici, sans broche et sans landiers,
> ça deviendrait du charbon!
> - Non pas, dit la petite Marie; je me charge de vous le
> faire cuire sous la cendre sans goût de fumée. Est-ce que
> vous n'avez jamais attrapé d'alouettes dans les champs,

et que vous ne les avez pas fait cuire entre deux pierres?
Ah! c'est vrai, j'oublie que vous n'avez pas été plumer
l'autre pour me montrer!

(*MD*, 67-8)

*Toward a Natural Symbolism: Meals as a Manifestation of
Rural Customs*

It was earlier stated that Sand uses the meal thematic in
order to transmit an ideological message whose purpose is
to demythify bourgeois values and to replace them with a more
simple peasant ethic. Certain gastronomical and culinary
practices of rural France depicted in her novels thus come
to symbolize a universal eating ethos which, according to the
author, is morally salubrious and therefore worth preserving.
Rural eating customs should function, then, as models for
appropriate social organization and behaviour. Certainly the
most fundamental symbol in this respect is the table, for it
is simultaneously a marker of social stability and of the
nuclear family. The table epitomizes the peasant's very existence: it is the locus of all social relations, a metonym
of the earth contracted to four legs, and, when it is replete
with food, an icon of the fields which the peasant labours.
  Sand's portraits of peasant meals, their gastronomical
elements, their daily rituals, their ceremonies, and their
attitudes toward food form one of the most interesting parts
of her work. Intimately familiar with the province of Berry,
Sand is at her best when describing these people at work and
at home. Her firsthand knowledge of the peasant and her belief in his natural virtues, especially as they relate to
Christian morality, account for her dual interest in depicting regional manners and their importance for her Christian
Socialist ideas. In many of her dining episodes Sand's interests centre on the obvious concern of providing local
colour and introducing rural life to the reading public of
her time. But these superficial cares pale before her most
basic humanitarian interests. Unlike many of her contemporaries, Sand rarely portrays intimate meals or highly stylized dinners; she uses meal situations not only to demonstrate the interaction between individuals and (above all)
between groups, but also to exploit ideologically the historical symbolic function of the meal in its ritualistic
context. In essence, Sand endeavours to transpose the agape
principle by superimposing the ancient symbolism of the
fraternal meal onto contemporary society. This transposition
then becomes the model for a new ideology.

Since work and food form the two poles of the peasant's existence, the family table and the community festival offer him his only respite from his ceaseless chores. At the table the ploughman can forget his daily toils and socialize no matter how simple the company. In *François le Champi*, for instance, a heavy workload keeps François away from Madeleine for most of the day, so, naturally, the table becomes the focal point in all their reunions: 'Mais il n'en faisait pas de chagrin, parce qu'en travaillant il se disait que c'était pour elle, et qu'il serait bien récompensé par le plaisir de la voir aux repas.'[4] As regards family life, all important decisions are debated and made at the table, with nuptial arrangements being among the most common topics discussed while supping. In *La Mare au diable*, le père Maurice ponders Germain's future as they eat; similarly, he had previously made plans for Germain to meet le père Léonard's daughter when the two dined together at an agricultural fair. However, in a variation on this theme, a turn of plot in *Les Maîtres Sonneurs* finds Joseph and Huriel in friendly rivalry for Brulette's hand, but the former's morose nature has led all concerned to prefer Huriel. The narrator, a participant in the events of the story, relates the scene: 'Quand je revins, je trouvai le Grand-Bûcheux [Huriel's father], Joseph et Huriel attablés ensemble. Ils m'appalèrent, et je me mis à souper avec eux, me prêtant à manger, boire, causer et chanter pour éviter l'éclat du dépit qui aurait pu s'amasser dans les discours dont Brulette aurait été le sujet' (italics mine).[5] A dispute ensues because of Joseph's refusal to give up his claim to Brulette; the argument is all the more unsettling because it occurs in an eating situation and, as such, violates normal codes of comportment. Such conditions cannot prevail at mealtime; the 'overturned' table must be set aright; stability must be restored. Appropriately, the family reconciles its differences during the next meal:

> Quand nous fûmes au repas, nous nous sentions tous soulagés de l'appréhension de la veille, par rapport à la fâcherie d'Huriel et de Joseph, et, comme Thérence montrait bien, soit en sa présence, soit en son absence, qu'elle n'avait pour lui aucun ressentiment, bon ou mauvais, du passé, je me trouvais, ainsi qu'Huriel et le Grend-Bûcheux, en idées riantes et tranquilles ... Nous étions là comme une seule famille ...
>
> (MS, 401)

George Sand draws many short sketches of peasant and rural eating customs to embellish the main portrait of meal scenes and to offset the connotations of Parisian bourgeois meals. In all these country dining episodes Sand pays little attention to social affectation so that she can give greater emphasis to the provincial table. She thus focuses her gaze on rural eating customs in the belief that there exists a natural correspondence between them and her own socialist ideology; consequently, by extension, she uses pastoral eating practices to symbolize peasant virtues. One of the main characteristics of the *Berrichon,* whose customs Sand knows intimately, is his lack of haste and a healthy respect for natural rhythms: 'Les paysans ne mangent pas vite, et le Petit Pierre avait si grand appétit qu'il se passa bien une heure avant que Germain pût songer à se remettre en route' (*MD*, 57). In *Jeanne*, a dinner at the home of Mme de Boussac serves the double purpose of ironizing aristocratic arrogance and idealizing peasant simplicity. The meal is taken in mixed company, and for the most part the interpersonal contacts at the table emphasize the gap between the classes whereas food and service show a delightful blend of unaffected elegance and natural charm:

> On était au dessert. C'était le départment de Jeanne. Elle entra apportant des corbeilles de pommes, de poires et de raisin admirablement conservés et arrangés avec art dans la mousse. Habillée en paysanne, avec beaucoup de propriété, les manches retroussées jusqu'au coude pour être plus adroite, elle allongea ses beaux bras blancs pour poser, au milieu de la table, un large fromage à la crême qu'elle venait de battre et de délayer à la hâte. Son teint était animé. Elle se pencha pour servir la table, sans méfiance et sans affectation ...[6]

In conformity with Sand's ideology, Jeanne is made to symbolize peasant modesty and informality; she is at once a capable culinary artisan and a refreshingly ingenuous person. All gastro-signs in this passage point to rural restraint, natural fare, and unpretentious conduct: on the one hand, they function to nullify aristocratic sophistication and snobbery; on the other, they operate as part of a suasive rhetoric which is used to propagate the socially exemplary attributes of the peasant.

The third element in the triad of symbols generated from rural eating customs may be labelled the nourishment principle

Essentially, it belongs to a metonymical system wherein food correlates not so much with currency as in Balzac's gastro-thematics but with work and physical activity. The emphasis peasants place on the nourishment principle in Sand's novels projects their knowledge that food is fuel: it enables one to work, to accomplish his daily task. In order to produce, one must consume. This elementary law of nature is repeated over and over again by Sand's characters. Moreover, being intimately related to the concept of work or physical activity, the natural appetite of her peasants lends itself to contrast with the sophisticated, often jaded, appetite of Balzac's characters. The narrator in *La Mare au diable*, for example, describes Germain's enthusiasm for food in relation to work, maintaining that he eats '... avec un appétit de laboureur ...' (*MD*, 69). Similarly, a rural truism has it that a child who eats with abandon shows signs of becoming a good worker.

Figuring as part of the food/work metonym, the journey is one of the most common activities with which the peasant associates hunger. Certainly, this concept is not unusual in any way, but the peasant custom of dining outdoors is radically different from the bourgeois and aristocratic custom of stopping at inns along the roadside. In a scene in *La Mare au diable* which finds Germain, Petit-Pierre, and la petite Marie en route to a distant village, the narrator takes the opportunity to comment on the natural inducement of appetite: 'Quand on eut avisé à cette précaution, Germain remit la jument au trot, et Petit-Pierre était si joyeux, qu'il ne s'aperçut pas tout de suite qu'il n'avait pas dîné: mais le mouvement du cheval lui creusant l'estomac, il se prit au bout d'une lieue, à bâiller, à pâlir, et à confesser qu'il mourait de faim' (*MD*, 55). A journey also provides the context for one of the meals depicted in *Jeanne*: when her guests arrive early following a long excursion, Mme de Boussac hastens the preparation of the meal because ' ... Les deux voyageurs étaient affamés' (*Jeanne*, 130). Conversely, when a traveller should normally show signs of hunger, his hesitation to eat reveals an inner preoccupation. After a long trip François le Champi is reunited with his family and served a hearty meal: 'Et voilà que, sans y songer, elle se mit à le servir fort honnêtement, à lui verser du meilleur vin gris de l'année et à le réveiller quand, à force de regarder Madeleine et Jeannie, il oubliait de manger. – Mangez donc mieux que ça, lui disait-elle, vous ne vous nourissez quasi point. Vous devriez avour plus d'appétit, puisque vous venez de si loin' (*FC*, 345). Finally, vigorous activity

usually induces hunger, so the fortitude of the 'superior
man' is signalled by the fact that he refuses to eat after
exerting himself: 'C'était un chasseur modèle; il n'avait
jamais ni faim ni soif, et les jeunes gens qui le suivaient
avec émulation maudissaient souvent son infatigable persévé-
rance' (*Jeanne*, 7).

In addition to the three primary symbolic functions of
food and eating just discussed, there exist in Sand's novels
two variations on the nourishment principle: the first recognizes the importance of food for maintaining a state of
good health: thus Sand often stresses the medicinal properties of certain victuals; the second belongs to an imagistic
system wherein non-edibles are regarded as sustenance in so
far as they provide nourishment for the soul. Food-as-medicine
coincides with the peasant attitude that food and drink restore health to the ill: food is nature's way of perpetuating
itself, restoring itself, curing itself. In *Les Maîtres
Sonneurs* the narrator and his father encounter a sickly
little girl during their travels; the father transforms
himself into a diagnostician of sorts when he comments on
the girl's condition 'Vrai Dieu, dit mon père, voilà un beau
brin de fille, et folle comme un jour, encore que la fièvre
l'ait blêmie. Mais ça passera, et avec un peu de nourriture,
ça ne sera pas une mauvaise défaite' (*MS*, 24). Similarly,
the triangle of friends consisting of Etienne, Brulette, and
Joseph forms an unlikely assemblage because of Joseph's bizarre nature. Brulette, however, shows her concern for him
by preparing food and reminding him of the necessities of
good nourishment: 'Et puis, elle prenait soin de lui comme
s'il eût été son frère. Elle avait toujours un morceau de
viande en réserve, quand il venait la voir, et, soit qu'il
eut faim ou non, le lui faisait manger, disant qu'il avait
besoin de se nourrir le sang et de se renforcer l'estomac'
(*MS*, 36). In *Le Meunier d'Angibault* cognac is used as a
resuscitative for an old man who has fainted, and is even
prescribed in medical fashion with precautions taken so as
not to disturb his chemical equilibrium because he is an
alcoholic:

Le meunier essaya de l'en détourner; mais le notaire,
qui avait trop étudié sa propre santé pour n'avoir pas
quelques préjugés en médicine, déclara que l'eau, dans
un tel moment, serait mortelle à un homme qui n'en avait
peut-être pas bu une goutte depuis cinquante ans ...

(*MA*, 332)

The second symbolic system related to food appears in the form of an image based on spiritual nourishment, as was earlier noted. In *Les Maîtres Sonneurs* the *Bourbonnais* woodsmen are renowned as expert musicians. A mysterious, somewhat diabolical, quality characterizes their music, which, they say, emanates from their very soul. Huriel, the son of the *Bourbonnais* chiefwoodsman, explains in alimentary terms the nature of his music to Joseph, the *Berrichon*, who has come to learn from the masters: 'La musique est une herbe sauvage qui ne pousse pas dans votre pays. Elle se plaît mieux dans nos bruyères, je ne saurais vous dire pourquoi; mais c'est dans nos bois et dans nos ravines qu'elle s'entretient et se renouvelle comme les fleurs de chaque printemps ...' (*MS*, 139). Clearly, in this scene the herbal properties of music are related to its medicinal qualities, since music has a restorative, revitalizing function. Huriel goes on to explain this his region is a source of inspiration where all aspiring musicians come to drink: ' ... ils viennent chez nous une fois en leur vie, et se nourissent là-dessus tout le restant ... Donc un jeune homme bien intentionné comme toi, disais-je à votre Joset, qui s'en irait boire à la source, s'en reviendrait si frais et gras nourri que personne ne pourrait se soutenir contre lui' (*MS*, 139). Music here becomes the equivalent of knowledge; the initiate must drink from its source in order to attain spiritual sustenance.

Ceremonial Meals

Not all meals, of course, have the sole function of satiating hunger or providing nourishment. Some of the most elaborate dining episodes appearing in Sand's novels, among them the regional ceremonials, offer the reader a profound insight into provincial rites. Outstanding in their documentation and local colour, these scenes often impart ethnological information, but Sand also uses them as symbols of universal eating customs and rituals with sacred origins which, she believes, should be preserved and practised. Two episodes of this type stand out above all others: the wedding ceremony occurring in the appendix of *La Mare au diable* and 'la fête de la Jaunée' taking place in *Les Maîtres Sonneurs*. At times Sand permits herself to be swept away in the ritual itself, its archetypal and mythological movements, momentarily forgetting the particular characters and events of the narrative. This occasional élan toward a spiritual domain prefigures her later concerns with the socio-philosophical implications of the concept of community.

La Fête de la Jaunée is a religious festival celebrated on the eve of June 22 by all villagers in the province of Berry.[7] Huriel, a visitor to the region, has the opportunity to watch and participate in a local festival. The ethnological aspects of the scene are emphasized because it is a ceremonial meal, and, as in most rural events, the primary activities consist of eating, singing, and dancing. The first phase of the meal finds a local woman, la mère Biaude, making preparations: 'La mère Biaude, voyant qu'il y avait là de l'ouvrage et du profit, avait fait apporter des bancs, des tables, du boire et du manger, et comme, de ce dernier article, elle n'était pas assez fournie pour tant de ventres creusés par la danse, un chacun se mit en devoir de livrer aux amis et parents qu'il avait là tout ce que son logis contenait de victuailles pour la semaine' (*MS*, 124). As usual, vigorous activity increases peasant appetites, and many other rural customs studied under separate heading also contribute to the significance of this meal. For example, all the participants donate food in a sort of symbolic gesture illustrating the concepts of brotherhood and sharing: 'Qui apportait un fromage, qui un sac de noix, qui un quartier de chèvre, ou un cochon de lait, lesquels furent rôtis ou grillés à la cantine vitement dressée. C'était comme une noce où les voisins se seraient invités les uns les autres' (*MS*, 124-5). Operative also is the practice of extending hospitality to strangers; in this particular scene each local family invites Huriel to dine at its table. The celebration itself continues throughout the entire night, and at sunrise, Huriel, in full appreciation of the earthly banquet, proposes a toast to the Great Provider: '-Amis, voilà le flambeau du bon Dieu! Eteignez vos petites chandelles, et saluez ce qu'il y a de plus beau dans le monde' (*MS*, 126). The festivity draws to an end as Huriel offers a prayer of thanks, thus setting an example for all to follow. Through Huriel, the mundane diversions of the celebration terminate in a sincere humbling of the soul, for he has not lost sight of the fundamental truths inherent in all religious festivals - those simple acts of humility which too often become obscured by the veneer of civilization. Within Sand's thematic, then, *la Fête de la Jaunée* has an ideological function since the meal complex contains all of the elements of a fraternal repast: sharing of victuals, commensality, and respect for the Divine.

The country wedding feast in the appendix of *La Mare au diable* on the other hand is a rich sociological digression on traditional marriage rites observed by the *Berrichons*. The occasion, the marriage of Germain and la petite Marie,

shows Sand at her best in documenting local ceremonial behaviour. The meal itself is portrayed in capsule form: 'On
remonta à cheval et on revint très vite à Belair. Le repas
fut splendide, et dura, entremêlé de danses et de chants,
jusqu'à minuit. Les vieux ne quittèrent point la table pendant quatorze heures. Le fossoyeur fit la cuisine et la fit
fort bien' (*MD*, 164). The customary activities include eating, singing, and dancing, but it is the fertility ritual
enacted for the newlyweds that occupies the primary niche
in this ethnological digression. This particular ceremony
falls under the general heading of the alimentary in so far
as the symbols employed in the ancient rites may be classified as foods or agricultural products. The ritual begins
with the placing of *la rôtie* (round of toast) in the nuptial
bed, a practice of which Sand does not approve, for she comments on the deleterious effect which the sexual connotations
of *la rôtie* produce on the morals of youth: 'Nous ne parle-
rons pas de la rôtie que l'on porte au lit nuptial; c'est
un assez sot usage qui fait souffrir la pudeur de la mariée
et tend à détruire celle des jeunes filles qui y assistent'
(*MD*, 165).

The central symbol in the enactment of the ceremony is
the cabbage (*la cérémonie du choux*), grown in and attached
to the earth by a sort of umbilical cord. This ritual has
its origins in ancient fertility rites derived from the
cults of Demeter and Dionysus, and the *Berrichons*, also an
agricultural society, glean their symbols of fertility from
their natural environment – the earth. Sand discourses on
the history of this pagan-Christian ritual and the development of its particular semiosis: 'De même que la cérémonie
des *livrées* est le symbole de la prise de possession du
coeur et du domicile de la mariée, celle du *chou* est le
symbole de la fécondité de l'hymen. Après le déjeuner du
lendemain de noces commence cette bizarre représentation
d'origine gauloise, mais qui, en passant par le christian-
isme primitif est devenue peu à peu une sorte de mystère,
ou de moralité bouffonne du moyen âge' (*MD*, 165). The reader may also detect similarities between this ritual and
those of the ancient Dionysian ceremonies,[8] especially in
the concept of the re-enactment, or the play, in which a
group of actors don masks and make sacred gestures: 'Car
c'est une véritable comédie libre, improvisée, jouée en
plein air, sur les chemins, à travers champs, alimentée par
tous les accidents fortuits que se présentent, et à laquelle
tout le monde prend part ... Le thème est invariable, mais
on brode à l'infini sur ce thème, et c'est là qu'il faut

voir l'instinct mimique, l'abondance d'idées boufonnes, la
façonade, l'esprit de repartie, et même l'éloquence naturelle de nos paysans' (*MD*, 167-8). The analogy between the
play (*la comédie libre*) and the feast is here made explicit
by the word 'alimentée': actors and amphitryons figure as
participants in a holy ritual; eating, by virtue of repetition and re-enactment, is a spectacle. Nowhere in Sand's
works is the theatricality of eating made more apparent
than in *la cérémonie du choux* wherein, by means of a total
participatory act, the celebrants momentarily cease to be
actors, transcend the mundane, and become the very substance
of the ceremony they are re-presenting.

Within the ceremonial re-enactment is an allusion to the
importance of productivity. The unproductive husband, a
drunkard, can be conceived of as the inverse of the peasant
woman's ideal; that is, instead of providing food for his
spouse through his work he symbolically devours her in an
economic sense. In the play she declares: 'Tu m'as mangé
mon pauvre bien, nos six enfants sont sur la paille, nous
vivons dans une étable avec les animaux; nous voilà réduits
à demander l'aumône, et encore tu es si laid, si dégoûtant,
si méprisé, que bientôt on nous jettera le pain comme à des
chiens' (*MD*, 167). The peasant is charitable but he is too
proud to accept charity; hence the importance of the *gagner
son pain* motif: being nourished by others reflects failure
and results in the loss of self-esteem.

Upon completion of the preliminary gestures, the actors
go out in search of the sacred cabbage, but only the drunken
husband is allowed to touch it:

> Sans doute il y a là un mystère antérieur au christian-
> isme, et qui rappelle la fête des Saturnales, ou quelque
> bacchanale antique. Peut-être ce païen, qui est en même
> temps le jardinier par excellence, n'est-il rien moins
> que Priape en personne, le dieu des jardins et de la
> débauche ...
>
> (*MD*, 170)

This pre-Christian reference is important because it elucidates some of the possible interpretations of the present
ceremonies which would be desirable in Sand's ideological
notions. For one thing, the feast of Saturnalia, held every
winter, embodied the idea that the Golden Age returned to
the earth during the days of its occurrence. Even more significant, however, was the fact that no war could be declared
(war is a symbolic form of autophagy) during this period of

brotherhood which found slaves and masters supping at the same table. In another sense this feast is a prototype of the communal banquets which Sand will use as models for an impending social rapprochement. The fundamental lesson to be retained from this episode is that commensality symbolized equality and community even before Jesus Christ. Unfortunately, during Sand's lifetime the practice of communal dining prevails only in the rural areas of France, and she obviously wants to revive and perpetuate it.

This so-called 'bacchanale antique' also resembles those festivals of Dionysus which took place during the five-day period in the spring in celebration of the vine. Blessed with peace and enjoyment, the celebrants gathered together for a play, a sacred performance in which all participated much as they do in the ceremony of the cabbage. The Dionysian festivals occurred many times during the year and commemorated the annual resurrection and ingestion of the god, the embodiment of the life force which, metonymically, becomes the fertility principle. The emphasis on the relation between the earth and fertility also appears in the person of Priapus, son of Dionysus and Aphrodite, who symbolizes both fecund virility and the fertility of the soil - thus the incarnation of the sexual and the agricultural.[9]

In the final stage of the ritual all the participants march to the bride's garden and choose the best cabbage. The groom then removes it from the earth (simulating childbirth) and they carefully plant it in a basket surrounded by fresh earth. At last, it is brought into the nuptial home where it is supposed to encourage prosperity and fecundity: 'Ainsi l'entrée triomphale et pénible du chou dans la maison est un simulacre de la prospérité et de la fécondité qu'il représents' (MD, 173). From there the groom carries it to the highest point on the roof of the house where it remains until nature destroys it. An early disappearance signifies sterility.

Aside from her personal interests in the traditions of her native province, George Sand makes an analogy between the ritual aspects of these ceremonies and their value as models for human unity and community. Implicit in these practices is the gradual transformation from regional gatherings to more universal means of reaching out toward one's fellow man. Sand's peasants have the necessary generosity of nature required to reconcile the differences between men: they are honest, virtuous, and gregarious. One immediately detects this concern for one's neighbour in the peasant custom of offering a gift of food as a sign of friendship. Sand's peasants, unlike many of her bourgeois characters, give food gratuitously as an expression of good will. In *La Mare au diable*, for example, le père Maurice instructs his son-in-law to bring a present to la veuve Guérin, whom Maurice wants Germain to marry: 'Tu mettras tes habits neufs, et tu porteras un joli présent de gibier au père Léonard. Tu arriveras de ma part, tu causeras avec lui, tu passeras la journée du dimanche avec sa fille, et tu reviendras avec un oui ou un non lundi matin' (*MD*, 36). In a similar incident la petite Marie offers Petit-Pierre some bread when she finds him eating sloes and mulberries. He will return the favour by giving her a flatcake showing that peasants often reciprocate with food. Let it suffice to say that culinary gifts and exchanges are quite common in Sand's novels, where their symbolical significance lies in the generosity of the act of giving, not in the implicit equation which the Bourgeois makes between food and money.

An interesting contrast between the characters of Balzac and those of Sand might also be made in order to illustrate the virtues of the peasant character. Those among Sand's peasants studied in this chapter belong mostly to the proletariat, yet they find pleasure in giving. Balzac's provincial characters are usually landowners who spend their lives hoarding. Herein lies the basic contrast between the respective visions of the two novelists: Balzac's world is based on differentiation, Sand's on assimilation; in Balzac's universe money separates men; in Sand's world love brings them together. Dining situations and attitudes about food are among the major areas in which this dichotomy manifests itself in the works of these two authors. Sand hopes for a society which will be reintegrated according to Christian-Socialist ideologies. She further seems to imply that an inherent analogy exists between the peasant's natural instincts and her own philosophical beliefs. Among the numerous virtues characteristic of the peasant, the willingness to sacrifice for others promotes an entire ideology of related concepts. As regards this particular study, Sand's ideological system rests firmly on four basic principles which form part of the peasant's code of conduct: hospitality, sharing, charity, and providing for the unfortunate.[10]

All these peasant characteristics belong to the same metonymical axis and share similar connotations, all relate in some way to both Christian and socialist philosophies, especially as promulgated by Pierre Leroux. In analysing these attributes, it would be appropriate to examine them separately with the understanding that the reader is well aware of their

mutual interdependence. Hospitality figures as a logical
extension of the food-as-gift custom, and it constitutes
the most basic code by which peasants live. Needless to say,
codes of hospitality are well rooted in Western culture;
thus it is only natural that Sand should wish to revive
ancient practices and to use them to set the ideological
tone of her message. In *La Mare au diable* le père Léonard
invites Germain to dinner in spite of the fact that the
young man is not interested in his daughter: 'Si vous voulez
sérieusement acheter mes bœufs, venez les voir au pâturage;
nous en causerons, et, que nous fassions ou non ce marché,
vous viendrez dîner avec nous avant de vous en retourner'
(*MD*, 103). Even the poor curé in *Jeanne* offers his meagre
provisions to the nobleman, Guillaume, at the time of his
visit: 'Il était près de quatre heures, et Guillaume, ex-
ténué de lassitude et de besoin, trouva que jamais hospitalité n'avait été plus opportune que celle dont il se voyait
l'objet. Presque sourd, malgré sa politesse habituelle, aux
empressements du curé, ce ne fut qu'après avoir dévoré,
avec un appétit de vingt ans, son modeste repas, qu'il se
trouva en état de l'écouter et de lui répondre' (*Jeanne*,
61). In contrast to the recipients of the curé's hospitality,
the antipathetic bourgeois, Marsillat, in *Jeanne*, requests
it, thereby illustrating a kind of transgression of the
peasant ethic: 'Curé, vous ne me refuserez pas l'hospitalité
d'un fagot et d'un verre de vin, car je suis glacé' (*Jeanne*,
67).

The expected hospitality between acquaintances notwith-
standing, Sand's peasants extend the same courtesy to strangers or foreigners. In *Les Maîtres Sonneurs* the arrival of
the *Berrichon* travellers at the home of le père Bastien,
the *Bourbonnais* woodsman, provides the opportunity for the
latter to be hospitable. Oddly enough the woodsmen have no
food to offer their guests as a sign of friendship; instead
they express their friendship itself. This eschewal of symbolization characterizes the *Bourbonnais* behaviour and demonstrates the propensity for natural simplicity which Sand
finds so admirable: 'Or donc, Tiennet, sois le bienvenu dans
nos forêts sauvages: tu n'y trouveras point du beau pain de
pur froment et des salades de toutes sortes comme dans ton
jardin: mais nous tâcherons de te régaler de bonne causerie
et de franche amitié' (*MS*, 178).

In Sand's novels peasant men and women often take on the
responsibility of an abandoned child, and in spite of the
fact that they have scarcely enough food for their own
children, these generous souls willingly share their food

with less fortunate folk, activating as it were the Christian virtue of sacrifice. *François le Champi* is the story of such a child reared by a peasant woman, Madeleine, who, even with a child of her own to feed, graciously accepts François into her home: ' - Ecoutez, dit la meunière: vous me l'enverrez tous les matins et tous les soirs, à l'heure où je donnerai la soupe à mon petit. J'en ferai trop, et il mangera le reste; on n'y prendra pas garde' (*FC*, 228). As in *François le Champi* a peasant woman, la Mariton, in *Les Maîtres Sonneurs* offers to take on the responsibility of two orphan children, Joseph and Brulette, yet a neighbour who is aware of la Mariton's sacrifice decides to take Joseph into his home in order to lighten her burden. Henceforth, all four sup together, signalling to the reader their bond of solidarity which is formed and maintained at the table: 'Tous quatre, d'ailleurs, mangeaient ensemble, la Mariton apprêtait les repas, gardant la maison et rhabillant les nippes, tandis que le vieux, qui était encore solide au travail, allait en journée et fournissait au plus gros de la dépense' (*MS*, 10).

As with hospitality and sacrificing, the code of sharing is not limited to acquaintances: the fundamental trust which the peasant holds in his fellow man becomes manifest by his willingness to share with strangers. In *Consuelo* the heroine arrives at a stream near a roadside where a young boy has stopped to eat. She becomes hungry as she watches him and offers to buy his bread, but he refuses, saying that he will give it to her: ' - Vous le vendre! s'écria l'enfant tout surpris et en rougissant: oh! si j'avais un déjeuner, je ne vous le vendrais pas! je ne suis pas aubergiste; mais je voudrais vous l'offrir et vous le donner.'[11] Similarly, in conformity with Sand's socialist ideals, Madeleine's culinary sacrifices in *François le Champi* serve as markers of charity and love for her fellow man:

> Madeleine pouvait, sans le fâcher, se priver de ses propres aises, et donner à ceux qu'elle savait malheureux autour d'elle, un jour un peu de bois, un autre jour une partie de son repas, un autre jour encore quelques légumes, du linge, des œufs, que sais-je? Elle venait à bout d'assister son prochain ...
>
> (*FC*, 267)

François does not fail to notice and appreciate these sacrifices on Madeleine's part, and he subsequently repays her in the only way he can: by work and devotion. Finally, this

idea of providing for intimates grows into the larger ethic
of working for the good of all mankind. In *Le Meunier d'Angibault* a Parisian worker sharing Sand's socialist beliefs
arrives at the mill of Grand Louis; the conversation between
the two men reveals the importance of human labour as it is
related to the nourishment theme:

> Ami, s'écria-t-il, le travail est beau et saint par lui-
> même; vous aviez raison de le dire en commençant! Dieu
> l'impose et le bénit. Il m'a semblé doux de travailler
> pour nourrir ma maîtresse; oh! qu'il serait plus doux
> encore de travailler en même temps pour alimenter la vie
> d'une famille d'égaux et de frères!
>
> (*MA*, 228)

In the most limited sense, the concept of work offers man
the opportunity to provide for his immediate family; however, Sand's cause is globalized here as the worker transforms the peasant ideal into the socialist notion of the
universal family of man. Equality and brotherhood result
from working for and eating with others. Grain and bread,
the noblest fruits of the earth according to Grand-Louis,
belong to those who reap and sow, not to those who acquire.
Sand's purpose in delineating these peasant characteristics
is to project them into the ideological domain of Christian
Socialism where they can serve as codes of conduct for all
men: these behavioural models taken in conjunction with the
pastoral feasts discussed earlier form the basis of the
fraternal order which Sand hopes to see realized in her
lifetime.

Communal Banquets: The Ultimate Expression of Group
Socialization

Perhaps the finest embodiment of this Christian Socialist
ethic occurs in the practice of communal dining. Above all
else the communal meal symbolizes the utopian ideal of fraternity: men working, sharing, and eating together. The
concept is hardly new, of course: the banquets and festivals
of the Greeks enjoyed a rich transformation under the influence of the early Christians. From the bacchanalia given
in honour of Dionysus, group feasts evolve to the agape
which Christians held together in memory of the Last Supper.
In Sand's social hierarchy it seems that the act of eating
together constitutes only the penultimate step on the road
to human solidarity, for the ultimate stage in the rapproche-

ment of the classes occurs after the meal, when a man and
a woman of different social classes sleep together. In any
event, the process of social assimilation becomes the desired goal, no matter by what symbolic gesture Sand chooses
to represent it.

The communal meal may be classified under three categories
in Sand's novels. Firstly, there are the natural or rustic
scenes which find peasants gathered at the same table either
for a ceremonial occasion or because that is their normal
mode of dining. Secondly, the socialist influence becomes
evident in the communal meals organized by workers' societies. Thirdly, the higher ideal of the Christian community
appears as the epitome of the spiritual banquet. Clearly,
Sand envisions the meal situation which promotes brotherhood
and sharing as the perfect force capable of destroying social barriers. A scene which finds noblemen and peasants
dining together, for instance, serves the double purpose
of changing formal social codes based on distinction and of
creating a forum where ideas can be freely discussed by all:
the table thus becomes the epicentre of the social revolution.

The first category of rapprochement meals, consisting of
pastoral feasts and ceremonies, may best be illustrated by
a set of contrasting episodes in *Les Maîtres Sonneurs*.
Taken together these meals function as a sociological contrast between the *Bourbonnais* and the *Berrichons*: virtually
the entire distinction between these two regional peoples
is based on their respective eating customs. Furthermore,
their attitudes about food and eating serve in part to reveal their lifestyles and local customs. But the contrast
also relies on ethnological and semiological elements made
all the more immediate because the characters present their
own opinions and viewpoints rather than those of the narrator, who is a participant in the action. This internal perspective lends both authenticity and objectivity to regional
peculiarities and reveals that the characters themselves
are aware of food and its rituals; in other words, they consciously use it as part of a semiotic exchange.

The first meal scene depicted finds Etienne, the *Berrichon*,
and Huriel, the *Bourbonnais*, discussing their respective
regional eating habits. In this particular case Huriel is
a guest of the *Berrichons*. For the most part, types of food
are not mentioned, nor are they important as signs here;
rather, Sand has her characters focus their attention on
the more superfluous elements of the dinner such as utensils
and tableware. The reader subsequently observes Huriel

admonishing the *Berrichons* for their useless luxuries:

> - Voilà des dressoirs, des tables, des chaises, de la
> belle vaisselle, des tasses de grès, du bon vin, une
> cremaillère, des pots à soupe, que sais-je? Il vous faut
> tout cela pour être contents; vous mettez à chaque repas
> une bonne heure pour vous lester; vous mâchonnez comme
> des b œufs qui ruminent.
>
> (MS, 101)

The emphasis placed on the manner of eating and the reasons
why the *Berrichons* dine as they do shows Sand's interest in
the anthropological aspects of meals. Since the meal is offered by a *Berrichon* to a *Bourbonnais*, Huriel's criticisms
of *Berrichon* customs implicitly indicate that his own people
eat differently and with less pomp. In addition to his critique of the sophisticated trivialities of *Berrichon* eating
customs, Huriel addresses himself to more fundamental issues
such as the duration of meals, the effects of food on digestion, and the problem of overweight:

> ... aussi, quand il vous faut remettre sur vos jambes et
> retourner à l'ouvrage, vous avez un crève-coeur qui revient
> tous les jours deux ou trois fois. Vous êtes lourds et pas
> plus gaillards d'esprit que vos bêtes de trait.
>
> (MS, 101)

Moreover, the *Berrichon* temperament, with its insistence on
diversion, is revealed by intemperate eating habits, the
moral being that eating customs exemplify lifestyles:

> Le dimanche, accoudés sur des tables, mangeant plus que
> votre faim et buvant plus que votre soif, croyant vous
> divertir et vous réconforter en vous indigérant, soupir-
> ant pour des filles qui s'ennuient avec vous sans savoir
> pourquoi ... vous faites, d'un jour de liesse et de repos,
> une pésanteur de plus sur vos estomacs et sur vos esprits;
> et la semaine entière vous en paraît plus triste, plus
> longue et plus dure.
>
> (MS, 101)

This scene, an obvious indictment of the dangers of too much
civilized living, accentuates the more superficial elements
in the lives of the *Berrichons* which Huriel - and through
Huriel, Sand herself - condemns: 'Oui, Tiennet, voilà la vie
que vous menez. Pour trop chérir vos aises, vous vous faites

trop de besoins, et pour trop bien vivre, vous ne vivez pas'
(*MS*, 101).

Huriel, by his insistence on needs as opposed to desires,
raises the contrast to a socio-economic level: all the ceremonial and stylized aspects of the *Berrichon* meal represent
the softness and insouciance which result from an overly
civilized life. These are practices which permit too much
luxury and leisure. In a more universal sense this critique
is designed to suggest society's misconstrued values about
social differentiation. Just as the novels of Balzac, and
of Flaubert as we shall see, often exploit the differences
between bourgeois and aristocratic tables and lower-class
tables, so this novel makes a similar distinction between
the peasant and the woodsman. The latter finds his pleasures
almost exclusively in nature and lives in temperance, without the need for luxury and diversion. He does not abuse
his body in gastronomical overindulgence nor does he reduce
food to a sign.

Much of the semio-sociological contrast developed by Sand
depends on the structural devices which illuminate it. Having chosen the dialogue to express the conflict, she can
naturally show the other side of the coin by having a
Berrichon answer Huriel's criticism. Etienne, in turn, de-
fends the values of his countrymen by engaging Huriel in a
series of questions destined to underscore the most egregious
deficiencies in *Bourbonnais* customs. Huriel chastises the
Bourbonnais for their coarse manners and crude eating habits,
implying that they lead a harsh life in order to economize
and accumulate wealth: 'Et quand tu auras mené cette dure
vie que tu vantes une vingtaine d'années, l'argent que tu
auras ménagé à te priver de tout, ne le dépenseras-tu pas
à te procurer une femme, une maison, une table, un bon lit,
du bon vin et du repos?' (*MS*, 102). Etienne's critique,
however, is a predictable result of conditioned social
mores: it represents civilization justifying itself. In
Sand's estimation, Etienne is obviously a victim of the
bourgeois fallacy: namely, the belief that social felicity
depends on how close one comes or does not come to realizing
middle-class values. Etienne can conceive of life only in
terms of his own ethic of acquisition and luxury; he thus
interprets Huriel's antagonism as envy.

Etienne's suspicions represent nature corrupted by society,
but Huriel's retort confirms the simplicity of his values
and reveals that they contain the most elementary truths
about life and happiness. Rather than *need* these luxuries
of the table because he has become accustomed to them, he

can enjoy them even more because he does not have them: 'Tu
me vois boire et causer, parce que j'aime le vin et que je
suis un homme. La table et la société me plaisent même beaucoup plus qu'à toi, par la raison que je n'en ai pas besoin
et n'en fais pas mon habitude. Toujours sur pied, mangeant
sur le pouce, buvant aux fontaines que je rencontre et dor-
mant sous la feuillée du premier chêne venu, quand, par
hasard, je trouve bonne table et bon vin à discrétion, c'est
fête pour moi, ce n'est plus nécessité' (MS, 102). Too much
civilized living and eating, according to Huriel, leads to
a jaded appetite. By contrast, he prefers a life of utter
simplicity - outdoor living and eating. On the more generalized level, an opposition exists between refinement, which
is based on need, and natural simplicity, which is predicated
upon contentment. The former concept, representative of bourgeois civilization, emphasizes external values, or the stylization of desire, whereas the latter idea recognizes the
importance of internal values, or spontaneous desire.

The second meal in the contrast, given by le père Bastien
in honour of Brulette and Etienne, acts as the counterpart
to the *Berrichon* meal. However, Bastien's meal interests us
here not for its ceremonial practices but rather for its
depiction of regional eating customs and the types of food
ingested. It is also significant to note, for both thematic
and analytical reasons, that Sand chooses to portray this
ethnological contrast in terms of meals and eating attitudes
rather than by means of other social activities of the *Berrichons* and *Bourbonnais*. In its most elementary function, food
sustains life, so it is somewhat ironic, if not surprising,
that such a basic act as eating has undergone a sophisticated
transformation in society. Because of this evolution, or, in
Sand's view, regression, from substance to sign, food and
gastronomical attitudes serve as excellent markers of the
degree of sophistication within a particular group. When the
emphasis shifts from the act of eating to the manner of eating the semio-cultural imperatives imposed upon the meal become apparent.

Whether for purposes of irony, didacticism, or both, Sand
delights in portraying the primitive culinary customs of the
Bourbonnais woodsmen in this meal scene. The sequence is
carefully divided into parts with each segment illustrating
a social or ethnological theme. The superstratum of this
particular episode accentuates regional differences between
the *Berrichons* and the *Bourbonnais* while the substratum
suggests the covert practice of social differentiation.
Furthermore, the accent on the communal aspects of the feast

and on the agape principle surpasses the more limited regional distinctions which prevail, thus generating and
modelling the context for Sand's idealized communal banquets.
  The immediately apparent differences between the *Berrichon*
meal and le père Bastien's feast concern setting and types
of food consumed. The woodsman's repast takes place outdoors,
in Nature's temple so to speak, whereas the *Berrichon* meal
occurs indoors. Similarly, the idea of sacrifice differs;
although both meals might be called communal eating scenes,
each participant at the *Fête* contributes food to the group,
sharing, but sacrificing nothing. Le père Bastien, on the
other hand, sets out his table before all his neighbours -
a gesture which signals both sharing and sacrificing. The
early stages of the description of Bastien's feast concern
the woodsmen's daily diet and the frequency of his meals,
but by far the most interesting aspects of this depiction
centre on the virtue of simplicity. In a sense the woodsmen
prove to be quite primitive by their habit of eating their
food cold:

> Ce n'était point avarice ni misère, mais l'habitude de
> simplicité, ces gens des bois trouvant inutile et ennuyeux
> notre besoin de manger chaud et d'employer les femmes à
> cuisiner depuis le matin jusqu'au soir.
>
> (*MS*, 188-9)

According to anthropologists, when fire civilized man he
showed his degree of refinement by cooking food, a practice
bespeaking the passage from the *cru* to the *cuit*, from the
exterior to the interior, which signifies his evolution from
primitivism to civilization. Moreover, the kinds of food
enumerated by the narrator and the almost animalistic rapid-
ity with which the *Bourbonnais* devours his meal are instrumental in producing the desired effect of culinary primitivism, at least by comparison with the more refined cooking
and eating practices of the *Berrichons*:

> On apporta de la viande grillée, des champignons jaunes
> très beaux, dont je ne pus me décider à goûter, encore
> que je visse tout ce monde en manger sans crainte; des
> œufs fricassés avec diverses sortes d'herbes fortes, des
> galetons de blé noir, et des fromages de Chamberat, re-
> nommés en tout le pays. Tous les assistants firent bombace,
> mais d'une manière bien différente de la nôtre. Au lieu
> de prendre leur temps et de ruminer chaque morceau, ils
> avalaient quatre à quatre comme gens affamés, ce qui,

chez nous, n'eut point paru convenable, et ils n'atten-
dirent point d'être repus pour chanter et danser au beau
milieu du festin.

(*MS*, 191-2)

The organic symmetry of these meals, then, adequately demar-
cates the differences between the *Bourbonnais* and the *Berrichons* by giving equal treatment to each region's customs.
Beneath the façade of Sand's impartial narrative persona,
there lies an admiration for the more primitive and spontaneous customs of the *Bourbonnais*. Living closer to nature
enhances their virtues and brings out their communal instincts. For Sand, these woodsmen are exemplary: they incarnate Rousseau's theory of the noble savage. In essence, they
may well set an example for the rest of society to follow so
that it can reorganize itself more equitably and morally.

In addition to endeavouring to activate the peasant ethic,
Sand attempted, under the influence of Pierre Leroux's social
philosophy, to lay the foundations for a society based on
the Christian principles of brotherhood, equality, and solidarity. Using the ideal Christian model of the meal - that
is, the Last Supper, the agape feasts, the Heavenly Banquet
- Sand hopes to make the table a paradigm for a future utopian society. Part of her ideological strategy consists of
reviving the past and imposing its socio-religious symbolism
on her contemporaries. Thus, in her novels, the equality
principle is elucidated by references to the religious conflicts in Bohemia in the fourteenth century.[12] Sand's
treatment of the wars between the Germanic empire, the defenders of papal authority, and the Bohemian sects, the
protectors of religious freedom, clearly places the problem
of oppression in both historical and gastronomical contexts.
The historical situation corresponds to the theme of universal oppression while the gastronomical reference is restricted
to religious oppression centring primarily on the question
of communion. By establishing her theme according to these
two ideas, that is, by maintaining the association between
freedom, equality, and solidarity, along with the possibility
of bringing them about at the table, Sand creates a model
for all her communal eating scenes.

Procope le Grand treats the religious wars between the
official Church, considered to be the oppressor, and the
Bohemian sects which were determined to exercise their
religious freedom of interpretation of the eucharistic rites.
The Bohemians are at odds with the Church over four principles

which they consider necessary to the practice of their
faith. Of the four only the first is pertinent here:
namely, the Bohemian demand that they be allowed to commune
in two kinds. The question is fundamentally one of equality
and freedom. The Bohemian sects wish to partake of both
the wafer and the wine, just as Christ preached and practised, but the Roman Catholic Church las long been communing under one kind (the wafer) and has literally 'retranché
le calice au peuple.'[13] The chalice then becomes the rallying cry and the symbol of oppression in the Bohemian's
battle for freedom. By virtue of its connotations, *la Coupe*
remains the symbol of equality; hence the oppressed view it
as a panacea for their ills. *La Coupe* may be identified
with the *Saint Graal*, or the eucharistic cup. Believing
the actual Grail had passed into Bohemia, the Taborites
assumed they were its defenders: moreover, they associated
it with the more general question of social equality.
Since the priests in the Roman Catholic Church communed in
two kinds, as opposed to the people who communed in one,
the latter began to envisage official Christianity as a
caste society:

Il est vrai que la Chrétienté officielle, c'était la
vieille société des castes, prêtes à se dissoudre et
que l'hérésie, la nouvelle Jérusalem, le nouveau saint
Graal, c'était le Peuple, son esprit, son symbole, son
avenir et ses destinées.

(*PG*, 6)

This equality principle based on the affective beliefs
surrounding *la Coupe* haunts Albert de Rudolstadt, a character in *Consuelo*, nearly four hundred years later. In one
episode he reflects aloud to Consuelo about the early eucharistic ritual of his ancestors, the Bohemians, explaining
the value of *la Coupe* as an instrument of social reorganization: 'La conquête de la coupe entraîna les plus nobles con-
quêtes, et créa une société nouvelle' (*Consuelo*, 133).
Albert's explanation of the struggles involved in the communion dilemma lies at the heart of Sand's social idealism
and reveals the connection between communal eating and the
Christian fraternity. According to Albert, equality itself
is holy; it is God's will that all men be equal and man's
responsibility to seek out and establish equality on earth.
For Albert's ancestors, moreover, communion became both
the symbol of equality and the catalyst for propagating it:

> Lorsque les peuples étaient fortement attachés aux céré-
> monies de leur culte, la communion représentait pour eux
> toute l'égalité dont les lois sociales leur permettaient
> de jouir ... La nation bohême avait toujours voulu obser-
> ver les mêmes rites eucharistiques que les apôtres avaient
> enseignés et pratiqués. C'était bien la communion antique
> et fraternelle, le banquet de l'égalité, la représenta-
> tion du règne de Dieu, c'est-à-dire de la vie de commun-
> auté, qui devait se réaliser sur la face de la terre.
>
> (*Consuelo*, 132)

For Albert the removal of the chalice from the people signifies a debasement of the eucharistic ceremony and serves
as a means of perpetuating social differentiation: '... ces
prêtres erigèrent l'Eucharistie en un culte idolâtrique,
auquel les citoyens n'eurent droit de participer que selon
leur bon plaisir ... et la coupe sainte, la coupe glorieuse
... fut enfermée dans des coffres de cèdre et d'or, d'où
elle ne sortait plus que pour approcher des lèvres du prêtre'
(*Consuelo*, 132). Equality could only be established by the
people's sharing in the eucharist, communing with both the
wafer and the wine. It is no wonder then that the rallying
cry of the people became 'La coupe! rendez-nous la coupe!'
(*Consuelo*, 132).

The fraternal repasts characteristic of the *compagnonnage*
movement are also used by Sand as prototypes of the communal
ethic. In the years prior to the Revolution of 1848 workers
were forced to organize in secret societies because of the
laws forbidding them to form unions. The purpose of these
organizations was to increase solidarity and thereby create
a labour force strong enough to be entitled to equal rights
and dignity within contemporary society. Recognizing the
dangers of the collective power of the working class, the
government forbade public banquets, so the workers established their own clandestine communities where they assembled
and dined together. These communities were formulated according to profession, consisting of carpenters, masons, and
various other groups which remained mutually exclusive. For
the most part, the *compagnons* comprised a brotherhood made
coherent by the equality principle. Appropriately, one of
the ritual acts signifying fraternal order was the practice
of communal dining. In *Le Compagnon du Tour de France* Sand
depicts a commensal workers' banquet at the inn of la
Savinienne in order to demonstrate how the equality principle operates among the members of the *Gavots*, a society
of carpenters:

Il y eut un moment de silence. La table était composée
de compagnons de trois ordres: compagnons *reçus*, compagnons *finis*, compagnons *invités*. Il y avait aussi bon nombre
de simples affilés; car chez les gavots règne un grand
principe d'égalité. Tous les ordres mangent, discutent
et votent confondus.[14]

Although such scenes occur frequently in *Le Compagnon du
Tour de France* it will not be necessary to discuss them in
detail since their ideological message is quite transparent.
As regards Sand's didacticism in this episode, it is important to note that whereas these meals demonstrate the principle of equality as symbolized by the practice of commensality, they are nevertheless ideologically incomplete because the guilds are mutually exclusive: a total form of
social assimilation remains to be articulated.

Once the individual elements of the equality principle
have been established, either in theory or in practice,
only the actual confrontation between the classes - and
their eventual reconciliation at the table - needs to be
realized. In many of her meal scenes Sand creates a situation in which people of different social backgrounds and
environments are forced to dine together. Here again, the
table proves to be the ideal symbol and locus of the process of rapprochement, particularly in view of the fact
that it had traditionally been a place of exclusion. Moreover, the characters involved in these confrontations are
quite aware of the symbolic significance of eating practices
and attitudes which had been developed for the purpose of
excluding others or distinguishing oneself: it is they who,
because of their awareness of the meal as semiosis, assume
the most important roles in the realignment of eating mores
by consciously endeavouring to change prevailing meal codes.

Sand is quite careful about the structural delineation of
her meals of confrontation. Frequently she uses parallel
situations, binary groupings of meals, or contrapuntal techniques in her effort to portray different perspectives of
the situation. In *Le Meunier d'Angibault*, for instance, she
employs a triple optic in order to reveal the respective attitudes of the peasant, the Bourgeois, and the aristocrat.
She presents the first major meal scene in the novel from
the peasant viewpoint: Grand-Louis, a miller by profession,
invites Marcelle de Blanchemont to have breakfast with him
and his mother. Sand constructs the prelude to the meal in
such a way that it becomes organically instrumental in revealing the socialist character of both Marcelle and Grand-

Louis. Their conversation, an odd one for a peasant and an aristocrat, evolves from the banal to the socially idealistic concept of equality, while the meal scene itself depicts the socialist principle of equality in practice. The table will be used here to test the validity of former beliefs and prejudices because it necessitates a cohesive action on the part of the diners as well as their awareness of the implication of this reconciliatory act. Following a short description of the courses - food is not an issue at all - Sand emphasizes the fraternal bond attained at the table:

> On avait mis le couvert des deux domestiques et des deux hôtes à la même table que madame de Blanchemont, et la meunière s'étonnait beaucoup du refus de Lapière et de Suzette, de s'asseoir à côté de leur maîtresse. Mais Marcelle exigea qu'ils se conformassent à l'usage de la campagne, et elle commença gaiement cette vie d'égalité dont l'idée lui souriait.
>
> (*MA*, 57)

At the conclusion of the meal Marcelle offers to pay for their services, but they refuse, saying they were given in good faith and with generosity. True charity is gratuitous. Instinctively, Marcelle extends an invitation to Grand-Louis to dine with her, a gesture which is of great significance because she belongs to the nobility. Grand-Louis does not accept the invitation at first for he fears the humiliation of social differentiation which aristocrats have imposed upon him. However, the rapprochement will indeed occur because Marcelle sincerely believes in equality and brotherhood:

> - Monsieur Louis, lui dit-elle, vous vous trompez sur mon compte. Ce n'est pas ma faute, si j'appartiens à la noblesse; mais il se trouve que par bonheur ou par hasard, je ne veux plus me conformer à ses usages. Si vous venez chez moi, je n'oublierai pas que vous m'avez reçue comme votre égale, que vous m'avez servie comme votre prochain, et, pour prouver que je ne suis pas ingrate, je mettrai, s'il le faut, votre couvert et celui de votre mère moi-même à ma table, comme vous avez mis le mien à la vôtre.
>
> (*MA*, 62)

Having examined the peasant-aristocrat relationship, Sand turns next to bourgeois attitudes. Again, she uses food and a meal situation to depict the bourgeois values of acquisition and preservation of wealth. The meal at Blanchemont castle, given in honour of Marcelle by the bourgeois Bricolin family, forms the counterpart to Grand-Louis' meal. The opposition exists on three levels: the structural, the social, and the economic. Since Sand's purpose is to reveal the respective attitudes of the classes in question, the social and economic differences may be treated in relation to their structural function. The first phase of the meal signals bourgeois miserliness and lack of grace: Mme Bricolin rarely serves dinner in her parlour for fear of damaging the furniture; the alteration in her routine at this meal makes her so inhospitable that during the second phase of the dinner her social prejudices surface and strain the atmosphere of gaiety. Learning that M. Bricolin has invited the miller to dine at their table, she reprimands him: 'Dis donc, monsieur Bricolin, est-ce que tu as perdu l'esprit, d'inviter ce meunier à dîner avec nous, un jour où madame la baronne nous a fait l'honneur d'accepter notre repas?' (MA, 103). This scene demonstrates a general tendency in Sand's novels – namely, that the true culprits of social differentiation belong neither to the peasant nor the aristocratic sphere but rather to the bourgeoisie. Most of her peasants and aristocrats, moreover, share noble instincts and social ideologies. It is Marcelle, for example, who insists that Grand-Louis be allowed to dine with them, and M. Bricolin also comes to the miller's defence by assuring his wife that Grand-Louis shows great honesty and integrity. In spite of the miller's virtues, however, Mme Bricolin violates the code of hospitality and thinks only in terms of economizing: ' – Et puis, comme il vient de loin, dit la fermière, vous vous croyez toujours obligé de l'inviter à dîner ou à goûter; voilà une économie!' (MA, 105).[15]

The final category of meal scenes exploiting the confrontation of the classes will manifest the potentials for brotherhood, as the confrontation between peasants and aristocrats, especially, evolves into a reconciliation on friendly terms. In *Le Marquis de Villemer* Sand again uses the theme of class conflict. In one episode Caroline, the governess of the Villemer family, receives an invitation to dine with them because the young marquis is in love with her. La marquise, his mother, offers Caroline a place at her table, but not without some anxiety about what might eventuate when the young lady is included at a meal attended entirely by aristocrats. On this particular occasion Caroline avoids possible embarrassment by rushing to her nephew's side when the latter becomes ill, a pretext for avoiding the dinner.

Nonetheless, a similar situation occurs when she and the
marquis decide to marry. Peyraque, a friend of the bride,
invites the couple to dine with him and, significantly,
the marquis accepts. No differentiation contaminates the
amiable ambience at this meal and the marquis even enjoys
watching Caroline perform the domestic chore of serving
the guests. The assimilation is consummated when the marquis's brother arrives, thus reconciling two nobles at a
bourgeois table and revealing their acceptance of a new,
more fraternal mode of existence:

> Quels cris de joie et de surprise remplirent la maison
> de Peyraque à l'apparition des voyageurs! Les deux frères
> se tinrent longtemps embrassés. Diane embrassa Caroline
> en l'appelant sa soeur. Il y en eut pour une heure à
> raconter à bâtons rompus, follement, sans se comprendre,
> sans savoir si on ne rêvait pas. Le duc mourait de faim
> et trouva exquis les mets de Justine, qui refit un dé-
> jeûner copieux, et que Caroline aidait toujours, riant
> et pleurant à la fois.
>
> (*Le Marquis de Villemer*)[16]

Perhaps it would be of some value to emphasize that the
most complete form of reconciliation between the classes
simultaneously involves a love plot. Certainly, many meals
exist which find men of different social backgrounds assembled
in order to debate their respective political ideologies:
in *Le Compagnon du Tour de France*, for instance, working-
class men break bread with bourgeois businessmen, air their
differences, and discuss the possibility of mixing the classes. Yet, the epitome of assimilation usually involves the
reader emotionally as well as intellectually. When Pierre
Huguenin, a carpenter, first dines at the home of the woman
he loves, one detects his embarrassment before an ostensibly
socially superior person:

> Il rougit comme un enfant, et se mit à déjeuner sans trop
> savoir ce qu'il faisait. Il acceptait et avalait tout ce
> qu'elle lui offrait, n'osant rien refuser, et ne craignant
> rien tant que d'échanger quelque parole avec elle dans ce
> moment-là. Cependant, à mesure qu'il mangeait (et il en
> avait grand besoin, car il était à jeun), il sentait rev-
> enir sa présence d'esprit.
>
> (*CTF*, 252)

The classic example of social assimilation also occurs in
Le Compagnon du Tour de France. After the marquise's coachman

has become inebriated and fallen from her carriage, Amaury,
a carpenter, offers to drive her home. This confrontation-
leading-to-a-reconcilation is set in motion by a gastronomical situation and is consummated on both the sexual and the
social levels. The entire rapprochement process begins when
Amaury shares his food with the marquise; his daily sustenance,
a loaf of rye bread, becomes the catalyst which leads the marquise to recall her past felicity. She then breaks bread with
him, completing a symbolical act of which both are well aware:

> Amaury ouvrit son sac et en tira le pain de seigle.
> Josephine le cassa, et lui en donnant la moitié: - J'espère
> que vous allez manger avec moi, lui dit-elle.
> - Je ne m'attendais pas à souper jamais avec vous, madame
> la marquise, répondit Amaury en recevant avec joie ce pain
> qu'elle venait de toucher.
>
> (*CTF*, 272)

With the barrier between them overcome, she tells Amaury to
abandon his forced respect for her, recognizes peasant instincts within herself, and even equates liberty with the
peasant's lifestyle. At this point the narrator intrudes and
underscores the importance of this mixed relationship: 'Il y
eut un moment de silence. Ce repas fraternal avait rapproché
bien des distances entre eux. En rompant le pain noir de
l'ouvrier, la marquise avait communié avec lui, et jamais
filtre formé avec les plus savantes préparations n'avait
produit un effet plus magique sur deux amants timides' (*CTF*,
272). Breaking bread together thus prefigures the ultimate
communion between two beings - the act of love.

George Sand's treatment of banquets and feasts is unique to
the extent that she develops her meal thematic almost exclusively in a provincial context. The geographical limitations
present in her novels (this chapter includes primarily her
rural novels) impose other restrictions on plot and charac-
terization, making it difficult for her to present an adequate cross-section of physical environments and social
milieux. The rural novels abound in scenes describing peasant life and pastoral simplicity, but they rarely depict
fashionable dinner parties in bourgeois or aristocratic
circles. For this reason, there are few situations which
portray hostility between opposing social spheres.
    In considering the limited nature of her subject matter,
the reader may conclude that Sand's meal scenes lack variety
and imagination, especially in contrast to the sumptuous
repasts earlier described in Balzac. After all, peasant

cuisine could hardly be called elegant, and farmers are renowned neither for their wit nor for their conversational
ability. All these factors would seem to indicate that rural
meals are rather dull, hardly worth the time to analyse in
depth; but fortunately, this cannot be said of Sand's delineation of country feasts. She uses eating situations in her
novels not necessarily for the sake of aesthetic balance, a
practice so prevalent in the novels of Flaubert, but because
they are at the centre of peasant life: working and eating
form the backbone of rural existence. These two elements are
part of a cycle in which the ploughman tills the soil so that
he may earn his bread, and then eats heartily in order to continue working. The entire process is a natural one, simple
and lacking any notion of superfluity or waste, since his
goal is not to amass wealth but to provide for his family.

By concentrating on the peasant, especially on his eating
customs and attitudes about food, Sand hopes to make her
readers aware of the virtue of simplicity. In a society which
had become so 'civilized,' she saw a deplorable disparity
between cultural sophistication and social morality. Much of
the division within the nation resulted from class distinction - equality and brotherhood were words shouted by zealous
young reformers but nowhere were they realities. Sand felt
that the peasant, often forgotten or ignored for one reason
or another, instinctively had these commendable qualities,
and that he manifested them particularly in his eating customs and practices. Consequently, she hoped to give her readers a glimpse of the ideal life much as Eugène Sue attempted
to do in *Les Mystères de Paris*, by exposing them to the rural
customs of providing and sacrificing for one's family, sharing one's food with one's fellow man irrespective of his
class affiliation, and being hospitable to all men.

It is certainly no coincidence that the peasant attributes
which Sand so admires are also characteristic of Christian
morality and socialist ideology, both of which enjoyed a considerable popularity during the years preceding the February
Revolution of 1848. Under the influence of Pierre Leroux,
Sand developed and explored socialist themes in her novels;
unlike the socialist theorists, however, she did not construct
theoretical utopias but integrated her progressive ideas into
already extant social structures - the rural peasant class
and the rising proletariat. They were to set the example for
all to follow for a reorganization of the society and a realignment of values: the peasants because of their inherent
virtue, the workers because of their insistence on fraternity,
solidarity, and community. All these qualities, ideas, and

tendencies which Sand endeavoured to portray are symbolized in her fictional meal scenes. Moreover, Sand's meal ethic progresses according to a spiritual plan: combining the moral instincts of the peasant with the fraternal inclinations of the worker, it develops from the pastoral festivals, with their links to ancient pagan and Christian rites, evolves to the communal spirit of the workers' banquets and the meals wherein social distinction ceases to exist, and culminates in a reconciliation of the classes. Equality, fraternity, community – all are characteristic of the agape, the supreme earthly banquet.

3 / SUE AND HUGO

An Alimentary Portrait of the Ghetto: The Meal as a Signal for Reform

The years 1830 to 1848 brought about a keen awareness in writers of the need for social reform. Novelists of the period - foremost among them George Sand, Eugène Sue, and Victor Hugo - were deeply committed to the idea that literature could well help the cause of progress and, in conformity with this conviction, placed their literary works in the service of humanity. Their response to rampant misery corresponds to a faith in Christian Socialism as the appropriate ideology to be adopted and transformed into viable new social institutions. For Eugène Sue and Victor Hugo especially, the fictional meal acquires entirely new connotations because the rigidly codified structure and the pervasive phenomenon of bourgeois cuisine cease to function in Parisian ghettos. The question confronting most of the characters in Sue's *Les Mystères de Paris* and Hugo's *Les Misérables* is not how well they will eat but rather whether they will eat at all. The very acquisition of food becomes the primary concern for characters in their novels because it is at a premium. These poor souls subsist at the absolute *degré zéro alimentaire*. Given these circumstances, the ideal 'system' is one which, first and foremost, keeps the people fed. Sue and Hugo directly confront the problem of starvation in their novels and endeavour to resolve it by focusing on the most primitive level of the gastro-alimentary sign, where the absence of food functions as a symptom of social disease and a signal for reform.

In *Les Mystères de Paris* Sue alerted contemporary society
to the horrors of the Parisian underworld and to the worsen-
ing problems of poverty. His sociological portrait of the
slums undoubtedly had an enormous influence on Hugo's *Les
Misérables*, and the success of *Les Mystères de Paris* undeniably encouraged Hugo to embark upon a similar adventure. In
view of the sweeping social frescos portrayed within the
body of their respective novels, Sue and Hugo may be called
popular novelists in the non-derogatory, strict usage of
the term. Yet they were also visionary romantics who used
their novels as vehicles of social transformation, calling
upon the literary sign, as it were, to affect the course of
history.

The great majority of eating scenes in *Les Mystères de
Paris* and *Les Misérables* affirm this commitment to social
reform and are thus designed to make the public aware of the
deplorable socio-economic conditions in the slums. It is
particularly worth noting that one of the major innovations
of both Sue and Hugo was to depict the eating habits and attitudes of ghetto inhabitants. Virtually all elements of
human refuse people their novels: the felonious, the disenfranchised, the poor. Moreover, according to both authors,
poverty, misery, and crime comprise an invidious trilogy of
social and cultural failure during the July Monarchy period,
the most egregious element of which is the perpetual threat
of hunger faced daily by the Parisian proletariat.

Sue and Hugo make an interesting contribution to the the-
matics of gastronomy in the nineteenty-century French novel
and to the use of meals as a gastro-sign, for they not only
employ the meal thematic as an index of substandard living
conditions but also initiate the reader into the kinds of
food which the poor are forced to eat. By virtue of its central and near-mythic nature, Paris occupies the centre of
Les Mystères de Paris and much of *Les Misérables*, enabling
the authors to underscore the Paris-as-Inferno motif which
was so prevalent in nineteenth-century French fiction. Paris
becomes a metonym and a microcosm of all budding industrial
societies burdened with increased centralization, ever-
widening disparities, and overpopulation.

Balzac, as we have seen, also explored and developed this
theme in *La Comédie humaine*, but he chose a different perspective by having the criminal penetrate the world of the
elegant. In Balzac's novels even the criminal is destined
for social success: there is little difference, morally
speaking, between a Vautrin and a Rastignac. On the other
hand, Sue and Hugo depict the poor in their own milieu in

order to effect, as Bory points out apropos of Sue's intentions, a 'démythification du beau monde' and a corresponding
'mythification du peuple.' Naturally this shift in perspective from *beau monde* to *bas-fonds* entails a correlative reversal in the semantic structure of meal scenes: '*Les
Mystères de Paris* assurent le passage entre le criminel
balzacien individuel, et comme minutieusement décrit, et le
criminel hugolien, obscure parcelle d'une foule obscure.'[1]
Food rarely differentiates between members of the ghettos
because total poverty reduces them all to a pitiful state
of equality. Meals, as may be expected under hardship, occur much less frequently than normal because most ghetto
residents cannot afford the luxury of indulgence in food
or adherence to conventional dining customs. Similarly,
restaurants and dinner parties have practically no relevance
whatsoever, nor do table etiquette, displays of silverware,
or elegant table settings. However, food itself becomes important in these novels by virtue of its very absence: to
a large extent, it determines behaviour, for its scarcity
leads people to steal or beg. Furthermore, conditions are
so bad in the slums that work is impossible to find; hence
both Sue and Hugo attenuate the theme of providing which is
so important in the novels of George Sand, for instance.
Earning one's bread and stealing one's bread cease to be
distinguished: a starving man will do anything he can just
to survive. Ultimately, dearth of food often leads the
characters peopling these novels to use food-substitutes
such as *absinthe* or *eau de vie* in an effort to provide minimal, though illusory, nutrition and momentary relief from
their misery.

Because the majority of characters in *Les Mystères de
Paris* and *Les Misérables* live at the poverty level, the
gastro-alimentary sign is reduced to its most elementary
types and functions. On the one hand, the prevailing type
of sign referring to food and meals used by Sue and Hugo
may be classified as a signal: by its scarcity or absence,
food impels characters to act or react in ways which are
not necessarily socially acceptable; they will do almost
anything for the promise of a solid meal. For this reason,
the semiotic structure of the gastro-alimentary thematic
in these novels belongs to the larger mechanism of stimulus-
response — the most basic and unsophisticated form of semiotic exchange. On the other hand, the sign-fuction of meals
and food in these novels operates at the ideological level
of the texts, where it is used to document the thesis that
poverty and crime are the direct results of an inequitably

organized social system. Thus, the semiotic matrix discussed
above is metonymically structured as a cause/effect relationship which, for purposes of this book, accounts for the number of documented instances used by both Sue and Hugo to
demonstrate that absence of food leads to crime or to other
nefarious forms of behaviour. In essence the biological
mechanism of stimulus/response is transformed into the
Christian Socialist hypothesis of cause/effect in order to
serve Sue's and Hugo's didacticism: namely, the utopian belief that conditions will be improved when the underlying
causes which produce them are removed or modified. Both writers, then, offer fresh responses to old problems in the hope
of persuading their compatriots to seek out new modes of action.

*'Le Ventre de Paris': Eating Practices of the Poor and
Disenfranchised*

Eugène Sue and to a somewhat lesser extent Victor Hugo use
documentary techniques of narration in their novels to portray eating practices in the urban milieu - particularly in
the slums of Paris. Documentation of total alimentary poverty doubles as a narrative strategy for arousing public
indignation and for inciting the prosperous to react and
improve the plight of their fellow man. Though the readers
of this book may well be aware of living conditions under
the July Monarchy, I should mention some of the most salient
material realities which plagued the capital during the
second quarter of the nineteenth century. The inference
that Paris was 'la cause et le coeur du crime' during the
July Monarchy period is well supported by Jean-Paul Aron's
comments on the poverty, unemployment, and overpopulation
which caused portions of the urban sector to deteriorate in
the midst of plenty. On Paris, Aron writes: 'Paris est gan-
gréné au XIXe siècle par une tragique misère. Les pénuries
de la Révolution, les guerres impériales ruineuses, le dé-
collage industriel dessinent grossièrement une situation
sillonnée, entre 1825 et 1850, de traits de plus en plus
sombres: l'invasion de la ville par les journaliers des
campagnes; la débâcle de l'artisanat; le défaut d'emplois
dans les fabriques récentes; le pullulement des désoeuvrés;
l'inflation des taudis, des cloaques, des espaces borgnes
et repoussants.'[2] On the ratio between demographic increase
and food consumption Aron observes: 'En résumé, tandis que
la population augmente, entre 1789 et 1846, dans la propor-
tion de 60%, la consommation générale demeure stationnaire

et la consommation par tête tombe de 67 kilos en 1789 à 50
en 1846' (*Aron*, 251). Finally, he comments on the *prima
causa* of this degradation of the many by the few: 'Triom-
phante, la bourgeoisie découvre à table l'Esprit que l'aris-
tocratie avait rencontré à la guerre et, mi-stupide, mi-
impudente, renvoie à la bestialité les ventres vides, les
producteurs réels auxquels, par politique, elle refuse le
droit au dîner' (*Aron*, 251).

In narrative terms, documentation of socio-historical
realities corresponds to the functional category called
informations, or explicit signification.[3] A predominance
of informational signs in a narrative further characterizes
the *récit* as belonging to the realistic mode. In the case
of Sue and Hugo, moreover, realism - precisely because it
reveals the living and eating conditions of the 'have nots'
- is further charged with the ideological function of rec-
tifying misery and malaise. Realism is thus transformed into praxis:[4] form is now used to shape a new content. The
degree to which substance is moulded by expression becomes
quite evident in *Les Mystères de Paris*, for this novel is
one of the early masterpieces of the feuilleton genre which,
by virtue of its length, allows for ample exposition and
documentation of poverty; so much so, in fact, that the
novel owes its impact to a veritable rhetoric of saturation.

It would be germane to this essay to outline some of the
sign-functions of *Les Mystères de Paris* as a *roman-
feuilleton*, not only because this genre encourages documentation and minute description but also because *Les Mystères
de Paris* opens with a meal scene which occupies the first
six chapters of the novel. This meal is too long to analyse
because it contains much extraneous material, but it is
worth mentioning that the meal context here serves as a
narrative cadre for the action which will follow. Consequently, it is by means of this initial meal scene that the
reader first encounters the main characters of the novel,
their personal backgrounds, and their common dilemma of
poverty, and that he is introduced to living conditions in
the ghetto. Depiction of the milieu thus establishes the
'underground' tone of the novel. At the centre of ghetto
life lurks the cabaret: Sue portrays it in Balzacian fashion
in order to underscore the intimate link between the characters and their environment. The cabaret - its unappealing
food, its solid metallic surfaces, its diluted yet colourful
spirits - becomes the metonymical extension of those who
inhabit the inner circles of Hell:

Le comptoir, plaqué de plomb, est garni de brocs cerclés
de fer et de différentes mesures d'étain; sur une tablette
attachée au mur, on voit plusieurs flocons de verre fa-
çonnés de manière à représenter la figure en pied de
l'empéreur. Ces bouteilles renferment des breuvages fre-
latés, de couleur rose et verte, connus sous le nom d'esprit des braves de ratafia de la colonne, etc., etc.[5]

The cabaret is both emblematic and symptomatic of life in
the ghetto: emblematic because it represents, microcosmic-
ally, the only locus of socialization in the slums; symptomatic because characters come to the cabaret to be cured of
their daily toils and disappointments: ' ... ils s'enivrent
au cabaret pour oublier les fatigues d'hier et celles de
demain' (Les Mystères, I, 255). Misery, in Les Mystères de
Paris, is indexed by the dearth of comestibles, and also
by the ubiquitous consumption of alcohol, which signals escape, forgetfulness, and boredom - a veritable spleen
baudelairien. Of necessity, imbibing supplants ingesting
in the slums: the poor avoid by drinking and drink in order
to avoid. In the presence of food, alcohol generally connotes congeniality and social rapprochement by dint of its
capacity to free inhibitions; in the absence of food, alcohol acquires an added connotation of hostility because it
now signifies withdrawal and dislocation from society.

The emphasis on the lack of food in Les Mystères de Paris,
and even in Les Misérables, leaves little room for authorial
attention to gastronomy itself: Sue and Hugo are reduced to
reporting basic alimentary facts. Naturally, food is mentioned in some of the more elaborate meal scenes, but they
are few in number; the profusion of courses so characteristic of bourgeois cuisine is replaced in slum dwellings by
a kind of gastro-penury. In spite of the need for culinary
and alimentary verisimilitude imposed on Sue and Hugo by
the economic situation of the proletariat, there are nevertheless several innovative references to food and to the
art of cooking. Sue undoubtedly assumes that the average
reader of Les Mystères de Paris is unfamiliar with the
foods he enumerates, for he not only lists the dishes or-
dered in one of the early scenes of the novel but also provides a footnote in order to describe the composition of
these dishes. When, for instance, le Chourineur, a character
in Les Mystères de Paris, orders an arlequin, Sue knows that
his public is not aware of the ingredients comprising the
dish and sets out to give documentary support to his reader

in a footnote which resembles an entry in a manual on contemporary cooking:

> 2. Un *arlequin* est un ramassis de viande, de poisson et
> de toutes sortes de restes provenant de la desserte de
> la table des domestiques des grandes maisons. Nous sommes
> honteux de ces détails, mails ils concourent à l'ensemble
> de ces mœurs étranges.
>
> (Les Mystères, I, 11)

The author's meta-commentary,[6] in which the gastro-sign
both conveys information to the reader and reveals Sue's
ideological posture, strikes us as being especially significant in the semiotic sense, for it is imbued with a triple
signification: first, the *arlequin* carries the economic connotation of poverty since it is destined for those who have
not even attained domestic status; second, it signals dislocation from the mainstream, from the prevailing culture,
in so far as the author deems it necessary to describe the
dish to his reading public; third, and most important, it
figures as a metonym of the ghetto, that is, of the hetero-
geneity obtained when people are thrown together by misfor-
tune only to form a 'ramassis,' an admixture of human refuse.
Sue inadvertently reveals his own cultural bias, which is
predominantly that of the bourgeoisie, by presenting le
Chourineur's description of the *arlequin* in an ironic tone
- with irony marking the social and ideological distance
between the author and his character:

> Quel plat! Dieu de Dieu! ... quel plat! c'est comme un
> omnibus. Il y en a pour tous les goûts, pour ceux qui
> font gras et pour ceux qui font maigre, pour ceux qui
> aiment le sucre et ceux qui aiment le poivre ... Des
> pilons de volaille, du biscuit, des queues de poisson,
> des os de côtelettes, des croûtes de pâté, de la friture,
> des légumes, des têtes de bécasse, du fromage et de la
> salade ...
>
> (Les Mystères, I, 12)[7]

Sue often has his characters discuss their eating habits
in an effort to inform the public of what the proletariat
eats, and also how much money workers and ghetto inhabitants
spend on food. Once again, these scenes are designed to accentuate the economic plight of the proletariat and the
deleterious effects of poverty. In the early pages of *Les
Mystères de Paris*, Rodolphe, the hero of the novel, poses

as a worker in order to familiarize himself with slum conditions. During a conversation with le Chourineur, he describes the worker's monetary allotments for food:

> - Avec ça, - continua Rodolphe - quatre sous de tabac,
> ça fait quatorze; quatre sous à déjeuner, dix-huit;
> quinze sous à dîner; un ou deux sous d'eau-de-vie, ça
> me fait dans les environs de trente-quatre à trente-cinq
> sous par jour.

> (Les Mystères, I, 13)

In a later episode Rodolphe queries Rigolette, a working-
class girl, about her living expenses:

> - Ecoutez bien: une livre de pain, c'est quatre sous;
> deux sous de lait, ça fait six; quatre sous de légumes
> l'hiver, ou de fruits et de salade l'été; j'adore la
> salade, parce que c'est, comme les légumes, propre à
> arranger, ça ne salit pas les mains; voilà donc dix sous;
> trois sous de beurre ou d'huile et de vinaigre pour as-
> saisonnement, treize; une voie de belle eau claire, oh!
> ça, c'est mon luxe, ça me fait quinze sous, s'il vous
> plait ...

> (Les Mystères, I, 366)

Two things are worth noting in this enumeration: the relation between the alimentary and the economic sign which is
made explicit in the statement 'quatre sous de légumes
l'hiver,' wherein food is quantitatively measured in terms
of money; and the socio-economic hiatus between character
and reader which is once again communicated by means of the
irony inherent in the viewpoint that 'une voie de belle eau
claire' is a luxury. Similarly, the reader cannot fail to
detect Sue's irony in a scene in which he has Rigolette
describe her favourite dish as a meal fit for the gods:
' - Je mets de belles pommes de terre jaunes dans le fond
de ma poêle quand elles sont cuites, je les écrase avec un
peu de lait ... une pincée de sel ... c'est un manger des
dieux ... Si vous êtes gentil, je vous en ferai goûter ...'
(_Les Mystères_, I, 366-7). Sue's irony is neither bitter nor
gratuitous, but rather has a didactic function in the text:
if Rigolette may be considered the eiron it is only for the
purpose of calling the contemporary reader's attention to
her deplorable existence, for his perception of the irony
of her statement depends on his privileged status as reader,
that is, as belonging to the socially superior class of

readers. The reader, by virtue of his own alimentary existence and culinary sophistication, recognizes the heterogeneous character of the dish described by Rigolette; he
implicitly understands that the ragout is an aggregate of
disparate elements and lacks the consistency, coherence,
and planning that characterize bourgeois cuisine: whereas
the latter signals a kind of cultural uniformity, the ragout,
because of its variegated combinations, connotes dissemina-
tion and discrimination, hence is the metonym of the ghetto
as the cauldron, as Hell.

Since life in an urban milieu produces its share of criminals, mental aberrants, and wayward children, it follows
that many unfortunate slum-dwellers will spend a large part
of their existence in prisons, mental institutions, or even
convents. Eugène Sue and Victor Hugo add a new dimension to
the thematic of food in the nineteenth-century French novel
by their interest in and depiction of eating practices in
institutions. From the ideological point of view there are
two reasons why Sue and Hugo render institutionalized life:
firstly, since utility and efficiency remain the major preoccupation of those who prepare and serve the food, institutionalized foods generally betray a lack of concern or
care for those who inhabit such places; secondly, both writers attempt to expose the irony, particularly as related
to prisons, of a situation in which food is provided free
of charge to the impecunious and to prisoners: the starving
commit crimes in order to enjoy the promise of a meal while
they are being detained. Such institutionalized practices
actually encourage crime. On the other hand, felons who
have money at their disposal are permitted to have food
brought in from the outside, a practice which makes deten-
tion pleasurable from a gastronomical viewpoint. When Maître
Boulard, a process-server in *Les Mystères de Paris*, is im-
prisoned, a friend visits him regularly and attends to his
needs. This episode initiates the reader into the 'prison-
paradise' motif. Supposing Boulard to be badly inconvenienced
by prison life, Bourdin assumes that his friend is unhappy:

> - Vous devez être horriblement mal ici, vous qui tenez
> tant à vos aises? Vous êtes à la pistole, j'espère?
> - Certainement; et je suis arrivé à temps, car j'ai eu la
> dernière chambre vacante; les autres sont comprises dans
> les réparations qu'on fait à la prison. Je suis installé
> le mieux possible dans ma cellule; je n'y suis pas trop
> mal: j'ai un poêle, j'ai fait venir un bon fauteuil,

je fais trois longs repas, je digère, je me promène
dehors.

(*Les Mystères*, I, 296)

For a *bon bourgeois* like Boulard, however, convenience alone
does not suffice; he expects to maintain his standard of
living even during confinement:

- Mais pour vous, qui étiez si gourmand, général, les
ressources de la prison sont bien maigres!
- Et le marchand de comestibles qui est dans ma rue,
n'a-t-il pas été créé comme qui dirait à mon intention?
je suis en compte ouvert avec lui, et tous les deux
jours il m'envoie une bourriche soignée ...

(*Les Mystères*, I, 296)

Before their conversation ends, Boulard asks his friend to
make sure the local merchant sends him an adequate supply
of *pâté* and a ' ... panier de vins composé ...' This scene,
with its references to the comforts of the good life, reveals to the astonishment of the reader that gastronomical
elegance and contemporary prison life are not wholly incom-
patible.

For the average inmate, moreover, food and dining are not
altogether intolerable either. Their circumstances differ
primarily with respect to the methods of distribution of
their food, not with respect to the types of food consumed.
For the most part, the prisoners' daily diet consists of
bread and meat, in addition to whatever they can procure
from the outside.

Chaque détenu recevait un morceau de bœuf bouilli désossé
qui avait servi à faire la soupe grasse du matin, trempée
avec la moitié d'un pain supérieur en qualité au pain des
soldats. Les prisonniers qui possédaient quelque argent
pouvait acheter du vin à la cantine, et y aller boire,
en termes de prison, la *gobette*. Ceux enfin qui, comme
Nicolas, avaient reçu des vivres du dehors, improvisaient
un festin auquel ils invitaient d'autres détenus.

(*Les Mystères*, II, 334)

So pervasive is the alimentary phenomenon that groups of
prisoners are permitted to assemble for dinner parties.
Sue depicts one such occasion which finds Nicolas, an inmate, and his friends gathered at the table to plot the
murder of Germain, a stool-pigeon:

Les convives du fils du supplicié furent le Squelette,
Barbillon, et, sur l'observation de celui-ci, Pique-
Vinaigre, afin de le bien disposer à conter. Le jambonneau,
les œufs durs, le fromage et le pain blanc dus à la
libéralité forcée de Micou le receleur furent étalés sur
un des bancs du chauffoir, et le Squelette s'apprêta à
faire honneur à ce repas, sans s'inquiéter du meurtre
qu'il allait froidement commetre.

(*Les Mystères*, II, 334)

Two reversals of normal eating codes prevail in this scene
and both are based on the counter-cultural mores of the
criminal element. Food is generally used as a sign to celebrate life, joy, and participation; here, the principle is
inverted and food becomes part of a death ritual. Similarly,
seating protocol usually conforms to an arrangement by which
the guests of honour occupy privileged stations at table by
virtue of their status; in this scene, the inmates adhere
to codes of protocol which are based on a hierarchy of bru-
tality. The murderer, by such standards, is the elite member
of the prison corps. Such a practice is the total inversion
and perversion of normal eating customs. The narrative depiction of the 'other side of the coin' doubles as an ideological weapon aimed at conventional society, for it confirms the vacuity underlying its cultural mythologies,
stripping them of any meaningful or transcendent status and
reducing them to arbitrary semiotic phenomena. If such is
the case, society can be restructured simply by imposing a
new semiosis on its members: socialism, as will be seen
later, alleviates the social oppositions and dichotomies
created by capitalism because it abolishes all forms of
distinction and private ownership and provides everyone with
food.

Two sketches of meals in other institutions merit brief
attention. The first takes place in a mental institution and
home for the aged. Sue's ostensible intention in depicting
this meal would seem to be that institutionalized meals can
work if care and concern accompany the preparation and distribution of food. The narrator of *Les Mystères de Paris*
echoes Sue's communal and commensal ideal in his description
of eating practices at the institution, where one finds '...
des réfectoires d'une admirable propreté où les pensionnaires
de Bicêtre prennent en commun une nourriture saine, abon-
dante, agréable, et préparée avec un soin extrême, grâce à
la paternelle sollicitude des administrateurs de cet étab-
lissement' (*Les Mystères*, II, 473). The second reference to

food in institutions occurs in *Les Misérables*. Unlike the
first, however, this scene imparts information on inferior,
often inhuman, eating habits. Hugo takes us inside the walls
of a convent in order to portray alimentary austerity. Meals
in the convent seem to violate the laws of nature: either
they are taken in total silence, thus nullifying the orality
of the eating act, or the Scriptures are read to the nuns
as they eat, forcing them to ingest as it were the underlying principles of their faith along with their food. Hugo
directs his satire at the severity of such a system and
finds it detrimental to the health of children:

> Les repas étaient revêches et la nourriture des enfants
> eux-mêmes sévère. Un seul plat, viande et légumes mêlés,
> ou poisson salé, tel était le luxe. Ce bref ordinaire,
> réservé aux pensionnaires seules, était pourtant une ex-
> ception. Les enfants mangeaient et se taisaient sous le
> guet de la mère semainière ...
>
> (*Les Misérables*, 510)[8]

As was mentioned earlier, one of the primary functions of
the gastro-alimentary sign in *Les Mystères de Paris* and *Les
Misérables* is to provide documentary evidence of extant social disparities: in brief, to force the reader to acknowledge
distance, dislocation, and dystopia as realities of his society. Many of the eating scenes in both novels, along with
the references to types of food consumed by the poor, to the
amount of money spent on alimentary needs, and to the very
locus of meals, comprise an inventory of the causes of crime,
corruption, illness, and despair. Neither Sue nor Hugo is
content, however, merely to state the existence of causes,
which were obvious to anyone who took the time to observe
urban life; rather they felt morally compelled to relate the
causes to their effects, thereby exonerating the destitute
of responsibility for their misfortunes while simultaneously
placing the blame on the bourgeoisie and the capitalist system.

*Actual and Virtual Effects of Starvation on Nineteenth-
Century French Society: Deprivation as Divergence,
Deprivation as Convergence*

Up to now, I have concentrated on the documentary functions
of food and eating practices in *Les Mystères de Paris* and
Les Misérables in order to accentuate the authors' thesis
that the social and economic infrastructure of the capitalist

system contributes to the malfunctioning of that system.
In other words, capitalism - because it engenders and perpetuates enormous disparities - becomes the cause of its
own destruction. Sue and Hugo were not content merely to
repeat this lesson, which was not quite so platitudinous
to their contemporaries as it is to ours, by inundating the
reader with evidence of deplorable social conditions; they
also drew a poignant inventory of the devestating effects
which poverty has on society. The portrayal of these effects
is all the more striking to the nineteenth-century reader
because of the kinds of responses they produced: in their
most passive form the effects of poverty might lead people
to beg, to withdraw, or even to destroy themselves; in their
most active form, however, they might provoke responses such
as crime or revolution which ultimately threaten all of society. In our discussion of effects, which also embraces
responses, we will examine how behaviour is coded in terms
of character typologies, socio-pathological syndromes, and
crime, and finally, how these effects are transformed into
new, socially acceptable causes.

It need not be re-emphasized at this point that food serves
as an index of character: examples of the relation between
food and temperament abound in all literatures of all times.
Nevertheless, when the food-character link is observed in
a collective rather than in an individual perspective, it
becomes evident that food is not only a passive marker of
the man; it is also an active agent which moulds men. Viewed
from this angle, the presence or absence of food tends to
create social types, groups of individuals who respond in
the same way to the alimentary phenomenon: hence, the abundance of victuals, along with the capital necessary for procuring them, inevitably produces a group which might be
called *bons vivants*, *gourmets*, or *gastronomes*; whereas the
copiousness of food, coupled with the financial incapacity
to obtain it, creates collectivities which might be described
by the epithets *misérables*, *affamés*, or *mal-nourris*. Essentially, social and economic oppositions of this kind may
broadly be subsumed under the headings 'haves' and 'have-
nots.' Prior to the nineteenth century, as readers conversant with French literature well know, the plight of the
'have-nots' was rarely depicted in novels: literature was
produced by and centred on the privileged classes. Sue and
Hugo attempt to reverse this tradition, but in order to underscore the fact of rampant poverty they had to eschew the
history of the individual, or rather they had to transform

the individual experiencing hardship into a collective type, a kind of by-product of the capitalist system. Both writers, then, have a tendency to classify their characters according to systems of binary opposition, both exaggerate segments of character to such an extent that individuals become stereotypes which are used for didactic purposes. In *Les Mystères de Paris* and *Les Misérables*, character oppositions are often established in relation to food or eating practices and appear as elements of three basic paradigms.

The first paradigm consists of the opposition between Good and Evil. Within its parameters, this paradigm contains an obvious moral component and a not-so-obvious metonymical component: the first is concerned with the question of food production (the motif of providing, to be exact), whereas the second relates to food consumption (specifically, the social context in which food is eaten). The best example of this type of opposition occurs in *Les Mystères de Paris* and it finds the Christlike hero, Rodolphe, contrasted with a diabolical child named Tortillard. Briefly speaking, providers are associated with Good, consumers with Evil. In the course of the narrative, Rodolphe, a wealthy aristocrat who has taken up the cause of the Christian Socialists, is portrayed as the Great Provider; he not only espouses socialist doctrines, he also practises them by devoting his wealth to the establishment of pastoral communes where food is abundant because everyone contributes to its production and dispersal. By virtue of his economic position, Rodolphe has always had more than enough to eat; following his conversion to socialism - an event which parallels Sue's own experience - Rodolphe thinks only of sharing his fortune and food with others. One of the members of the commune describes the 'master' in the following terms: ' - Figurez-vous qu'un jour notre maître s'est dit: "Je suis riche, c'est bien; mais comme ça ne me fait pas dîner deux fois ... si je faisais dîner tous ceux qui ne dînent pas du tout, et dîner mieux de braves gens, qui ne mangent pas à leur faim"' (*Les Mystères*, I, 251).

The contrast between Rodolphe's inherent goodness and Tortillard's fundamental iniquity is made evident during one of the meals served at the Bouqueval commune. Tortillard's father has come to Bouqueval to enjoy a life of serenity and penitence; for his wicked ways he has been blinded by Rodolphe and is now wholly dependent on others. His son, however, is a product of the slum environment and, until recently, has often been abused by his father. It is germane to this essay that Tortillard's enmity toward his father should be revealed at the table, since eating is

usually accomplished in an ambience of rapprochement and
congeniality. On the surface, Tortillard appears to be an
indulgent and generous son: 'Tortillard lui préparait ses
morceaux, lui coupait son pain, lui versait à boire avec
une attention filiale' (*Les Mystères*, I, 248). Under the
table, however, the sadistic young rascal subjects his
father, nicknamed le Maître d'école, to inhuman treatment:

> Ceci était le beau côté de la médaille, voici le revers.
> Autant par cruauté que par l'esprit d'imitation naturel
> à son âge, Tortillard trouvait une jouissance cruelle à
> tourmenter le Maître d'école, à l'exemple de la Chouette;
> ainsi qu'elle, il trouvait un charme extrême à avoir, lui
> chétif, pour *bête de souffrance* un tigre muselé ... il
> eut de plus la méchanceté de vouloir raffiner son plaisir
> en forçant le Maître d'école à supporter ses mauvais
> traitements sans sourciller, et compensa chacune de ses
> attentions ostensibles pour son père supposé par un coup
> de pied souterrain particulièrement adressé à une plaie
> très ancienne que le Maître d'école, comme beaucoup de
> forçats, avait à la jambe droite ...
>
> (*Les Mystères*, I, 248)

The 'underside of the table,' which is visible only to the
reader and not to those present at the meal, figures as a
metonym of the opposition between Good and Evil, for it calls
attention to the hidden forces which motivate certain individuals and groups. Deception, illusion, and manipulation
prevail in this scene: metonymically speaking, the table
represents society; it is a *point de repère*, a stabilizing
force, the centre of gravity in the life of an individual
or a nation. This table, however, stands on weak legs, for
the head and the heart are cut off from the sexual organs
and the legs, undermined as it were by the lower-body principle wherein the dark forces abide. The ideal space of the
table is utopian, euphoric, unified; it is the locus of an
equilibrium between the upper- and the lower-body principles.
The disequilibrium which is here metonymically expressed as
'le beau côté de la médaille' and 'le revers' is more than
just a character marker, it also marks an underlying disjunction in French society, a dystopia. According to Sue,
the overturned table must be set aright, it must stand on
firm legs, it must be grounded in an ethic of unity and community.

The dislocation of the individual self from the collective
self, the search for an underlying unit of purpose, forms

the basis of the second paradigm of character oppositions
centring on the psychological syndrome of alienation. The
coordinates of this paradigm derive from Sue's conception
of what constitutes normal as opposed to abnormal behaviour,
in so far as eating practices are concerned. The norm in
this case would be the commune, whose eating ethic is above
all founded on the principle of commensality. Sue often has
his characters digress on the virtues of living in communes
where they enjoy a sense of belonging and well-being because
they participate in a selfless, productive process. During
a meal at the farm the intellectual spokesman of the group
speaks of the benefits of the communal spirit:

> - Eh bien, c'est tous les jours comme ça: bon travail et
> bon repas, bonne conscience et bon lit; en quatre mots,
> voilà notre vie; nous sommes sept cultivateurs ici, et,
> sans nous vanter, nous faisons autant de besogne que
> quatorze, mais aussi on nous paye comme quatorze ...
> (Les Mystères, I, 250-51)

Similarly, the model farm provides its members with handsome
culinary and financial rewards: 'On devait être payé comme
nous le sommes, c'est-à-dire comme des princes, nourri mieux
que des bourgeois, et partager entre tous les travailleurs
un dixième des produits de la récolte ...' (*Les Mystères*,
I, 255).
  The abnormal, on the other hand, is defined in terms of
a deviate, disjunctive, divergent principle; it is comprised
of individuals or groups who are cut off from the mainstream
either because of heinous deeds or malevolent intentions.
One of the characters whom Rodolphe meets in the early
stages of *Les Mystères de Paris* is aptly called le Chourineur
because of his obsession with cutting. He becomes so intoxi-
cated with the act of slaughter that he forgets his need for
food and drink, symbolically cutting himself off from life:
'D'abord ça avait commencé par m'écœurer d'égorger ces
pauvres vieilles rosses qui ne pouvaient pas seulement m'al-
longer une ruade; mais quand j'ai eu dans les environs de
seize ans et que ma voix m'a mué, c'est devenu pour moi une
passion, un besoin, une rage ... que de *chouriner*! J'en per-
dais le boire et le manger ...' (*Les Mystères*, I, 28). The
hunger for an inexplicable vengeance is not confined to obviously disturbed or deprived individuals; it also extends
into the domain of so-called normal behaviour when, for instance, primal instincts emerge under extraordinary circumstances. There is an unforgettable scene in *Les Mystères de*

Paris where the execution of two murderers is symbolically
transformed into a grotesque parody of a cannibalistic ceremony. By acting out their cannibalism, their thirst for human blood, the individuals comprising the mob momentarily
suspend their humanity: their descent into Hell is echoed
in the frenzied pitch of their voices as they await the
execution of fellow human beings. The allusions to stupor,
delirium, and intoxication suggest a satanic ritual: 'Bientôt, pour ces têtes exaspérées par le vin, par le mouvement,
par leurs propres cris, ce ne fut plus même de l'ivresse,
ce fut du délire, de la frénésie ... ' (*Les Mystères*, I,
545). Sue's preoccupation with cannibalism is not gratuitous,
nor is cannibalistic symbolism merely an inference of the
reader, for the narrator in *Les Mystères de Paris* makes an
explicit comparison between cannibals and this mob in order
to underscore the transgressional, self-annihilating character of eating human flesh, whether figuratively or literally:

> Ces railleries, ces menaces de *cannibales*, accompagnées
> de chants obscènes, de cris de sifflets, de huées, augmen-
> taient encore lorsque la bande du Squelette eut fait, par
> violence impétueuse de son impulsion, une large trouée
> au milieu de cette foule compacte.
>
> (*Les Mystères*, I, 545)

Metaphorically speaking, capitalist society is a system in
which the poor are devoured by the rich: to live is to eat
or be eaten.

The third, and by far the most pervasive, paradigm consists of the opposition between 'haves' and 'have-nots.'
There is nothing new or profound about uncovering this contrast, even as it is expressed in terms of gastronomical or
alimentary imagery, since food has always been one of the
primary signs of economic status in reality as well as in
fiction. What is novel, however, is the fact that Sue and
Hugo have chosen to transmit the message from the perspective of the 'have-nots'; most prior depictions of literary
meal scenes had painted a portrait of plenitude. In describing the eating practices of the 'have-nots' Sue and Hugo are
attempting to ally the sympathy of the largely bourgeois reader and to rally him to the cause of Christian Socialism. Such
a strategy would be undermined were they to focus solely on
unsympathetic criminal types, mental aberrants, and the like;
instead, both novelists chose to delineate characters who are
victimized by society for no apparent reasons, characters who
might be generally described as unfortunate social types.

Many of these types will be treated in subsequent sections of this essay: for the time being, let it suffice to sketch out two of society's typical victims, both of whom are raised to the level of social species in Hugo's repertory of characters. Hugo evokes Gavroche who represents the ubiquitous *gamin parisien* and who is best characterized by his perpetual mien of hunger and malnutrition: 'Le gamin de Paris est respectueux, ironique et insolent. Il a de vilaines dents parce qu'il est mal nourri et que son estomac souffre ...' (*Les Misérables*, 602). Marius, the student, is another type destined to a life of hardship and potential hunger; Hugo also describes him by his eating habits:

> ... ou il balayait son palier, ou il achetait un sou de fromage de Brie chez la fruitière, ou il attendait que la brume tombait pour s'introduire chez le boulanger, et y acheter un pain qu'il emportait furtivement dans son grenier, comme s'il l'eut volé. Quelquefois on voyait se glisser dans la coucherie de coin ... un jeune homme gauche portant des livres sous le bras, qui ... demandait une côtelette de mouton, la payait six ou sept sous, l'enveloppait de papier, la mettait sous son bras entre deux livres, et s'en allait. C'était Marius. Avec cette côtelette, qu'il faisait cuire lui-même, il vivait trois jours.
>
> (*Les Misérables*, 694)

These particular characters manage to survive quite well, and even respectably, in spite of their difficulties in procuring food. Often, as is true with students, their predicament is temporary and transitional: they can hope for a change in the future. Such characters may be classified as documentary cases of hardship who usually bear with their condition and eventually overcome it. However, there exists another, more wretched group of characters who appear in narrative situations in which the documentary function of the food thematic coalesces with its ideological function. For these characters, who do not fall into typical groupings, poverty and starvation are permanent factors in their lives, so much so in fact that they become causes of undesirable behaviour patterns. In effect, indigence is imbued with a pathological connotation, poverty is now viewed as a social sickness who symptoms are, among other things, physical and mental illness, degradation, child abuse, inhuman working conditions, and crime. Accordingly, in their depictions of starving individuals, Sue and Hugo transcend the documentary

function of the food sign in order to propose an ideological function and to provoke a practical response to the
horrors of starvation.

Unlike Balzac, who chose only to describe or reproduce
various social spheres, Sue and Hugo attempt, perhaps with
some ironic intentions, to nullify extant forms of social
differentiation and to replace them with new social structures.[9] To this extent, most allusions to the food and the
eating habits of the impecunious may be read in a negative
sense - as metonyms of the void. Both writers thus portray
starvation as *le creux*: hunger signals an emptiness, a spatial separation from the object of one's desire. This distance is restated metonymically on the social level, where
the hungry are isolated from the well fed. Focus on disen-
franchisement serves as an ideological weapon which forces
the reader, i.e. the well-fed, well-bred individual, into
a sort of complicity with the author: it appeals to his compassion, to his capacity for action; it entreats him to
overturn the tables of distinction and to break prevailing
social codes.
    Prosperous humanity cannot deny the fact of starvation,
but it can choose to avoid action. This problem is especially acute because it is inescapable, though not necessarily irresolvable: slum-dwellers are condemned to the vici-
ous circle of hunger; children, especially, become its unfortunate victims. The overwhelming importance of this
problem in France during the Industrial Revolution forms
the basis of Hugo's introduction to *Les Misérables*:

> Tant qu'il existera, par le fait des lois et des moeurs,
> une damnation sociale créant artificiellement, en pleine
> civilisation, des enfers, et compliquant d'une fatalité
> humaine la destinée qui est divine; tant que les trois
> problèmes du siècle, la dégradation de l'homme par le
> prolétariat, la déchéance de la femme par la faim, l'at-
> rophie de l'enfant par la nuit ... tant qu'il y aura sur
> la terre ignorance et misère, des livres de la nature de
> celui-ci pourront ne pas être inutiles.
>
> (*Les Misérables*, 2)

For obvious ideological and moral reasons, both Sue and
Hugo present many examples of the deleterious effects of
starvation and hunger on children. In one passage from *Les
Misérables*, for instance, Jean Valjean reminisces about his
childhood; like all the unfortunate people of this earth

his early existence was predicated on the possibility of
starvation: '... les enfants Valjean, habituellement affamés, allaient quelquefois emprunter au nom de leur mère une
pinte de lait à Marie-Claude, qu'ils buvaient derrière une
haie ou dans quelque coin d'allée, s'arrachant le pot, et
si hâtivement que les petites filles s'en répandaient sur
leur tablier et dans leur gourlotte' (*Les Misérables*, 89).
The same problem burdens Fleur-de-Marie, an abandoned child
in *Les Mystères de Paris* who recounts how she was taken in
by the cruel la Chouette and forced to sell food in order
to earn money for her 'benefactor.' La Chouette deprives
Marie of her meals if she fails to earn at least ten *sous*
daily: the threat of starvation forces the child to submit
to abuse. In such circumstances, food becomes an instrument
of coercion, a means by which children are exploited. The
entire ethic of the nourishment principle is here subverted;
once again, poverty and starvation become the *prima causa*
of degradation, exploitation, and even crime. The evils of
child abuse are made explicit when Fleur-de-Marie describes
the meagre daily ration of food given to her so that she may
keep working:

- Le lendemain matin la borgneuse me donnait la même ration
  pour déjeuner que pour souper, et elle m'envoyait à Montfaucon chercher des vers pour amorcer le poisson; car,
  dans le jour, la Chouette tenait sa boutique de ligne à
  pêcher près le pont Notre-Dame ... Pour un enfant de sept
  ans qui meurt de faim et de froid, il y a loin, allez ...
  de la rue de la Mortellerie à Montfaucon.

                                        (*Les Mystères*, I, 15)

By comparison with Fleur-de-Marie, le Chourineur had no substantial food at all. As a child he frequently had to eat
non-nutritional parts of vegetables, scraps, and garbage
just in order to relieve his hunger. Probably the most egregious example of child abuse takes place when Fleur-de-Marie
must beg for food while la Chouette prepares *fritures* on
the Pont-Neuf. As a gastro-sign the *fritures* underscore the
evils of child abuse and attest to the disparity between
spaces within the same economic sphere: a dichotomy is established between the hungry and the starving. La Chouette's
neglect of Marie's needs contradicts the providing ethic
characteristic of rural folk, which slum inhabitants often
share, and results in a complete loss of charity. The dearth
of food, Sue would have it, initiates a kind of egocentrism
wherein humaneness ceases to exist, a moral vacuum in which
crime is bred.

In many cases the need for food becomes so intense that
the poor will go to any extreme to make edible whatever is
available. Edibility, then, becomes the minimum requirement
for survival. When these measures fail the impoverished do
what they can to make even the smallest quantities of food
last for lengthy periods of time, or they resort to the ingestion of non-nutritional parts of meats and vegetables.
In *Les Misérables* the extreme poverty of the inhabitants of
Dauphiné leads them to prepare their bread so that it will
be suitable for eating during the winter: 'C'est comme cela
dans tout le pays haut de Dauphiné. Ils font le pain pour
six mois, ils le font cuire avec de la bouse de vache séchée.
L'hiver ils cassent ce pain à coups de hache et ils le font
tremper dans l'eau vingt-quatre heurs pour pouvoir le manger'
(*Les Misérables*, 14-15). If food cannot be made edible, many
of these people will resort to eating decaying vegetables,
putrefied flesh of animals, or garbage. In actual fact, food-
stands in the ghettos were not averse to selling such products.[10] 'Des étalages de charbonniers, de fruitiers, ou de
revendeurs de mauvaises viandes occupaient le rez-de-chaus-
sée de quelques-unes de ces demeures' (*Les Mystères*, I, 1-2).
Similarly, in his flight from starvation le Chourineur takes
up a despicable trade: he slaughters diseased animals in
order that their flesh may be sold on the open market. His
disregard for life is symbolized in the contaminated earn-
ings he gleans from his trade: 'Quand j'avais égorgé mes
bêtes, on me jetait pour ma peine un morceau de la culotte
d'un cheval crevé de maladie ...' (*Les Mystères*, I, 26).
Hugo, too, delivers a message in an incident ememplifying
the degradation of children. In a very poignant scene in
Les Misérables a young bourgeois child absent-mindedly
throws his *brioche* into a basin as food for the swans; two
starving children who had been watching him immediately
rush to the pool, fish out the soaked pastry, and devour it:

> Comme les Cygnes arrivaient, la baguette toucha le gâteau.
> L'enfant donna un coup vif, ramena la brioche, effraya
> les cygnes, saisit le gâteau et se redressa. Le gâteau
> était mouillé; mais ils avaient faim et soif. L'aîné fit
> deux parts de la brioche, une grosse et une petite, prit
> la petite pour lui, donna la grosse à son petit frère,
> et lui dit:
> - Colle-toi ça dans le fusil.
>
> (*Les Misérables*, 1250)

In *Les Mystères de Paris* and *Les Misérables* stealing is
often the solution to the problem of hunger. The reader's

first encounter with Rodolphe and le Chourineur in *Les
Mystères de Paris* occurs when the latter attempts to mug
the hero in order to get money for food and drink. Yet, le
Chourineur explains that he has very mixed emotions about
theft; he would rather starve than steal food; ' - Souffrir
la misère et la faim plutôt que de voler ... c'est avoir du
cœur et de l'honneur ...' (*Les Mystères*, I, 28). This incident is not reported without a certain irony, for the refusal to steal frequently leads the more virtuous characters
in the novel into a form of slavery. La Petite Marie, following her release from prison, becomes the slave of l'Ogresse. In return for her services she receives food and
lodging, and more than her share of abuse: 'Les habits que
je porte appartiennent à l'ogresse; je lui dois pour mon
garni et pour ma nourriture ... je ne puis pas bouger d'ici
... elle me ferait arrêter comme une voleuse ... je lui ap-
partiens ... il faut que je m'aquitte' (*Les Mystères*, I,
24). In examining the circumstances which force the poor
into bondage so they can eat, one can easily detect that
the real crime is the oppressive machinery within society
itself. People must eat: to force them into slavery to do
so is inhuman and vulgar. Reduced to this lowly state man
is easily manipulated; he will tolerate almost any humiliation for the slightest promise of food. Louise, a character
in *Les Mystères de Paris* who works as a domestic, speaks of
the abuse imposed upon her by her master who subjects her
to gastronomical temptations: '... la femme de charge con-
tinua de me tourmenter; elle me donnait à peine ce qui
m'était nécessaire pour me nourrir, enfermait le pain sous
clef; quelquefois par méchanceté elle souillait devant moi
les restes du repas qu'on me laissait, car presque toujours
elle mangeait avec monsieur Ferrand' (*Les Mystères*, I, 400).
When Mme Séraphin, the housekeeper, decides to feed Louise,
she offers her bread accompanied by adulterated wine. The
poor creature is further disgraced when a soporific is
mixed with her ration of wine in order to facilitate a sexual assault. The misuse of food and drink as related by Sue
and Hugo accentuates the bondage issue and the oppression
of the weak by the strong.

If starvation may be considered an effect of impecunious
social conditions, it is also true that the desire to eat,
or rather to survive, can become a cause in its own right
to the extent that it prompts the starving to sate their
hunger in any way possible. Only too often this means re-
sorting to crime. Possibly the greatest contribution Sue and

Hugo made to the role of meals in the novel can be found in the emphasis they placed on the relation between food and crime. Their ideas clearly coincide with the socialist ideology on this point because they undeniably assert and affirm the cause-effect argument between the absence of food and incidence of crime. Hugo even inserts a statistic on the subject in *Les Misérables*: 'Une statistique anglaise constate qu'à Londres quatre vols sur cinq ont pour cause immédiate la faim' (*Les Misérables*, 93). Moreover, both authors add an interesting dimension to this problem by their belief that criminals are made, not born. A starving man, with no money to provide for his children, has no alternative but to steal. By placing the blame on society rather than on the individual, Sue and Hugo have a tendency to attenuate 'crimes' of this sort. In fact they frequently invoke cases of sympathetic characters who must daily face the humiliation of their poverty. One example of this type occurs in *Les Mystères de Paris* in a scene where the poor, who have been depriving themselves of food so their children can have more to eat, go to market only to witness the affluent buying superfluous snacks:

> Les malheureux supporteraient peut-être allégrement leur sort s'ils croyaient qu'un chacun est comme eux. Mais ils vont à la ville ou au bourg le jour de marché, et là ils voient du pain blanc, d'épais et chauds matelas, de enfants fleuris comme des rosiers de mai, et si rassasiés qu'ils jettent du gâteau à des chiens ...
>
> (*Les Mystères*, I, 255)

Society, that is bourgeois society, is the ogre, and, in the end, it alone will suffer for its indifference either by being victimized by crime or transformed by revolution: in both cases, there occurs a shift in perspective from eater to eaten. It is equally important to note that actual hardened thieves also steal to eat, a fact witnessed particularly by Sue, who in no way contradicts his thesis that criminals are made not born but who attempts to convince society that by perpetuating inequities it is doing irreparable damage to itself; it is, in essence, subverting its own ethic. Ironically, one of the major meal scenes in *Les Mystères de Paris* depicts a celebration which takes place in the home of a family of brigands and murderers who have gathered round the table for the purpose of revelling in their latest felony. So pervasive is the cultural practice of supping and celebrating that it remains operative even when other social codes cease to function. Nonetheless, the inversion of so-called normal eating rituals appears in other subcodes of this particular meal which reflect the transgressional aspect of criminality. In the first place the mother figures as the ringleader of the clan, and familial unity results from mutual participation in crime: the bond of solidarity between clan members becomes stronger as their propensity for crime increases. In conformity with this inverted ethic, Martial, the one honest son, is regarded as an outcast in his own family; his children are, moreover, deprived of food and made to haul the heavy bounty stolen earlier while their relatives adorn the table with it and sup in transitory luxury: 'Restée seule, la veuve s'occupa des préparatifs du souper de la famille, plaça sur la table des verres, des bouteilles, des assiettes de faïence et des couverts d'argent' (*Les Mystères*, II, 46). The bad influence of such criminals on children becomes a paramount social issue for Sue: deprivation of food and subsequent relief through crime are a constant menace to the honest upbringing of children. The author convincingly demonstrates how the machine, once set in motion, transforms a potentially useful commodity into a socially pernicious one.

Secondly, as the meal progresses through its various stages the image of the table as the centre of family unity totally disintegrates and the normal eating code of conviviality degenerates into animosity when Nicolas unsuccessfully tries to start a quarrel with his brother Martial. When this measure fails, the others attempt to make Martial's meal as unpleasant as possible. Perplexed by their inability to unnerve him, la Veuve orders one of her daughters to clear the table in a blatant suppression of the codes of table etiquette:

> – Calebasse, ôte le vin, – dit la veuve à sa fille.
>   Celle-ci se hâtait d'obéir, lorsque Martial dit:
> – Attends ... je n'ai pas fini de souper.
> – Tant pis! – dit la veuve en enlevant elle-même la bouteille.
>
> (*Les Mystères*, II, 56)

In this brief episode the table has been transformed from a place of harmony into one of hostility: the socio-ideological implications of such a transformation are particularly dangerous to a society organized on the model of the nuclear family because of the impending threat to the entire society when the nucleus dissolves.

This meal among thieves is the antipole of those meals served at the communal farm at Bouqueval. Whereas the Bouqueval community adheres to the principle of working to eat, the family of culprits refuses work in favour of crime. The members of the Bouqueval community live in peace and harmony, sharing with their comrades and enjoying the gastronomical fruits of their mutual efforts. Unity and self-esteem characterize their association; they eat festively on a daily basis. The entire process is self-generative and beneficial to all. By contrast, the widow's family of thieves lacks the spiritual unity of Bouqueval and remains intact only out of necessity. The criminal act, like work, constitutes a mutual effort, but one which is always in danger of disruption by a greedy member. In the dark recesses of the 'underside of the table,' to state the situation metaphorically, a latent hostility prevails and manifests itself in acts of cruelty and inhumanity; children, especially, are its victims.

An essential conclusion about the contemporary socio-economic system as it affects food and eating might be drawn from the semiotic network of meals in *Les Mystères de Paris*. It can be stated in the form of a cause/effect metonym: if indulgence in luxuries on the part of aristocrats and Bourgeois leads to dissipation resulting from superfluity, and if the desire for luxuries induces the 'have-nots' to engage in a life of crime, then superfluity and indigence form two poles on the same axis. The remedy to this dilemma must be sought in a new system wherein no dichotomies exist.

The now-classic example of the rapports between starvation and crime is the story of Jean Valjean, the protagonist of *Les Misérables*; it is imperative to understand that his entire life is determined by a single response to hunger. In the early pages of the novel Jean Valjean symbolizes all the oppressed people of the earth, all the victims of capitalism; he is a paradigm of suffering, unemployment, and poverty. When the very subsistence of his family was threatened by lack of food, Jean Valjean stole a loaf of bread in order to keep them alive: 'Il arriva qu'un hiver fut rude. Jean n'eut pas d'ouvrage. La famille n'eut pas de pain. Pas de pain. A la lettre! Sept enfants!' (*Les Misérables*, 89). For his crime he was condemned to a five-year sentence of forced labour. Hugo finds this inequity so gross that he embarks on a digression which reveals his own ideological stance on the matter; he bears no animosity toward the criminal who steals to eat, and even feels a certain sympathy for him: 'Peut-on attendre quand on a faim?' (*Les*

Misérables, 94). Moreover, as Hugo attempts to convince the
reader, not only does the lack of food induce a man to steal
but the fact that he has stolen can prevent him from obtain-
ing food in the future. In order to illustrate this thesis,
Hugo introduces the reader to Jean Valjean in an episode which
uses a meal situation to berate society's attitudes toward the
convict. The stigma surrounding former inmates is the result
of an unenlightened and inhuman attitude which perpetually condemns a man for his past. A minor infraction of the criminal
code, for instance, is sufficient to make a man a social outcast with no hope of reintegrating himself into society.

When the reader first encounters Jean Valjean in *Les Misérables* the ex-convict is wandering near the village of Digne
in search of food and lodging. Stopping at an inn, he witnesses a typical scene in the life of the establishment,
evoking the *chaleur-repos* motif so familiar to most nineteenth-
century readers:

> L'homme se dirigea vers cette auberge, qui était la meil-
> leure du pays. Il entre dans la cuisine, laquelle s'ou-
> vrait de plain-pied sur la rue. Tous les fourneaux étaient
> allumés; un grand feu flambait gaiement dans la cheminée.
> L'hôte, qui était en même temps le chef, allait de l'âtre
> aux casseroles, fort occupé et surveillant un excellent
> dîner destiné à des rouliers qu'on entendait rire et par-
> ler à grand bruit dans une salle voisine.
>
> (*Les Misérables*, 64-5)

This sketch of the activities of the inn is a necessary prelude to the change in mood which will ensue when Jean's
identity is revealed to the innkeeper. In the opening sequences of this passage the atmosphere is gay and festive;
consequently, when Jean enters and requests dinner the host
graciously offers to serve him. No discrimination occurs at
this point even though Jean has a ragged and fierce appearance. However, when someone in the room recognizes him and
informs the innkeeper that he is a convict, the latter refuses to serve him. The stigma, then, imposes a blatant exclusion of the convict: he is degraded, humiliated, refused
the most basic courtesies. None of Jean's supplications
soften the host: 'Ah bah! mais je meurs de faim, moi. J'ai
marché dès le soleil levé. J'ai fait douze lieues. Je paye.
Je veux manger' (*Les Misérables*, 66). A social exile, Jean
wanders the streets of Digne until he finds another cabaret,
but once again he is turned away, denied the commensal
privilege, banished from the table.

In recounting this episode Hugo has constructed a didactic irony in order to expose the plight of the convict. If the abundance of food and the means to obtain it keep a man honest, a society which refuses a man food is creating a criminal. With all means of procurement exhausted, the starving have no recourse but to steal in order to eat. The stigma of the convict actually encourages crime: society, moreover, perpetuates the problem in the name of propriety and morality. And here it might be noted that society unwittingly inverts the work ethic: condemning criminals to forced labour induces hunger, yet the meagre rations of food doled out to the inmate are disproportionate to the quantity of work he must perform. Eternally cast as the villain, as the *pharmakos*, the criminal has no alternative but to act out his 'crimes' against those who have placed him in this double bind.

By reinverting the perspective, that is, by placing Jean Valjean in a situation where he is made to feel accepted, Hugo lays the foundation for a transformation in the convict's character and thus permits him to embrace the Christian ethic. The symbolic act by which one confirms his belief is an eating ritual: Christ enters the heart in the practice of communion. The central meal of the novel, and the one which prefigures Jean's espousal of Christianity, takes place at the home of Monseigneur Bienvenu, the bishop of Digne, and it stands in direct contrast to all the situations in which Jean endured starvation or exclusion from the table. The transition from exclusion to inclusion occurs when Jean happens upon the home of the bishop and discovers, much to his surprise, that the latter welcomes him into his house and makes preparations to have an additional place set at his table. From the very inception of this scene Christian generosity prevails and presents itself in relation to food and dining: Bienvenu's hospitality astounds Jean as does his refusal to accept money for the meal. The bishop's charity contrasts sharply with the inhospitality of the innkeepers whom Jean had met earlier; Bienvenue does all in his power to make Jean feel comfortable: 'Madame Magloire, dit l'évêque, mettez ce couvert le plus près possible du feu. Et se tournant vers son hôte: – Le vent de nuit est dur dans les Alpes. Vous devez avoir froid, monsieur?' (*Les Misérables*, 81). The coalescence of fire and fare marks the passage from outsider to insider, from *pharmakos* to communicant, for in this archetypal conjunction of images, hearth (fire) becomes co-substantial with heart (love). The very essence of the Christian spirit of brotherhood

and equality, here symbolized by the hearth motif, receives
its best expression in the words of the bishop:

> L'évêque, assis près de lui, lui toucha doucement la main.
> - Vous pouviez ne pas me dire qui vous étiez. Ce n'est pas
> ici ma maison, c'est la maison de Jésus-Christ. Cette porte
> ne demande pas à celui qui entre s'il a un nom, mais s'il
> a une douleur. Vous souffrez; vous avez faim et soif;
> soyez le bienvenu.
>
> (*Les Misérables*, 81-2)

The religious and ideological implications of the *faim et
soif* metaphor are made transparent in Bienvenu's parable:
to starve is to seek the Wisdom, to eat is to know the
Divine, to ingest is to assimilate the Godhead into one's
very being. The invitation to dine which the bishop extends
to Jean Valjean doubles as the latter's introduction and
initiation into the Christian faith.

Bienvenu's meal is unusual given the context of the other,
subsistence-level meals described in *Les Misérables*. In this
scene Hugo relates the gastronomical elements of the meal,
the unfolding of the sequence of courses, and even the table
setting; this emphasis on gastronomically descriptive elements, so inconsistent with the narrative techniques Hugo
uses in other meal delineations, forces the reader to focus
his gaze on the symbolic and connotative aspects of food
and ritual which are employed as a kind of subtext to communicate the Christian message. The first stage of the description of the meal consists of an enumeration of the ingredients of the soup served by Madame Magloire: 'Cependant
Mme Magloire avait servi le souper. Une soupe faite avec de
l'eau, de l'huile, du pain, du sel, un peu de lard, un morceau de viande de mouton, des figues, un fromage frais, et
un gros pain de seigle' (*Les Misérables*, 82). As usual, the
bishop's meal is frugal, the food simple: the spirit of commensality counts above all else. Hugo, in recounting this
meal, mentions the seating arrangement - normal seating protocol in the nineteenth century signals differentiation and
social hierarchization - in order to accentuate the fact
that Jean receives the same treatment as any other guest at
Bienvenu's table; that is, he enjoys equal status with the
host, a mark of the Christian ethic. Before serving Jean,
the bishop says a prayer of thanks then asks Mme Magloire
to adorn the table with silver setting and crystal china.
This last action has a double significance: on the one hand,
it serves to elevate Jean's self-esteem and thus help him

escape the social stigmas which had been forced upon him;
on the other hand, it poses a problem - namely, the temptation to steal the silverware. Jean is made to face a dilemma
which, ideologically speaking, aligns him with the Christian
who must choose of his own free will. Essentially, the table,
here a metonym of the choices open to Jean - communion with
men as opposed to disjunction from men - acts as a catalyst
for Jean's redemption.

Every reader knows that Jean Valjean chose the Christian
path, and in so doing he serves as a model for all mankind.
Hugo clearly offers the possibility of solace to all destitute peoples, and a message of hope by reassuring them that
perseverance and right actions will ultimately be rewarded.
Crime does not pay; but neither is one forever condemned
for his past. Following his espousal of the Christian ethic,
Jean's life acquires an exemplary character. Among his many
charitable acts the one which most concerns us here is his
willingness to accept responsibility for an abandoned child,
to become her surrogate father. Cosette, like Jean before
her, led a life of hardship. It is only fitting then that
those who became or remained virtuous in the face of tremen-
dous adversity should one day be rewarded. Cosette's recom-
pense, and Jean's ultimate felicity, occur on her wedding
day and are epitomized in the sumptuous nuptial meal which
Jean is able to provide for the newlyweds. Symbolically,
this meal represents a sort of compensation for the hard-
ships which these characters have endured: by virtue of
their faith and tenacity, Jean, Cosette, and Marius, her
bridegroom, have truly earned the right to eat profusely.
Hugo's narrative technique of composing the feast in parts,
using a variety of tones and including most of the activities and habits normally associated with the table, makes
it different from other meal descriptions in the novel:
minute attention to culinary and gastronomical detail is
impossible in a description of near-starvation.

The narrative depiction of Cosette and Marius' wedding
feast, though brief, places it clearly in the context of bourgeois supping to the extent that it emphasizes a spirit of
revelry, abundance of fare, and china, crystal, and silverware. In spite of his espousal of the people's cause, Hugo
reveals himself to be, at least in his admiration for *aisance*
and *plaisance*, quite bourgeois at heart. Virtue is rewarded
and felicity attained in the ethos of the bourgeoisie:

Un banquet avait été dressé dans la salle à manger.
Un éclairage à giorno est l'assaisonnement nécessaire

d'une grande joie. La brume et l'obscurité ne sont pas
acceptées par les heureux.

...

La salle à manger était une fournaise de choses gaies.
Au centre, au-dessus de la table blanche et éclatante,
un lustre de Venise à lames plates, avec toutes sortes
d'oiseaux de couleur, bleus, violets, rouges, verts,
perchés au milieu des bougies; autour du lustre des gir-
andoles, sur le mur des miroirs-appliqués à triples et
quintuples branches; glaces, cristaux, verreries, vais-
selles, porcelaines, faïences, poteries, orfèvreries,
argenteries, tout étincelait et se réjouissait.

(*Les Misérables*, 1339)

Perhaps the deep significance of this meal is to be sought
in its imagistic patterns, for at the metaphorical level
the meal is equated with artistic creation: the first part
metaphorically allies light with joy, and, ultimately, with
the divine presence which infuses the life of the newlyweds;
the second part develops around the image of the *fournaise*
wherein all activities are contained and harmonized, blended
as in the process of cooking itself, until they become one.
In its aesthetic aspect this meal supersedes the bourgeois
ethos which centres on material comforts and social differentiation, and attains a level of cosmological harmony and
unity.

*Transitions and Transformations: Meals as Models of
Convergence*

The foregoing discussion demonstrated that in the semiotic
apparatus of fictional meals, food and character, the starvation syndrome, and the relation between dearth of food
and incidence of crime were narrative strategies for elucidating the social distances and hierarchies in French society. In essence, all three analytical categories reflect
a fundamental dispersal or divergence of social energies
and practices. The fact that Sue and Hugo chose to evoke
this reality by recording eating practices in the ghetto
attests not only to the all-pervasiveness of food-as-sign
but also to the ideological efficacy of fictionalizing food,
for *la chère* is at once a symbol and an existential phenomenon, a sign-substance as it were. As substance, as immediate reality – or rather, as substance *in abstentia* for
the poor – food entreats society to exploit its symbolic
value (it is well to remember when discussing the concept

of 'want' that a symbol stands for something which is 'missing') in order, one day, to replace the symbol with the substance, to transform the ideological into the edible. The question which is implicit in Sue's and Hugo's statements regarding the scarcity or absence of food is: how can the gastro-alimentary sign, heretofore used to signal disparity, distance, and divergence, be charged with a new semantic function so that it can operate as a sign-praxis to produce commensality, confluence, and convergence?

Their answer to this problem resides, on the one hand, in investing the gastro-alimentary sign with new connotations borrowed from contemporary socialist theory and, on the other hand, in offering model fictional solutions which correspond with the cause/effect hypothesis which both authors advocate in their respective narratives. The two cases recently cited, the family of brigands in *Les Mystères de Paris* and the Jean Valjean story in *Les Misérables*, both illustrate and confirm the cause/effect hypothesis. However, the first case remains unresolved: hunger breeds crime and, once bred, crime perpetuates itself (i.e. crime as solution) unless a new element is introduced to break the chain of events. The insertion of a new logic of circumstances is precisely what happens in the Valjean story: the initial phases of Jean's hardship parallel those of the criminals in *Les Mystères de Paris* in so far as he resorts to crime as a response to hunger just as they did. In Valjean's case, however, the transition from excluded to exonerated occurs when the Christian ethic of charity and equality is put into practice by the Bishop of Digne: material hunger is transformed into spiritual hunger. Jean Valjean repents his sins, is converted to Christianity, leads a virtuous life, and is thus rewarded gastronomically and spiritually at the end of his story.

The models of transition offered by Sue and Hugo range from the simple to the complex, though all belong to the thesis of cause and effect. Perhaps the most simplified, if not simplistic, solution occurs in *Les Mystères de Paris* wherein Sue suggests that behaviour can be modified by conditioning: in reality, the situations he describes for the reader do not constitute cases of classical conditioning in the psychological sense but rather illustrate the process of code switching. The first example finds the hero of *Les Mystères de Paris*, Rodolphe, switching from a socially superior form of behaviour to a more vulgar response when in the ghetto milieu. One would expect a character faced with the eating manners and practices in the slums to adopt similar customs. In *Les Mystères de Paris* and *Les Misérables* inferior habits among the poor are implied but the reader can only deduce this because the narrators in both novels usually depict only the good habits with which more vulgar practices contrast. The infrequent special courtesies paid by ghetto inhabitants to their superiors constitute a form of obsequiousness; among familiars, however, special treatment rarely takes place. Poor service, moreover, usually typifies cabaret customs yet, in one instance, after Rodolphe has defeated the local strongman in a fight, his newly acquired prestige induces the hostess of the *Lapin blanc* to show her estimation of him by switching to a socially superior *formule de politesse*:

> L'ogresse, enfin, adressant à Rodolphe l'un de ses plus gracieux sourires, chose inouïe, exorbitante, fabuleuse dans les fastes du *Lapin blanc*, se leva de son comptoir pour venir prendre les ordres de son hôte, afin de savoir de lui ce qu'il fallait servir à sa *société*; attention que l'ogresse n'avait jamais eu pour le Maître d'école ou le Squelette, terribles scélérats qui faisaient trembler le Chourineur lui-même.
>
> (*Les Mystères*, I, 9)

In a similar scene Thomas and Sarah, two characters in *Les Mystères de Paris*, betray their noble background by their gracious actions in the ghetto milieu. Their dress, demeanour, and manners are anomolous at the *Lapin blanc*; consequently, when Thomas addresses l'Ogresse as 'madame' her own civility increases, activating Sue's belief that good actions promote good actions: 'La mère Ponisse, flattée de cette courtoisie, se leva de son comptoir, vint gracieusement s'appuyer à la table des nouveaux *consommateurs* et dit: – Voulez-vous un litre de vin ou une bouteille cachetée?' (*Les Mystères*, I, 38). These seemingly insignificant details figure as part of Sue's semiotic apparatus in *Les Mystères de Paris*, for, cumulatively, they belong to the metonymic structure of cause and effect. The example cited above simply confirms Sue's thesis that a change in the paradigm of causes produces a change in the paradigm of effects: rancour breeds rancour, civility breeds civility.

Another transitional situation, which was alluded to earlier, also amounts to a modification of causes. According to the principle involved here, a change in the locus of the meal, from Paris to Province, will have salubrious effects. In one scene of *Les Mystères de Paris* the benevolent

Rodolphe offers to take Fleur-de-Marie away from the misery of the city and place her on his country farm: he obviously becomes the spokesman for Sue in his description of the pastoral setting and life on the farm:

> Sans doute; il y a justement un pont de bois sur la rivière. Au retour, il est, ma foi, six ou sept heures: dans ce temps-ci, comme les soirées sont déjà fraîches, un bon feu flambe gaiement dans la grande cuisine de la ferme; vous allez vous réchauffer et causer un moment avec les braves gens qui soupent en rentrant du labour. Ensuite vous dînez avec votre tante. Quelqufois le curé ou un fermier voisin se met à table avec vous.
>
> (*Les Mysteres*, I, 64)

In describing life on the model farm, Rodolphe echoes Sue's belief that circumstances and character can be altered by introducing slum inhabitants to a new environment. Perhaps his thinking is too idealistic to be convincing; nevertheless he is quite aware of the need to impose a new semiotic convention on the downtrodden as a catalyst for change. All of the negative connotations of ghetto meals (absence of a fixed locus of the meal, absence of the *chaleur-repos* affect, absence of congenial companions) are here transformed into their positive counterparts, permitting the character to pass from outsider to insider, from patient to agent, from famished to fulfilled. Sue shares Sand's beliefs in the virtues of communal eating and thus relates the positive aspects of hunger to life in the country. The farmers at Bouqueval, the model farm in *Les Mystères de Paris*, eat heartily because they work hard, a concept which stands in direct opposition to life in the ghetto. Furthermore, Sue's advocacy of Christian Socialism, like Sand's, manifests itself in the providing principle: collective effort leads to self-respect and mutual enjoyment of the fruits of the earth; earning one's bread enables the worker to derive pleasure and pride from his work. By design, then, Rodolphe assigns Marie to the task of preserving food because it offers her compensation for her prior life of alimentary penury.

Many effects of the living conditions in the slums are detrimental to the health and happiness of the inhabitants, yet one should not lose sight of the good qualities which characterize the more generous element. In conformity with the Christian ethic, both Sue and Hugo appeal to the intrinsic virtue of the individual for bringing about change.

Thus, the Bourgeois's abuse and mistreatment of children
by depriving them of food or making them work long hours
to earn their meals find their counterpart in the gratuitous acts of kindness and generosity of the poor. The reader might remember the young Parisian boy in *Les Misérables*
who fished a *brioche* out of a swan basin and gave half of
it to his brother. Gavroche, another character in *Les
Misérables*, singularly exemplifies the principle of sharing;
he will steal to eat if need be but when he has money to
buy food he offers to share his purchase with hungry children:

> Et il tira d'une de ses poches un sou. Sans laisser aux
> deux petits le temps de s'ébahir, il les poussa tous deux
> devant lui dans la boutique du boulanger, et mit son sou
> sur le comptoir en criant:
> - Garçon! cinq centîmes de pain.
> (*Les Misérables*, 968)

Charity, a virtue associated with peasants in Sand's novels
and with the poor in Hugo's works, also plays a role in *Les
Mystères de Paris*. In Morel, Sue portrays a man who is so
destitute that his family often has to go without food for
several days on end; he is even forced to witness the slow
death by starvation of one of his children. Mademoiselle
Rigolette, a neighbour, permits each of Morel's children
to dine with her on a rotating basis:

> - Les pauvres gens sont donc meilleurs qu'eux tous,
> puisqu'ils s'entreaident ... Cette bonne petite mademoi-
> elle Rigolette, qui nous a si souvent veillés, moi ou
> tous les enfants, pendant nos maladies, a emmené hier
> Jérome et Pierre pour partager son souper. Et son souper,
> ça n'est guère: une tasse de lait et du pain. A son âge
> on a bon appétit; bien sûr, elle ne sera privée ...
> (*Les Mystères*, I, 332)

Like Sand, Sue also thematizes the act of providing.
Rodolphe, the Christlike hero of *Les Mystères de Paris*,
embodies the charitable ideal and becomes the saviour of
the humble, the poor, the sinners. Born a nobleman, he uses
his massive wealth to aid his fellow man and often mingles
with the inhabitants of the ghettos in order to show them
the path to social progress and rehabilitation. He builds
a model farm where they can work and provide for their own
needs. As might be expected, food is plentiful on the farm

because the members of the community have produced it with
their own labour. Finally, in his portrait of Monseigneur
Bienvenu, the bishop of Digne who also serves as a transitional model, Hugo dwells on some of the bishop's eating
habits in order to accentuate his saintly preoccupations
and his temperance vis-à-vis food. Deeds come first in the
priorities of Bienvenu: 'Il passa toute la journée et toute
la nuit près de lui, oubliant la nourriture et le sommeil,
priant Dieu pour l'âme du condamné et priant le condamné
pour la sienne propre' (*Les Misérables*, 17). Christianity
emphasizes humility, simplicity, and the virtues of poverty;
it comes as no surprise, therefore, to find the bishop imposing these codes upon himself, especially by keeping his
daily meals frugal and untainted with culinary excesses:

> Sa messe dite, il déjeunait d'un pain de seigle trempé
> dans le lait de ses vaches.
> A midi, il dînait. Le dîner ressemblait au déjeuner.
> Le soir à huit heurs et demie, il soupait avec sa sœur,
> Mme Magloire debout derrière eux et les servant à table.
> Rien de plus frugal que ce repas. Si pourtant l'évêque
> avait un de ses curés à souper, Mme Magloire en profitait
> pour servir à Monseigneur quelque fin gibier de la mon-
> tagne. Tout curé était un prétexte à bon repas; l'évêque
> se laissait faire. Hors de là, son ordinaire ne se com-
> posait guère que de légumes cuits dans l'eau et de soupe
> à l'huile. Aussi disait-on dans la ville: *Quand l'évêque
> ne fait pas chère de curé, il fait chère de trappiste*
>   (*Les Misérables*, 20-1)

Sue and Hugo deliver an appropriate finale to the deplorable socio-economic conditions manifested in this study in
so far as they reflect food and dining at the proletariat
level. If degrading conditions for one segment of society
are a result of oppressive and unjust institutions, then it
follows that too much gastro-alimentary degradation will
lead the poor to change those institutions. Much of the
poverty and misery documented by Sue and Hugo was used to
make the public aware of social problems, particularly of
starvation and its effect on children and slum-dwellers.
For the most part the meals described in these novels differ radically from those portrayed by the other authors
treated in this book: firstly, because the meal scenes and
gastronomical references in *Les Mystères de Paris* and *Les
Misérables* accentuate the problem of hunger, not satiation;
secondly because the lack of sufficient food leads many

penniless souls to a life of crime. The contemporary reading
public might have reacted with contempt for the poor, or
indifference. Or, perhaps, the more enlightened members of
society might have been aroused into a course of action
aimed at eliminating rampant poverty. Certainly, Sue and
Hugo would favour the latter form of response: Sue addresses
himself to this more active group when he advocates a solution based on the communal principle, which is fictionally
embodied in the model farm at Bouqueval; Hugo, on the other
hand, envisions disaster for the more recalcitrant segment
of society, because if their mythos should prevail revolution would inevitably result.

The problem of food scarcity, when intense and ubiquitous,
demands immediate response. This concept is extremely important because it gives birth to the theory that revolutions
emanate directly from material conditions, starvation being
the most acute dilemma faced by the masses:

> Dans les cas les plus généraux, l'émeute sort d'un fait
> matériel; l'insurrection est toujours un phénomène moral.
> L'émeute, c'est Masanielle; l'insurrection, c'est Sparta-
> cus. L'insurrection confine à l'esprit, l'émeute à l'es-
> tomac. Gaster s'irrite; mais Gaster, certes, n'a pas tou-
> jours tort ... Nourrir le peuple est un bon but, le mas-
> sacrer est un mauvais moyen.
>
> (*Les Misérables*, 1079)

Hunger forces the masses to rebel; the germs of destruction
are implanted by the inequities of the system; people will
feed on these inequities. The ultimate expression of the
crisis between 'haves' and 'have-nots' is metonymically
transposed into an antagonism between alimentary superfluity
for one group and the inaccessibility of necessary victuals
for another. When the masses are reduced to the point of
starvation, theft and revolt cease to be moral questions:
they are metamorphosed into necessities, conditions for
survival. Man is a predator; in the end, he will kill to eat.

Revolution, however, is not the only solution to the problem of starvation. Sue, like many of the contemporary socialist theorists, championed peaceful change and endeavoured
to ameliorate the situation by following the principles of
Christian Socialism. The reader can readily detect the influence of a Cabet or a Fourier on Sue's conception of the
model farm at Bouqueval, so it might be appropriate to conclude this particular analysis on a positive note by showing
the reader a small slice of communal life at Bouqueval.

Harmony, which for purposes of this book may be defined
as that blissful state of equilibrium between appetite and
desire, becomes most apparent at mealtime. The communal
feasts at Bouqueval represent the epitome of the socialist
ideal, the rewarding side of life to which society's out-
casts may aspire. Bouqueval comprises an ideal community
where men and women earn their keep through work and mutual
cooperation. It admits any fugitive from society who shows
promise of salvation through fraternal living, charity, and
sacrifice. Moreover, it prepares the workers for a construc-
tive social life once they have gone back into the world.
In an attempt to demythologize bourgeois eating rites and
customs, Sue has established this community in a pastoral
setting. As in Sand's novels, characters placed in natural
surroundings integrate Nature's harmony into their very
moral fibre. If Sand paved the way for a value system based
on peasant simplicity and communal instincts, Sue valorized
the activities of an agricultural commune by using the meal
as a symbol and a paradigm of total community.

From the narrative viewpoint the workers' dinner at Bouqueval is the most elaborately developed meal scene in *Les
Mystères de Paris*. Representing the apex of Sue's socialist
thinking in this particular novel, it consists of carefully
structured parts, descriptive passages saturated with culinary references, and enlightening digressions on the aims
and purposes of such communities. All these elements combine
to produce an effect of social harmony, a veritable earthly
paradise. To a large extent, the narrator's presence is emphasized so that his sensitivity and his omniscience can
inform the reader about the subtle implications of brotherhood. The narrator recounts the first phase of the meal,
making the reader his accomplice, inviting him to enjoy the
harmonies of the kitchen at mealtime.

> Est-il quelquchose de plus réjouissant à voir que la cui-
> sine d'une grande métairie à l'heure du repas du soir,
> dans l'hiver surtout? Est-il quelquechose qui rapelle
> davantage le calme et le bien-être de la vie rustique?
> On aurait pu trouver une preuve de ce que nous avançons
> dans l'aspect de la cuisine de la ferme de Bouqueval.
>
> (*Les Mystères*, I, 242)

Having allied our sympathies by conjoining the motifs of
repos, *chaleur*, and *unicité*, the narrator then paints a
sensual portrait of the kitchen equipment, enhancing the
brilliant and reflective properties of the copperware and

china in order to convey to what extent the 'extrême propreté' of the table mirrors life at Bouqueval:

> De grand marmites et des casseroles de cuivre rouge
> rangées sur des tablettes étincelaient de propreté, une
> antique fontaine du même métal brillait comme un miroir
> ardent non loin d'une huche de noyer, soigneusement cirée,
> d'où s'exhalait une appétissante odeur de pain chaud.
> Une table longue, massive, recouverte d'une nappe de
> grosse toile d'une extrême propreté, occupant le milieu
> de la salle; la place de chaque convive était marquée
> par une de ces assiettes de faïence, brunes au dehors,
> blanches au dedans, et par un couvert de fer luisant comme
> de l'argent.
>
> (*Les Mystères*, I, 242-3)

These opening passages are stylistically and thematically
symmetrical in so far as the first part illustrates the
affective aspects of the meal, that is, the collaboration
between narrator and reader, whereas the second part exemplifies the descriptive elements and culinary attractions in
a mode reminiscent of the tableau style. The passage cited
above comprises one element of the tableau, depicting as
it does the delicate blend of colours, lighting, and odours
and thereby creating a sort of aesthetic harmony. The second
scene in the tableau portrays the virtuous elements of communal eating: cleanliness and undifferentiated seating. The
third part captures the beauty of copious culinary delights:

> Au milieu de la table, une grande soupière remplie de
> potage aux légumes fumait comme un cratère et couvrait
> de sa vapeur savoureuse un plat formidable de choucroute
> au jambon et un autre plat non moins formidable de ragoût
> de mouton aux pommes de terre; enfin un quartier de veau
> rôti, flanqué de deux salades d'hiver, accosté de deux
> corbeilles de pommes et de deux fromages, complétait
> l'abondante symétrie de ce repas.
>
> (*Les Mystères*, I, 243)

During the next phase of the meal the narrator shifts
from aesthetic preoccupations to sociological digressions.
Here he develops the theme of the virtues and benefits of
communal eating; joy and felicity become the leitmotifs of
this description wherein commensality has a salubrious effect on the mood of the participants:

> Après avoir terminé les apprêts du souper et posé sur
> la table un broc de vin destiné à accompagner le *dessert*
> la cuisinière de la ferme alla sonner la cloche. A ce
> joyeux appel, laboureurs, valets de ferme, laitières,
> filles de basse-cour, au nombre de douze ou quinze, en-
> trèrent gaiement dans la cuisine. Les hommes avaient
> l'air mâle et ouvert; les femmes étaient avenantes et
> robustes, les jeunes filles alertes et gaies; toutes ces
> physionomies placides respiraient la bonne humeur, la
> quiétude et le contentement de soi; ils s'apprêtaient
> avec une sensualité naïve à faire honneur à ce repas
> bien gagné par les rudes labeurs de la journée.
>
> (*Les Mystères*, I, 242)

This meal typifies the fundamental sociability of the act
of eating: food has been transformed into ideological substance and sustenance, its connotations and rituals form
the combinatory elements of a socialist semiosis. *La chère*
is honoured because it is earned. Founded upon the sowing
and reaping philosophy, this social system allows for only
slight distinctions of degree, not of kind, among members
of the community at Bouqueval. Yet the reader comes to understand that a kind of patriarchy exists even among social
equals, for le père Châtelain, the oldest and most venerated
worker, sits at the head of the table. To him goes the honour
of intoning the evening prayer, which is an important part
of the ritual of communal eating because it allies socialism
with Christianity, food with religion. Moreover, the convergence of social and religious contexts is enhanced and complemented by another ritual gesture:

> Après avoir dit le *Bénédicite* à haute voix, le père Châte-
> lain, suivant un vieil et saint usage, traça une croix sur
> un des pains avec la pointe de son couteau, et en coupa un
> morceau représentant *la part de la Vièrge* ou la part du
> pauvre; il versa ensuite un verre de vin sous la même in-
> vocation et plaça le tout sur une assiette qui fut pieuse-
> ment placée au milieu de la table.
>
> (*Les Mystères*, I, 244)

For Eugène Sue, the communal banquet symbolizes the perfect
state of harmony, fraternity, and equality to which man
can aspire in this lifetime. Placed unequivocally in the
Christian Socialist tradition, this meal, like the ultimate repast toward which Sand was evolving in her pastoral

novels, constitutes the early version of the Heavenly Banquet.

The socialist movement which began in the 1830s encouraged many novelists to preach reform in their fictions and even induced some of them to transform into actions the principles they were upholding in their work. Eugène Sue and Victor Hugo belong among those authors who attempted to improve social and economic conditions both in fiction and in practice. In their novels both men responded to the problems faced by the masses: certainly, no dilemma was more acute for the impoverished proletariat during the years from 1830 to 1848 than the threat of starvation. Sue and Hugo often used the meal thematic to illustrate this predicament. Their most serious innovations as regards gastro-alimentary themes centre on the portrayal of deplorable eating conditions, the devastating effects of malnutrition, and the undeniable correspondence between the absence of food and the presence of crime. But, out of the chaos comes light. Neither Sue nor Hugo paints a picture of total despair. In the estimation of both authors dearth of food inevitably creates positive forms of response: Hugo envisions revolution as the logical extension of those social disparities which have resulted in poverty and starvation, while Sue foresees a more peaceful solution to the problem in the establishment of pastoral communes. Both writers demand that the masses be given the right to eat with dignity. In any event, thanks to the efforts of Sue and Hugo, the emphasis on food as an alienating factor which so characterized the early years of the nineteenth century is replaced in later years by the idea of food and community, though it should be noted that not all distinctions disappear, since to a well-fed reading audience the portrait of starvation which both authors paint is an unfamiliar and often ignored one.

Essentially, Sue and Hugo endeavour to enlighten the contemporary reader by leading him to an awareness of the virtualities of the cause-effect hypothesis. Readers are thus forced into the Sartrian position of choosing to act or choosing not to act: should they opt for action society could be ameliorated by the adoption and implementation of socialist communal models, but should they decide on a course of inaction society would be violently, perhaps radically, transformed by revolution. In either case the reading public is made to bear the responsibility for the outcome.

4 / FLAUBERT

Aesthetic and Ideological Coalescence in the Alimentary Sign: *Madame Bovary*

Even the most superficial reading of *Madame Bovary* reveals a high frequency of eating scenes, allusions to food, and alimentary imagery. Indeed, it seems that the novel is truly organized around the table: all the major characters of the novel are depicted, in large part, by their alimentary habits and attitudes; events unfold between the three major banquets, which serve as turning points in the evolution of Emma's life; and even the major themes of the novel are somehow imbricated and reflected in its alimentary discourse. Therefore, in assessing the semiotic role of the meal complex in *Madame Bovary* it will be necessary to account for, or in some way explain, this phenomenon of alimentary, culinary, and gastronomical saturation which is so characteristic of Flaubert's narrative but which does not characterize the other novelists I have discussed. Certainly, the novels of Balzac, Sand, Sue, and Hugo contain, as we have seen, an impressive number of meal scenes with functions analogous to those of Flaubert's. There exists, then, a fundamental sameness as far as the sign-functions of their fictional meals are concerned: all of the novelists included in this study tend to transcode cultural, economic, psychological, and sociological phenomena into alimentary discourse in their narratives. However, the underlying difference between Flaubert and the others in this regard is that Flaubert makes the so-called practical, utilitarian, and transparent ideologies of his fellow artists subservient to the more ideal-istic, 'useless,' and hermetic concerns of Art.[1]

The tension between alimentary banality and gastronomical
sublimity in *Madame Bovary* manifests itself as a series of
oppositional transforms or analogues which occur throughout
the novel and which permeate its stylistic, thematic, characterological, and organizational structure. Other than the
fact that Flaubert makes extensive use of gastro-alimentary
discourse in *Madame Bovary*, inundating the novel with eating
scenes and references to food, there is nothing significantly
innovative about his dining episodes as most resemble - in
their formal presentation, anyway - those meals described
by Balzac, Sand, Sue, and Hugo. Perhaps one should seek to
differentiate Flaubert from the others not in terms of the
means he employs to evoke food and dining but rather in relation to the ends he pursues, for certainly the other
novelists were all recorders of reality to varying degrees,
i.e. all portrayed social differentiation and stratification,
and, especially as far as Sand, Sue, and Hugo were concerned,
the meal was used to signify an extant ideology or it was
put in the service of an emerging ideology. Flaubert's goal,
paradoxical though it may seem, was to re-present faithfully
the semio-ideological surface of the meal context - the meal
as a material bourgeois phenomenon - in order, at a deeper
semantic level, to subvert the bourgeois ethos by poeticiz-
ing and transforming it in the work of art. In *Madame Bovary*
the meal, to the extent that it is elevated to the level of
aesthetic artifact, serves to undermine its heretofore ideological function in the nineteenth-century French novel.
This position is, as many critics have observed, not without contradictions, since Flaubert's ostensible anti-
ideological stance amounts to little more than a counter-
ideology in which practical and utilitarian concerns cease
to be priorities in favour of aesthetic and artistic pur-
suits.

L'Art pour l'art as practised by Flaubert constitutes an
ideology in itself: with regard to the gastronomical and
alimentary discourse in *Madame Bovary* such a theory is reflected in a breach between the surface structure of Flaubert's meal scenes and their underlying semantic structure.
For, indeed, Flaubert evokes lavishly - and not without some
complicity of values - the bourgeois eating ethic. Meal
scenes in *Madame Bovary* are highly repetitive and mimetic
structures, mimesis being an apparent approval of the established order of things whether they be meals or social and
political practices. Yet Flaubert's fundamental intention
is to destroy, or somehow transcend, the very phenomena he
so carefully and artfully constructs. The dilemma - if it

is a dilemma - poses itself primarily at the anecdotal and descriptive levels of his novel where art appears to imitate reality. This same dilemma is resolved, however, at the actantial and diegetic levels of the text in so far as nearly every meal scene in *Madame Bovary* contains an implicit irony, hence a negative judgment on the part of the narrator. This for several reasons: first, in his rather conventional use of the meal as a character index, Flaubert emphasizes the negative aspects of personality, e.g., Charles' mediocrity, Homais' pompousness, Emma's pathology; second, by alternating interior and exterior perspectives when relating a specific eating event he produces a disparate vision of the reality of that event whose clarification depends on the omniscient narrator's reliability and distance; third, several of the supping scenes in *Madame Bovary* are focused through Emma (the interior perspective) with the result that the reader's own perceptions of the meal context are distorted because Emma views meals as signs, not as substances (one is thus drawn into the artifices of gastronomy at the expense of alimentary reality); and, finally, Flaubert's characters, particularly the Bourgeois, are generally very aware of the semiotic nature of food and eating practices; consequently they use, or rather misuse, the food sign to manipulate or ostracize others.

As a general rule the reader bears witness to a double encoding procedure when deciphering the significance of Flaubert's dining episodes in *Madame Bovary*. On the one hand, characters in the novel use the meal and dining rituals as signs when interacting with other characters: for the most part these characters belong to the bourgeoisie or they accept its values as the norms of gastronomical comportment. Under these circumstances the semiosis surrounding the meal tends to emphasize *la gastronomie*, that is, the stylization of appetite and desire rather than the nutritional functions of eating.[2] On the other hand, the bourgeois eating ritual would appear quite normal to contemporary readers were it not for the narrator's method of reporting routine dining situations as well as banquet scenes in *Madame Bovary*, i.e., via interior and exterior perspectives. In the first instance the meal is usually focused through Emma, who is a victim, an eiron of the semiotic game being played out before her *eyes*; references to her *palate* are in fact rare. In the second instance, however, the narrator subtly conveys to the reader Emma's sense of disproportion and illusion in decoding events around her. At this level of narration the sign-function of the meal and its ritual is made transparent for the reader, enabling him to perceive the scene in an ironic dimension. Gastronomy thus reveals itself as a proliferation of form upon substance. The artist, however, rises above this distortion by means of his artistic creation, wherein he restores the balance between form and substance. Material bourgeois values are thus offset by the artist's search for an essential, aesthetic integrity. Art, as Flaubert would have it, is a more elevated form of semiosis than economic exchange and the bourgeois production-product mentality, for art simultaneously surpasses the latter and acts as a meta-commentary upon it. In short, it de-mythologizes bourgeois cultural practices and their concomitant effects upon individuals like Emma Bovary who are victims of the bourgeois fallacy.

Returning now to the structural characteristics of dining scenes in *Madame Bovary*, I would like to suggest an analytical approach that would do justice to the alimentary, culinary, and gastronomical discourse which informs this fiction. So pervasive is the *fait alimentaire* in *Madame Bovary* that Victor Brombert, an eminent contemporary critic, has commented that the entire novel could be explicated on the basis of its alimentary and gastronomical elements: 'In *Madame Bovary*, food, the ritual of meals, deglutition and rumination play a particularly important role. One would almost be tempted to explicate the entire novel in terms of its gastronomic and digestive imagery.'[3] Such an analysis would be too ambitious for this chapter, yet something of the sort will be undertaken for what might be considered the semiotic parameters of the novel which serve to elucidate Emma Bovary's character - or, at least, her *Bovarysme* - and for its significant structural features: its stylistic, organizational, characterological, and ideological components. Although I do not intend to embark upon a formal structural analysis of the gastro-alimentary sign in *Madame Bovary*, I believe that it is relevant to approach the subject from a structural perspective because of the density and frequency of the gastro-alimentary sign and also because of the overlapping and interweaving of the meal phenomenon at all levels of the text.[4]

'Bovarysme' and the Alimentary Sign

In *Madame Bovary* meals have a very important psychological function as indices of Emma's temperament and as symptoms of her pathology. For the most part major banquets serve to highlight her ephemeral periods of ecstasy whereas daily meals taken at home parallel her moods of despair. In short, the entire complex of meal episodes in *Madame Bovary* functions as a metonymic extension of what has come to be known as *Bovarysme*, or that '... pouvoir départi à l'homme de se concevoir autre qu'il n'est ...'[5] *Bovarysme*, because it marks a distintegration of personality, a distance between self and self-conception, may be described, in general terms, as a psychopathological syndrome, or, in semiotic terms, as a cleavage between form and substance, as a fragmented sign.

But *Bovarysme* also manifests itself as an alimentary attitude. The form it appropriates for its expression is coded metonymically as the dialectic between appetite and desire: in this regard Emma's appetite is never sated, for her desire far exceeds her capacity to become congruent with her *self* and her surroundings. Brombert clearly perceived the alimentary nature of *Bovarysme* when he wrote:

> Food plays an extraordinary role in his [Flaubert's] novels: feasts, orgies, bourgeois meals, peasant revels. This concern for appetite and digestion corresponds unquestionably, as Richard suggests, to the larger themes of his work: the 'appetite' for the inaccessible, the voracious desire to *possess* experience, the preoccupation with metamorphoses, the tragedy of indigestion, and ultimately the almost metaphysical sense of nausea as the mind becomes aware that not to know everything is to know nothing. The very essence of *bovarysme* seems involved in this frustrated gluttony.
>
> (Brombert, 49)

Whether viewed from the perspective of the alimentary, the psychological, or the semiotic, *Bovarysme* is, quite obviously, a binary phenomenon which becomes actualized in the thematic matrix of the novel, in its many dichotomies and oppositions. There exists, for instance, an implicit contrast between the reporting of meal-events in the novel and Emma's distorted perception of them. Thus, one of the underlying intentions of the narrator in his depiction of the major banquets is to reveal not only Emma's psyche but also the realities at table - social superiority to name but one - which tend to set her fantasies in motion. Because her appetite for the romantic and the luxurious obscures her relishing of the real, Emma's experience with food rarely entails a knowledge of gastronomy or an indulgence in a moment of alimentary bliss but rather it is associated with the semiotic paraphernalia of the meal, with the stylized elements of feasting such as sparkling silverware, ornate table settings, and the grandeur of the gentry. As regards the evolution of Emma's personal psychology the major banquets in *Madame Bovary* represent summits of happiness which correspond in large measure to her flights from reality; occationally, the pivotal meals, as they will also be called, reveal psychological dynamics of a less personal nature: namely, elements of socialization and intra-group rivalry among the rural bourgeoisie and aristocracy. Fundamentally, the antagonisms depicted in these eating episodes have a larger social and economic basis, but they are frequently played out in the theatre of Emma's mind. In any event meals in *Madame Bovary* bear witness to the close association between the psychology and the sociology of the novel.

Bovarysme comprises a kind of psycho-textual norm to which characters and events conform or contrast, becoming as it were sources of pleasure or pain, felicity or despair for Emma. Her distorted view of reality would demand that the ephemeral magnificence of a Vaubyessard ball be transformed into a permanent occurrence; anything less - the *repas de ménage*, for instance - becomes a deplorable deviation from the sublime. Following the logic of *Bovarysme*, meals either serve as indices of conflicting social practices and customs in rural Normandy or they can be interpreted as symptoms of Emma's psychopathology. So embedded is the *vision bovaryste* in the narrative that, even before Emma's appearance in the story, the narrator introduces the reader to the principal characters by describing their eating habits and gastronomical attitudes and thus prepares him for the effects they will later have on Emma. In order to understand Emma's eventual dilemma the reader must first comprehend how the insipid personality of Charles will affect her. The narrator introduces Charles in the first chapter of the novel: an anomaly among his peers at school, he invariably takes his meals in the refectory so that his mother can save a few extra pennies. The reader soon learns that Charles' mother dominates him to such an extent that she even chooses his first wife, forcing him deeper into submission and bourgeois domesticity. His eating habits reflect the routine nature of his marriage and serve to remind the reader of the tasteless daily diet which so pleases him - 'Il lui fallait son chocolat tous les matins'[6] - but which will later place him in sharp contrast with Emma when they become betrothed. Perhaps the closest Charles ever comes to a state of revolt against the blandness of his diet is when his first wife dies and he suddenly acquires a new feeling of independence that manifests itself in a change of eating habits: 'Il y pensa moins, à mesure qu'il s'habituait à vivre seul. L'agrément nouveau de l'indépendance lui rendit bientôt la solitude plus supportable. Il pouvait changer maintenant les heures de ses repas ...' (*Madame Bovary*, 20).

The narrator also introduces Mme Bovary *mère* by alluding to her alimentary attitudes, particularly the economic implications of meals. Besides forcing Charles to sup in the refectory at school in order to economize, she reveals her frugality by sending him cheap cuts of veal from time to time. The one extravagance she permits her son is the dinner given in honour of his graduation. Although this particular meal plays a very small role in the narrative itself, it signals the importance provincial bourgeois families attach to success. For Mme Bovary, especially, the meal represents the attainment of status and respect to the extent that it signifies public recognition of Charles' achievement as a student.

In keeping with the pattern of oppositions established early in the novel, certain meals tend to reveal two characters with similar personalities at the same table with others whose personality traits differ from their own. On the day of their arrival at Yonville, Emma and Charles are invited to dine at a local restaurant, the *Lion d'Or*. The guests at their welcoming dinner include the pharmacist, Homais, and a young inhabitant of the town, Léon. The conversation during and following the meal is especially significant because it sets the tone for the personal affinities of character between the romantics, Emma and Léon, as opposed to the realists, Bovary and Homais.

At this point in the narrative the relationship which will eventuate between Emma and Léon is only foreshadowed, whereas the ponderous reality of the bourgeois temperament is foregrounded. During their first winter in Yonville, the Bovarys invite Homais to dinner on several occasions. The frequent intimate meals at the Bovary table described by the narrator provide a fairly complete elucidation of Homais' character. He pretends to be an eminent man of science whose knowledge approaches omniscience. The elements of his character are put into relief at the Bovary table, where he delights in discussing health as it is related to food and where he all too often embarks on pseudo-scientific discourses: 'Parfois même, se levant à demi, il indiquait délicatement à Madame le morceau le plus tendre, ou se tournant vers la bonne, lui adressait des assaisonnements; il parlait arôme, osmasôme, suc et gelatins d'une façon à éblouir'

(*Madame Bovary*, 91). Homais also reveals an avid interest
in culinary matters by describing the recipes he collects,
and his skills seem endless as he advocates new methods of
conserving cheeses and wines:

> La tête, d'ailleurs, plus remplie de recettes que sa
> pharmacie ne l'était de bocaux, Homais excellait à faire
> quantité de confitures, vinaigres et liqueurs de cale-
> facteurs économiques, avec l'art de conserver les fromages
> et de soigner les vins malades.
>
> (*Madame Bovary*, 91)

The narrator does not report this coalescence of the culinary and the scientific so characteristic of nineteenth-
century hygienic attitudes without a certain irony, at least
as far as Homais' knowledge is concerned, since the allusion
to his professional competence in the passage above seems
to indicate a plenitude of form signalling an emptiness of
content. Similarly, Homais' pompousness also becomes the object of the narrator's irony when the former delivers a
tirade on his affection for sophisticated restaurants or
for dining with famous contemporaries. In one incident the
narrator uses alimentary image and substance to ironize
Homais' infatuation with appearance: 'Homais *se délectait*.
Quoiqu'il *se grisât* de luxe encore plus que de bonne chère,
le vin de Pommard, cependant, lui excitait un peu les facultés, et lorsque apparut l'omelette au rhum, il exposa sur
les femmes des théories immorales' (*Madame Bovary*, 259-60;
my italics). So ensconced is he in bourgeois *paraître* that
in the final pages of the novel, as Emma lies dying, Homais
ceases to occupy himself with her distress because his propensity for ostentation, for rubbing elbows with the great,
leads him to think only of the honour of dining with the
renowned Dr Larivière, who has come to treat Emma in her
ultimate agony: 'Le pharmacien les rejoignit sur la place,
Il ne pouvait, par tempérament, se séparer des gens célébres.
Aussi conjura-t-il M. Larivière de lui faire cet insigne
honneur d'accepter à déjeuner' (*Madame Bovary*, 298).
  Certainly, this tendency to view the major characters of
the novel as eirons even before Emma's appearance would
subtly coerce the reader into sympathizing with the heroine's
viewpoint on events when she finally does enter into the action of the novel. *Bovarysme*, then, by virtue of the fact
that it constitutes the very essence of the protagonist, is
tentatively established as the psycho-textual norm for the
reader's perception of actors and actions in *Madame Bovary*:

moreover, because events are frequently focalized through Emma, the *norme bovaryste* imposes itself so forcefully that the reader, too, partially appropriates her vision without necessarily sharing her delusion. In the early stages of the novel, and even throughout its evolution, the dichotomous nature of *Bovarysme* often manifests itself in the heroine's alimentary attitudes and in her disaffection with country life. At the real and symbolic centre of the peasant's existence stands the kitchen, for kitchens were and are romantic and magic places. Because of the kitchen's ambivalent symbolism, however, because it is at once the poetically charged '... lieu privilégié de la métamorphose'[7] and the prosaically centred locus of the most routine chores, it serves as an excellent signifying device for exposing the polarities of *Bovarysme*, for the kitchen in *Madame Bovary* has the structural function of acting as the site of the initial meetings between Emma and Charles, then between Emma and her later lovers, and it also has the semiotic function of signalling social and economic status to Emma as well as to the reader. Kitchens are signs, class markers.

With regard to the structural function, it is worth noting that when Charles Bovary first goes to the Rouault farm to set the fractured leg of Emma's father he enters the house through the kitchen. In this first instance the kitchen serves the double purpose of bringing about the initial encounter between Emma and Charles and simultaneously indexing her character and her peasant background:

> Une jeune femme, en robe de mérinos bleu garnie de trois volants, vint sur le seuil de la maison pour recevoir M. Bovary, qu'elle fit entrer dans la cuisine, où flambait un grand feu. Le déjeûner des gens bouillonait alentour, dans des petits pots de taille inégale. Des vêtements humides séchaient dans l'intérieur de la cheminée. La pelle, les pincettes et le bec du soufflet, tous de proportion colossale, brillaient comme de l'acier poli, tandis que le long des murs s'étendait une abondante batterie de cuisine, où miroitait inégalement la flamme claire du foyer, jointe aux premières lueurs du soleil arrivant par les carreaux.
>
> *(Madame Bovary*, 14)[8]

This descriptive evocation of a typical Norman kitchen exploits the motif of the hearth, which suggests congeniality, and implies, by means of reference to fire, flames, and

reflections, that the kitchen mirrors peasant life. Moreover, having met Emma in the kitchen, Charles gets further
acquainted with her in the dining room only to learn that
'Mlle Rouault ne s'amusait guère à la campagne ...' (*Madame
Bovary*, 15). Emma stands in opposition to this hearth motif,
for indeed the kitchen is a metonym of the country life
which she so detests; this scene, then, prepares the reader
for the incompatibilities between Charles and Emma which
will surface in subsequent depictions of domestic meals following their marriage.

It would also be helpful to point out that the kitchen
serves as the initial meeting place for Emma and her future
lovers. When the Bovarys first arrive at the village of Yonville the proprietess of the *Lion d'Or* invites them to dinner, and just as Emma enters the kitchen of the inn she notices Léon, the young man with whom she will later have an
affair: 'Mme Bovary, quand elle fut dans la cuisine, s'ap-
procha de la cheminée ... De l'autre côté de la cheminée,
un jeune homme à chevelure blonde la regardait silencieuse-
ment' (*Madame Bovary*, 74). The ensuing meal further develops
the similarities between Emma and Léon, who finds the boardinghouse atmosphere intolerable because he must dine with
people whose company he does not enjoy. When Léon leaves
Yonville, Emma's loneliness makes her ripe for a liaison
with another local man, Rodolphe. Paying a professional visit
to Charles one afternoon, Rodolphe sees Emma at work in the
kitchen, speaks with her, and makes plans to seduce her.
Emma eventually submits to his advances and agrees to go
horseback riding with him: appropriately, she leaves the
house through the kitchen when embarking on her first amorous escapade.

The second function of kitchens was earlier described as
semiotic because Emma clearly perceives kitchens as signs;
that is, she invariably notices the contrast between kitchens she visits for the first time and her own kitchen.
Generally, the more extraneous elements in the narrator's
descriptions of kitchens, such as details about the décor,
cookware, and sometimes the dishes being prepared, all serve
as indices of socio-economic status to Emma. At the centre
of this semiosis is situated the kitchen on the Rouault
farm, the one which subconsciously haunts her whenever she
enters another kitchen, for, she believes, kitchens signal
social rank.

Emma marries Charles in order to escape from the kitchen
(i.e. the fate of the peasant woman) and is quick to hire a
domestic servant to do the cooking when she and Charles

settle into their new home. Nevertheless, she often has the opportunity to enter bourgeois homes now that she has ascended in social rank; during such visits she directs her attention to the well-equipped kitchens in these fastidious dwellings. Calling on M. Guillaumin to request financial aid, she is escroted to the dining room which is adjacent to the kitchen; as she looks around the room she contrasts it with her own more modest dining area:

> Un large poêle de porcelaine bourdonnait sous un cactus qui emplissait la niche, et, dans les cadres de bois noir, contre la tenture de papier de chêne, il y avait la *Esméralda* de Steuben, avec le Putiphar de Schopin. La table servie, deux réchauds d'argent, le bouton des portes en cristal, le parquet et les meubles, tout reluisait d'une propreté méticuleuse, anglaise; les carreaux étaient décorés, à chaque angle, par des verres de couleur.
> - Voilà une salle à manger, pensait Emma, comme il m'en faudrait une.
>
> (*Madame Bovary*, 280)

This scene is important because it marks Emma's discontentment with her own life: she constantly seeks escape from the reality of her existence (symbolized by the kitchen) by wishing for better material surroundings. Her unfulfilled desires, figuratively described as a perpetual state of hunger, always lead her to make contrasts, particularly in circumstances related to food or to rooms associated with food. Emma never quite comes to accept elegant food and kitchens for what they are, but rather views them as signs of a way of life which she desperately wants to lead, thus creating in herself an unbridgeable space between her 'appetite' and its satiation.

The fact that the three men in Emma's romantic life first make contact with her in the kitchen is no coincidence, nor is it fortuitous that Emma has a propensity for viewing kitchens as signs. Indeed, the multiplicity of kitchen scenes in *Madame Bovary* poses two important critical questions: firstly, are the two functions of the kitchen previously described related to one another? secondly, are these functions subsumed in a larger narrative code? I would like to suggest that both these questions can be answered positively, and furthermore, that kitchens fit into the thematic structure of the novel as a whole. In response to the first question it may be said that the kitchen, in addition to its structural function as locus for character encounters, also operates at the symbolic level of the text, for the narrator intentionally uses it to underscore Emma's dichotomized life, her *Bovarysme*, her oscillation between appearance and reality. Emma's romanticism is, in fact, actualized in her love affairs, and her flights from the banalities of domestic life are symbolized by the kitchen, itself an ambivalent sign, a door simultaneously opening on adventure and closing on domesticity: this explains why she meets her lovers in the kitchen and also why she sets out on amorous affairs from the kitchen.[9]

The use of the kitchen as a symbol revealing polar oppositions of a pathological nature in the heroine parallels its use as a symbol pointing to France's transformation from an agricultural society to a modern industrial state. Flaubert's personal nostalgia for the past, his antipathy toward the Bourgeoisie, betrays itself in his propensity for describing what one historian of cuisine has called the 'romantic kitchen':[10] such kitchens were worlds unto themselves, centres of family life, symbols of unity, strength, and endurance. But the invention of the modern gas stove near midcentury signals the end of an era. No more would kitchens have this socializing and integrating function: because of the more compact gas stove, kitchens would occupy less space, thereby forcing the family into other rooms, diffusing them spatially, separating them from the hearth. Flaubert's nostalgia for 'romantic kitchens' undermines his doctrine of *impassibilité*, for clearly his aesthetic evocations of the 'romantic kitchen' and the ironies underlying his descriptions of the elaborate kitchens of the rich betray his hatred for the Bourgeoisie. Flaubert's implicitly ideological posture as revealed in his attitudes about kitchens brings me to my final point: namely, that kitchen scenes belong to the semiotic apparatus of the novel as a whole. Kitchens are part of the larger thematic structure of *Madame Bovary* to the extent that they function semantically to echo the central theme of the novel (i.e. the conflict between romanticism and realism), but at the same time they operate at the ideological level of the text because they reflect Flaubert's own ambivalence vis-à-vis ineffective sentimentalism and bourgeois practicality.

Though kitchen scenes occur early in the novel and are interspersed throughout, Emma first begins to emerge as the primary actor in the events at that point in the narrative when her wedding to Charles takes place. It is interesting to note in this respect that one of the first indices of her

Bovarysme as made evident through her own actions belongs
to the network of signs centred on the novel's alimentary
and gastronomical discourse. The earliest manifestation of
the conflict between romanticism and realism surfaces in
Emma's discussion with her father about arrangements for
the nuptial meal; contrary to le père Rouault's wishes to
celebrate the wedding in traditional country fasion, Emma,
the romantic, requests that the ceremony unfold at midnight:

> Dans les visites que Charles faisait à la ferme, on cau-
> sait des préparatifs de la noce, on se demandait dans
> quel appartement se donnerait le dîner; on rêvait à la
> quantité de plats qu'il faudrait et quelles seraient les
> entrées.
>   Emma eût, au contraire, désiré se marier à minuit, aux
> flambeaux; mais le père Rouault ne comprit rien à cette
> idée. Il y eut donc une noce, où vinrent quarante-trois
> personnes, où l'on resta seize heures à table, qui recom-
> mença le lendemain et quelque peu les jours suivants.
>   (*Madame Bovary*, 24)

Emma's attraction to flamboyant fare is made apparent in the
dispute with her father: the scene serves to establish her
character in the reader's mind and to prepare him for the
fluctuations in her temperament which occur when, as a house-
wife, she becomes immersed in the daily tedium of uncere-
monious meals.

The bland *repas de ménage* consumed at home in the presence
of Charles are thus made to function as metonyms of Emma's
character and of her malaise and also as symptoms of her
pathology, which arises out of an excessive desire to escape
from the banalities of existence: 'Ainsi, la haine du réel
se confond, chez Mme Bovary, au centre même de sa personalité,
avec le pouvoir de se concevoir autre qu'elle n'est ...'
(de Gaultier, 31). Domestic meals, in particular, attest to
the breach between reality and illusion, for they mark Emma's
dissatisfaction with her marriage and her abhorrence of routine. The first series of meals signalling negative or pathological states of mind occurs just after the wedding feast
when she and Charles arrive at their new home in Tostes: 'La
vieille bonne se présenta, lui fit ses salutations, s'excusa
de ce que le dîner n'était pas prêt, et engagea Madame, en
attendant, à prendre connaissance de sa maison' (*Madame Bovary*,
29). The striking contrast between the previous ceremonial
feast at the wedding banquet and the return to prosaic activity is suggested by this meal which is not yet ready.

Everything in the Bovarys' new home becomes a semiotic
extension of the personality of its master and, therefore,
contributes to the adverse effect it produces on Emma. Dis-
contented with her domestic life, she often daydreams, re-
experiencing her wedding day which becomes more precious
and vivid in memory than it was in reality. What now could
be more of a letdown, more indicative of her malaise, than
the intimate meals with Charles? For him, however, the domestic repasts lead to a kind of bovine contentment: '...
le cœur plein des félicités de la nuit, l'esprit tranquille,
la chair contente, il s'en allait ruminant son bonheur,
comme ceux qui mâchent encore, après dîner, le goût des
truffes qu'ils digèrent' (*Madame Bovary*, 32). By contrast
with Emma, Charles is oblivious to the semiotic character
of meals: he delights in the taste of good food rather than
its appearance. Whereas his failure to manipulate the gastro-
alimentary sign might well attest to a lack of intelligence
on his part, it also signals a wholeness, a sense of belonging in the world, a stasis.

Emma's only escape from a life of total mediocrity is the
occasional *plat coquet* she serves to dinner guests. The routine meals at home, on the other hand, tend to enhance, at
least as far as Emma is concerned, Charles' lack of finesse
and interest in refined dining: '... il mangeait le reste
du miroton, épluchait son fromage, croquait une pomme, vidait
sa carafe, puis s'allait mettre au lit, se couchait sur le
dos et ronflait' (*Madame Bovary*, 40). As a result of this
eventless life Emma soon falls victim to severe spells of
bordeom. It is precisely at this moment that she is lifted
out of her ennui by a change in routine: Emma and Charles
are invited to dine at the chateau of the Marquis d'Andervilliers at Vaubyessard.

Although emotional peaks such as the Vaubyessard ball and
banquet offer Emma sporadic respites from her boredom, they
also entail such rude returns to reality at their conclusion
that Emma's condition gets progressively worse. In the series
of meals which occur after the Vaubyessard ball the psychopathology of the heroine clearly coincides with the manic/
depressive syndrome and reflects itself in her alimentary
attitudes and habits. When Emma returns home after the ball
she has difficulty in readapting to the realities of her
existence much as was the case in more attenuated form when
she moved into her new home after her wedding. Once again,
she begins to fantasize, to create visions of aristocratic
gatherings, to dream of distant lands. In one such revery
she uses a map of Paris as a catalyst to conjure up visions

of life in fashionable Parisian restaurants: 'Dans les
cabinets de restaurants où l'on soupe après minuit riait,
à la clarté des bougies, la foule bigarrée des gens de lettres et des actrices' (*Madame Bovary*, 55). By contrast,
Charles becomes even more intolerable in his eating habits:

> Elle se sentait, d'ailleurs, plus irritée de lui. Il
> prenait, avec l'âge, des allures épaisses; il coupait,
> au dessert, le bouchon des bouteilles vides; il se passait,
> après manger, la langue sur les dents; il faisait en
> avalant sa soupe, un gloussement à chaque gorgée, et,
> comme il commençait d'engraisser, ses yeux, déjà petits,
> semblait remonter vers les tempes par la bouffissure de
> ses pommettes.
>
> (*Madame Bovary*, 58)

Deeply ensconced in bourgeois mediocrity, Emma constantly
anticipates another invitation to Vaubyessard, which never
comes. Consequently, she regresses emotionally and is once
again consumed by boredom. As her despair intensifies her
meals at home grow all the more unbearable until that moment, often referred to by critics, when her very life is
reflected in her dish:

> Mais c'était surtout aux heures des repas qu'elle n'en
> pouvait plus, dans cette petite salle au rez-de-chaussée,
> avec le poêle qui fumait, la porte qui criait, les murs
> qui suintaient, les pavés humides; toute l'amertume de
> son existence lui semblait servie sur son assiette, et,
> à la fumée du bouilli, il montait du fond de son âme
> comme d'autres bouffées d'affadissement.
>
> (*Madame Bovary*, 61)

Following this existential dilemma Emma's appetite deteri-
orates rapidly, causing erratic changes in her eating habits.
Just prior to her relapse into depression, her indecision
and her anxiety take the form of compulsive eating episodes:
'Emma devenait difficile, capricieuse. Elle se commandait
des plats pour elle, n'y touchait point, un jour ne buvait
que du lait pur, et, le lendemain, des tasses de thé à la
douzaine' (*Madame Bovary*, 62). Her need for change, for a
state of equilibrium, becomes so intense that she purposely
encourages illness by diet. Her psychological condition
reaches its paroxysm when she can no longer eat at all:
'Dès lors, elle but du vinaigre pour se fair maigrir, con-
tracta une petite toux sèche et perdit complètement l'appétit'

(*Madame Bovary*, 63). At this point in the narrative it has become evident that the space between Emma and the world is carved out by an excess of appetite, by an incapacity to satisfy her hunger: 'La voracité flaubertienne se montre alors dans son vrai jour, qui est tragique. Car l'échec de la digestion n'empêche pas sa faim de [la] pousser vers de nouveaux objets: ...' (Richard, 124). This scene stands as a prelude to Emma's ultimate rejection of life for, symbolically speaking, the stomach *is* the person; Emma's ingestion of vinegar foreshadows her suicide to the extent that the gastro-intestinal contractions incurred by drinking it figure as a metonym of her shrinking away from life.

Appropriately, the narrator evokes Emma's final decline by concentrating on her loss of appetite. Obsessed with the idea that Charles should become a famous physician, she despairs when he fails in his attempt to glorify the Bovary name by curing a clubfoot. For the first time in her life Emma contemplates suicide: once again, her retreat from existence is signalled by her rejection of food: 'Et il fallut descendre! il fallut se mettre à table! Elle essaya de manger. Les morceaux l'étouffaient' (*Madame Bovary*, 192). Emma's temperament, her *Bovarysme*, proves to be destructive in the end because it prevents her from incorporating the real world. Food is life, and Emma refuses to eat; her need for escape and for a life of illusion is a thinly disguised death-wish. Given the enormous importance of food and meals as they reflect mood and character in *Madame Bovary* it is not surprising that Emma's death actually results from a perverted ingestive process: refusing the food of life, she inverts the nutrition principle - ingestion and digestion of food as assimilation and acceptance of existence - by swallowing poison. Her renunciation - or rather, expurgation - of life is symbolically expressed in her body's violent and convulsive protest against extinction: reality is rejected in a cataclysm of *vomissures*.[11]

In *Madame Bovary* attitudes about food and eating do not always indicate extreme states of psychopathology, even as far as Emma is concerned. Many of her milder neuroses also receive expression through the postures she assumes in situations indirectly related to alimentary and gastronomical practices. Emma leads many lives, in imagination if not in fact. One of her more innocuous illusions consists of adopting the habits of a saint in order to compensate for her lover's recent departure. Unable to find material and psychological felicity, she hopes to attain spiritual satisfaction

by means of abstinence and acts of charity. In her saintly
role she offers food to the poor: 'Alors, elle se livra à
des charités excessives. Elle cousait des habits pour les
pauvres; elle envoyait du bois aux femmes en couches; et
Charles, un jour en rentrant, trouva dans la cuisine trois
vauriens attablés qui mangeaient un potage' (*Madame Bovary*,
201).

The romantic temperament often associates setting with
mood, and Emma Bovary is a classic victim of the pathetic
fallacy. During her liaison with Léon she spends an illusory
honeymoon with him in Rouen, an event that is highlighted
by the couple's excursion to a nearby island where they partake of a meal in a primitive and exotic environment:

> Ils se plaçaient dans la salle basse d'un cabaret, qui
> avait à sa porte des filets noirs suspendus. Ils mange-
> aient de la friture d'éperlans, de la crème et des cérises.
> Ils se couchaient sur l'herbe; ils s'embrassaient à
> l'écart sous les peupliers; et ils auraient voulu, comme
> deux Robinsons, vivre perpétuellement dans ce petit en-
> droit, qui leur semblait, en leur béatitude, le plus
> magnifique de la terre.
>
> (*Madame Bovary*, 238)

One final conclusion might be drawn about Emma's attitudes
toward food: namely, that in all her emotional states of
mind she characteristically ignores the value of food as a
substance in itself. She allies it, rather, with a feeling,
an illusion, or a dream, and never enjoys the simple taste
of a good meal.

Yet other characters, mediocre as they may be, enjoy food
as substance and ceremony: '... la cérémonie alimentaire
change de climat selon la situation et l'atmosphère propre
de chaque roman, mais elle demeure toujours cérémonie, et
toujours la table se dresse entre les hommes comme un lieu
de rencontre, presque de communion' (Richard, 119). These
felicitous meals, while significant and interesting in themselves, place Emma's neurosis into relief, and, although
they do not actually constitute a major meal thematic in
the novel, they nevertheless serve to restore the balance
in the indigestion/digestion metonym. They clearly represent
the average or mediocre character's capacity to regard food
as both sign and substance, and thus to embrace and, in fact,
assimilate life's inconsistencies by incorporating them into
the body where they will be processed and subsequently transformed into wholesome modes of response to reality: 'Digestion,

rumination, ces métaphores alimentaires évoquent un processus de transformation intérieur par lequel la sensation devient non plus seulement mienne, mais moi' (Richard, 123).
Emma is not the only character in the novel whose emotive
states are portrayed in relation to dining situations.
Charles delights at the wedding feast and the reader will
remember how he ruminates in contentment at Emma's home-
cooked dinners. Léon, the young man who will become Emma's
lover, also enjoys the positive effects of congenial company once the Bovarys arrive in Yonville and dine with him
at the *Lion d'Or*. Somewhat morose before their arrival,
Léon's attitude changes after having supped with a lady:
'Le dîner de la veille était pour lui un événement considér-
able; jamais jusqu'alors, il n'avait causé pendant deux
heures de suite avec une *dame*' (*Madame Bovary*, 80).

  Traditionally, meals play an important role with respect
to social rituals. Special ceremonial meals are often re-
served for happy occasions: when Charles feels that he has
successfully completed the operation on the clubfoot, he
naturally decides to celebrate with a dinner:

> Puis, Charles ayant bouclé son malade dans le moteur
> mécanique, s'en retourna chez lui, où Emma, toute anxieuse,
> l'attendait sur la porte. Elle lui sauta au cou; ils se
> mirent à table; il mangea beaucoup, et même il voulut,
> au dessert, prendre une tasse de café, débauche qu'il ne
> se permettait que le dimanche lorsqu'il y avait du monde.
> (*Madame Bovary*, 165)

Customarily, perhaps pardoxically, meals also celebrate moments of relief and respite from life's tragedies. Incongru-
ous though it may seem, the meal following Emma's death enables Homais and Bournisien, heretofore enemies, to regain
their equilibrium and to put an end to former hostilities:

> Félicité avait soin de mettre pour eux, sur la commode,
> une bouteille d'eau-de-vie, un fromage et une grosse
> brioche. Aussi l'apothicaire, qui n'en pouvait plus,
> soupira, vers quatre heures du matin:
> - Ma foi, je me sustenterais avec plaisir! L'écclésiasti-
> que ne se fit point prier; il sortit pour aller dire sa
> messe, revint; puis ils mangèrent et trinquèrent, tout en
> ricanant un peu, sans savoir pourquoi, excités par cette
> gaieté vague qui nous prend après des séances de tristesse;
> et, au dernier petit verre, le prêtre dit au pharmacien,
> tout en lui frappant sur l'épaule:

- Nous finirons par nous entendre!

(*Madame Bovary*, 310)

But this ostensibly reconciliatory repast has an underlying symbolic function which outweighs its surface significance of bringing two former adversaries together, for essentially it signals a return to the living, an integration into the mainstream of life, hence a triumph over *Bovarysme*. In this short scene the pleasures of ingestion and the stabilizing function of the meal as a *point de repère* amidst life's vicissitudes re-establish the unity of vision which is experienced by the emotionally stable no matter how 'mediocre' they may be. There is both an irony and a reassurance in the fact that the seemingly inconsequential acts of being (form and substance united) prevail over the grandiose gestures of appearance (form and substance divided). In the end *être* predominates over *paraître* - and Homais and Bournisien sup while Emma sleeps.

The Major Banquets of Madame Bovary: A Confluence of Codes

Up to now meal scenes have been discussed primarily in relation to those psychological codes of the novel which centre around the phenomenon of *Bovarysme*, particularly as it reveals itself in Emma's attitudes about routine dining at home. For the most part the domestic meals correspond to the depressive component of Emma's psychopathology: her ennui, her disaffection with country life, her revulsion before banality and mediocrity. The manic side of her personality, on the other hand, is placed into relief in the major banqueting scenes of the novel, but in these instances her character constitutes only one of several signs in the coding systems associated with gastronomical and alimentary discourse. In these revels and repasts the reader witnesses a kind of semiotic convergence of the novel's psychological, sociological, ideological, and narrative codes: all is subsumed in the aesthetic principle of structuration; coherence evolves not so much from the story told but rather from the telling of the story.

In order to familiarize the reader with the multiple structural functions of meal episodes in *Madame Bovary* a general theoretical statement on the novel's gastro-alimentary structuration would be appropriate at this point. An analysis of the various eating scenes in *Madame Bovary* demonstrates that Flaubert uses the same narrative techniques in depicting the pivotal banquets (the wedding feast,

the Vaubyessard ball and banquet, the *Comices agricoles*)
that he uses when describing routine meals taken in the
Bovary home or in restaurants. Moveover, it should now be
made apparent that whereas those semiotic phenomena related
to *Bovarysme* fall into binary groupings – *Bovarysme* is in
effect a bipolar syndrome – the larger aesthetic discourse
of the novel occurs as a series of ternary structurations:
there are, for instance, three macro-meals whose stylistic,
organizational, and anecdotal elements themselves unfold in
a tripartite exposition. Finally, three fundamental structural and narrative strategies emerge from Flaubert's meal
depictions: first, meals form an integral part of the structural rhythms and modulations of the novel to the extent
that the pivotal banquets are carefully counterpoised with
the routine repasts; second, the evocation and unfolding of
individual dining episodes conform to a rather uniform stylistic patterning, and; third, macro-meals are presented in
a similar, often identical, manner.

From what we have learned so far about the gastronomical
and alimentary discourse in *Madame Bovary* it should be quite
evident that all repasts in the novel may be broadly classified as macro- or micro-meals, and that the former correspond to the positive aspects of eating and the latter to
the negative. It is important to note that this formal opposition also reflects the novel's principal thematic and
actantial categories: Emma's dichotomized personality, for
example, or its metonym, the opposition between romanticism
and materialism. For the most part macro-meals mark the summits in the heroine's life, moments of elation, flights from
reality, contacts with the aristocracy, in short the manic
pole of her personality. The micro-meals, on the other hand,
are associated with the banal pole of existence for Emma:
they unmask the pallid face of reality and figure either
as signs or as symptoms of the depressive syndrome in her
character. In effect, the antithetical structure of meal
scenes in *Madame Bovary* becomes the metonymic transform of
the pathology of the heroine.

The stylistic pattern used for all the major banquets also
parallels its organizational structure in so far as it consists of contrasting stylistic contexts. The descriptive
passages which precede the meal episode comprise a kind of
macro-context in which banality, boredom, and routine are
accentuated. The banquets themselves, however, form a micro-
context which is stylistically saturated with references to
food, feelings, and felicity: generally, the narrator evokes
Emma's elation during the various stages of the micro-sequence.

Following his hyperbolic description of the meal itself the
narrator employs once again a neutral stylistic context
which marks Emma's return to, and discontentment with, reality.

Similarly, the narrator's manner of presenting the banquet
scenes within the micro-context may also be reduced to a
ternary formula. It consists of a *preparatory phase* comprising, among other things, the arrival of the guests, a description of their clothing and mannerisms, references to the
décor, and an enumeration of the social activities preceding
the meal; the *actual meal-event* wherein the narrator centres
his attention on the silverware, the table setting, the
seating protocol, the dishes served, and such codified practices as table etiquette, duration of the meal, and the socialization process; the *sequel*, which includes those activities normally following the meal - dancing, conversing,
and gambling. Also, depending on the effect that the narrator wants to produce on the reader, this entire sequence of
events is presented either from an exterior perspective (the
omniscient narrator) when he decides to throw customs, social practices, or gastronomy into relief for their own sake,
or from the interior perspective (usually focalized through
Emma) when he seeks to emphasize the emotional impact of the
meal on a particular character. Finally, within a given
micro-context, the narrator usually alternates the perspectives and varies the rhythms of the three phases much as a
dramatist would do in order to compensate for the introduc-
tory, expositional, and conclusive restraints imposed upon
him by the exigencies of classical form.

The feast provided by le père Rouault to honour his daughter's
betrothal constitutes the first major banquet described in
Madame Bovary. The narrator places it between two low-key
or neutral chapters in order to make it all the more resplen-
dent: such is the pattern he will continue to use for similar meal-events throughout the novel. In conformity with the
formula for the presentation of macro-meals, the preceding
chapter deals with the events leading up to the marriage
while the following chapter gradually releases the reader
from the aesthetic experience of the nuptial meal and eases
him back again into the routine existence Charles and Emma
fall into from the very beginning of their marriage. The
effects of the wedding feast may also be considered stylistically as regards the preceding and following chapters: the
reader observes an opposition between the hyperbolic descriptive context of the nuptial revel and the more monotonous

tones of daily repasts and activities. In contrast to the
splendour of the wedding party, the description of the
Bovary home in Tostes, for example, evokes the domesticity
and blandness which will characterize much of Charles and
Emma's connubial life: 'Derrière la porte se trouvaient
accroché un manteau à petit collet, une bride, une casquette
de cuir noir, et, dans un coin, à terre, une pair de house-
aux encore couverts de boue sèche. A droite était la salle,
c'est-à-dire l'appartement où l'on mangeait et où l'on se
tenait' (*Madame Bovary*, 30).

In the depiction of the wedding feast the formal techniques put into relief both the aesthetic subtleties of feasting and the customs of peasants. It is quite apparent that
this meal is a kind of ritual or ceremonial dinner which
serves an important function in the lives of the betrothed
and in rural society as a whole. On the one hand, it is
deeply rooted in contemporary anthropological and sociological practices and, on the other hand, it also belongs to the
tradition of ancient, even archetypal, rural wedding ceremonies.[12] The description of the banquet proper radiates
like a *pièce de résistance* surrounded by lesser dishes,
placed as it is in the centre of the other wedding activities. Within the formula established for macro-meals, this
feast itself constitutes the micro-context, which the narrator opens by describing the setting, the table, and the fare.

The banquet sequence begins with an allusion to the location of the table and to some of the courses being served:
'C'était sous le hangar de la charretterie que la table
était dressée. Il y avait quatre aloyaux, six fricassées de
poulets, du veau à la casserole, trois gigots et, au milieu,
un joli cochon de lait rôti, flanqué de quatre andouilles à
l'oseille' (*Madame Bovary*, 26). The outdoor setting and the
dishes clearly place this revel in the world of provincial
cookery; the distribution of the food on the table asserts
the regional character of the meal while simultaneously accentuating its Norman flavour: 'Aux angles, se dressait
l'eau-de-vie, dans des carafes. Le cidre doux en bouteilles
poussait sa mousse épaisse autour des bouchons et tous les
verres, d'avance avaient été remplis de vin jusqu'au bord.
De grands plats de crème jaune, qui flottait d'eux-mêmes au
moindre choc de la table, présentaient, dessinés sur leur
surface unie, les chiffres des nouveaux époux en arabesques
non-pareille' (*Madame Bovary*, 27).

The narrator elaborately evokes the important sociological
and festive aspects of the meal in that now classic scene
wherein he describes a very stylized *pièce montée*. Such an

occasion warrants an unusual course, one that does not figure in the daily lives of farmers and peasants; thus Rouault,
in order to make it known that he is not indifferent to
lavishness and pomp, in order to reveal that he, too, perceives the value of food as a sign, has a pastry cook brought
in from the city to prepare the wedding cake. In a beauti-
fully sumptuous and memorable scene which unveils at once
Flaubert's formidable culinary knowledge and his authorial
irony, the reader is treated to a poetically charged description of the cake:

> A la base d'abord, c'était un carré de carton bleu figu-
> rant un temple avec portiques, colonades et statuettes
> du stuc tout autour, dans des niches constellées d'étoiles
> en papier doré; puis se tenait au second stage un donjon
> en gâteau de Savoie, entouré de menues fortifications en
> angélique, amandes, raisins secs, quartiers d'orange; et
> enfin, où il y avait des rochers avec des lacs de confit-
> ure et des bateaux en écales de noisettes, on voyait un
> petit Amour, se balançant à une escarpolette de chocolat,
> dont les deux poteaux étaient terminés par deux boutons
> de rose naturelle, en guise de boules, au sommet.
>
> (*Madame Bovary*, 27)

This scene is one of the best examples of culinary stylization in French literature, for indeed the alimentary value
of the *pièce montée* is metonymically displaced only to be
replaced by an artistic and symbolic significance which
transcends the mimetic aspect of the description. Essentially, the raw material of food undergoes a double aesthetic
transformation: in the first mimetic phase, the ingredients
for the wedding cake are moulded by the culinary artist,
the *pâtissier*, into an architectural edifice, an alimentary
artifact; in the second phase the literary artist, Flaubert,
transposes the verbal character of his description into an
icon, a visual analogue. This process of double encoding,
which creates a space between the represented and the re-
presentation, endows the *pièce montée* with an existence of
its own: it becomes an aesthetic entity that transcends
time and region to be immortalized in literature.

In the next descriptive sequence the narrator concentrates
on the unfolding of the various stages of the meal. Timing
is essential, for the activities that take place between
the courses give the reader a glimpse into the world of
rural customs and behaviour. It is particularly appropriate
that the narrator reports these different moments in an

enumerative style and that he alternates eating episodes
with social activity:

> Jusqu'au soir, on mangea. Quand on était trop fatigué
> d'être assis, on allait se promener dans les cours ou
> jouer une partie de bouchon dans la grange, puis on
> revenait à table. Quelques uns, vers la fin, s'y endor-
> mirent et ronflèrent. Mais, au café, tout se ranima;
> alors on entonna des chansons, on fit des tours de force,
> on portait des poids, on passait sous son pouce, on
> essayait à soulever les charrettes sur ses épaules, on
> disait des gaudrioles, on embrassait les dames.
>
> (*Madame Bovary*, 27)

The activities described during the intervals of the meal
exemplify the rural way of life and serve as a contrast to
the banquet that will take place at Vaubyessard. In this
outdoor revel, however, the narrator emphasizes eating as
vitality, as energy, as overt and wholesome activity revealing a certain congruence between man and nature. At the
Vaubyessard ball, on the contrary, he foregrounds the function of food as sign, as class marker, as clandestine code
of which only the happy few are cognizant.

In the concluding passages of the wedding feast the narrator shifts his focus from integrated activity - the con-
fluent rituals of peasants and farmers - to divisive actions
- the divergent behaviours occasioned and imposed by a hier-
archical social organization. At this point the narrative
perspective changes from global view to close-range focus,
with the result that the reader now has the opportunity to
witness the reactions of certain important participants at
the feast. In his endeavour to portray the social psychology
of this particular group the narrator centres his attention
on various individuals, beginning with Emma as she refuses
the traditional wedding prank: 'La mariée avait supplié son
père qu'on lui épargnât les plaisanteries d'usage' (*Madame
Bovary*, 27). By rejecting peasant tradition Emma symbolically renounces her way of life; in spite of her recalcit-
rance, a cousin decides to play the trick anyway, much to
the chagrin of le père Rouault. Although he belongs to
rural society and conforms to its traditions, he asks the
cousin not to carry out the ritual prank because of extenu-
ating circumstances - the presence of the socially superior
Bovary family. Such a breach of codes of conduct inevitably
results in a feeling of animosity between le père Rouault
and the offended cousin.

The animosity activated by this incident becomes the dominant psychological motif during the remainder of the description of the wedding feast and contrasts sharply with the
ambience of gaiety which preceded the incident. At the epicentre of this hostility lurks the unstated but invidious
practice of social stratification: the animus of the cousin
thus engenders a more pervasive feeling of malaise and rancour among many of the guests. Food itself becomes an instrument of provocation; in one scene the furious cousin is
seated at the table with some other guests who are angry because they were served unsuitable slices of meat: 'En dedans
de lui-même, il accusa le père Rouault d'être fier, et il
alla se joindre dans un coin à quatre ou cinq autres des
invités qui, ayant eu par hasard plusieurs fois de suite à
table les bas morceaux des viandes, trouvaient aussi qu'on
les avait mal reçus, chuchotaient sur le compte de leur hôte
et souhaitaient sa ruine à mots couverts' (*Madame Bovary*,
28). They mistakenly assumed that the finest cuts went to
the most important guests, an assumption which is certainly
understandable considering the semiotic hierarchies established for various cuts taken from the same animal and then
coordinated with larger social and economic stratification.
In this particular scene, food functions as a social metonym
for the offended guests, for certainly their animosity results not from the taste or the quality of the meat they
receive but rather from its connotative value as gastronomical sign: they perceive a homology between social and alimentary structures when in fact the resemblance is only coincidental.

Charles' mother, too, regards herself as having been ill
received by the Rouault clan because she was excluded from
the culinary corps which planned and prepared the meal. A
social code thus becomes manifest in her attitude: as a member of the upper bourgeoisie she finds herself alienated
from the peasants, farmers, and *petits bourgeois* who attend
the banquet. As she envisages it, her only role in this
ceremony is a passive one: she is expected to be in atten-
dance at the wedding ceremony and to sup at the banquet,
nothing more. Consequently, having been excluded from the
Rouault group, she in return excludes herself by leaving
the table prematurely and retiring, a gesture which obviously
signals her displeasure: 'Mme Bovary mère n'avait pas des-
serré les dents de la journée. On ne l'avait consultée ni
sur la toilette de la bru, ni sur l'ordonnance du festin;
elle se retira de bonne heure' (*Madame Bovary*, 28). It might
be pointed out that Mme Bovary's behaviour is coded orally,

as well as gastronomically, in the few passages which describe her at the wedding table, for the buccal symbolism of the *dents serrées* would imply a rejection and exclusion in itself, especially within the framework of Freud's theories on orality. In this particular case Mme Bovary mère refuses to incorporate what she considers to be *le bas monde*, just as the offended guests in the preceding passages declined *les bas morceaux de viande*.

M. Bovary père also distinguishes himself from the group of provincials by adopting an attitude of gastronomical snobbery: he sips a drink unknown to the other guests, knowing all the while that this action will enhance his stature: 'Son époux, au lieu de la suivre, envoya chercher des cigares à Saint-Victor et fuma jusqu'au soir, tout en buvant des grogs au Kirsch, mélange inconnu à la compagnie, et qui fut pour lui la source d'une considération plus grande encore' (*Madame Bovary*, 28).

For the primary significance of the wedding feast the reader must understand the social and psychological interactions among the guests. No single character, not even Emma, receives more attention from the narrator than another in this scene: its success depends on the conflicts established between the insiders, or rural peasant group, and the outsiders, or the provincial bourgeoisie. The animosity discussed earlier results from the co-presence of divergent ideologies and from the incompatibility of the two groups' codes of conduct. The action which triggered the animosity opened a familiar wound. On the one hand, the group of insiders shares a somewhat collective identity based on region, customs, and class; it enjoys a sense of total participation in the activities, it relies on a code of intra-group association with little differentiation between its members. On the other hand, the outsiders, namely the Bovarys, lack this feeling of belonging to the group of revellers; in fact they actually cultivate this lack by increasing the social distance between themselves and their hosts. For them, intimacy on the social scale would constitute a form of debasement; consequently, they exclude themselves from the group by means of offensive actions and attitudes: theirs is a transgression of codes which manifests itself in terms of gastronomical and alimentary signs.

It is both surprising and significant that Charles and Emma receive so little attention during the wedding banquet. The reader can easily understand the narrator's neglect of Charles' actions because of his mediocrity; Emma's situation, however, would seem to demand more development. After all, this is her wedding day and it would be natural for the narrator to depict the events of the banquet through her eyes, as he will do at the Vaubyessard ball. The minimal focus on and through Emma can undoubtedly be explained by the narrator's ironic posture vis-à-vis his heroine: for a romantic like Emma the joy of the feast occupies the imagination either in the form of anticipation and revery or in the memories which the event provides. Immersion in the reality of the moment rarely impresses her. *Bovarysme*, which is here made apparent in Emma's non-participation in peasant rituals and in the enmity this behaviour generates among the guests, implies distance and dissonance. Feasting, on the other hand, implies incessant renewal and flux, a concert of actions and events culminating in a state of harmony and constant participation. The narrator does not fail to evoke, if only implicitly, the state of integration which archetypal feasting engenders, the unanimity and wholeness in which time is suspended and the world forgotten. Revellers and farm animals alike conjoin in celebratory praise of the earth's bounty: 'Le soir, pour partir, les chevaux gorgés d'avoine jusqu'aux naseau eurent du mal à entrer dans les brancards; ils ruaient, se cabraient, les harnais se cassaient, leurs maîtres juraient ou riaient ...' (*Madame Bovary*, 27). In the closing passages of the wedding feast the narrator creates a carnival-like atmosphere wherein he portrays the universal elements of feasting. The continuous display of festivities and actions - the *parade*, once set in motion, continues throughout the night in a seemingly timeless succession: '... et toute la nuit, au clair de la lune, par les routes du pays, il y eut des carrioles emportées qui couraient au grand galop ... Ceux qui restèrent aux Bertaux passèrent la nuit à boire dans la cuisine. Les enfants s'étaient endormis sous les bancs' (*Madame Bovary*, 27).

Chronologically speaking, the aristocratic banquet at La Vaubyessard is the second pivotal feast in *Madame Bovary*, yet it is certainly the first in importance in its effect on the heroine. The wedding revel offered Emma few memories and left her relatively uninspired because it was, after all, a familiar part of her world. In one sense it epitomizes peasant reality, the very condition Emma so desperately tries to avoid. Traditionally a wedding day remains a coveted memory, the ultimate day of bliss in a woman's life; for Emma, however, it is the Vaubyessard ball which occupies the most cherished niche in her memory. Yet, in spite of the

fact that this scene represents the one instance in the
novel wherein a confluence occurs between the mythos of
aristocracy and the ethos of mediocrity, Emma is treated
somewhat ironically because she fails to perceive the vacuity implicit in aristocratic opulence; instead, she stands
in distant and speechless awe of the spectacle without
fully participating in it.

Using the same technique as for other macro-meals, the
narrator opens the Vaubyessard sequence with a description
of the chateau of the Marquis d'Andervilliers: viewed from
the outside, as Emma and Charles would see it upon their arrival, the marquis' residence radiates an aura of splendour,
elegance, and refinement. These early descriptive phases set
the tone for the meal by making the reader aware that the
chateau and the immensity of the lawns, the gardens, and
the stables impress Emma in their grandeur and prepare her
for the marvels yet to come. In the opening sequences of
this scene, then, the narrator has opted for an exterior
perspective – the firm setting of the milieu in the mind of
the character and reader – precisely because of the power
of such patrician surroundings to produce strong feelings
in Emma.

The psychological point of view adopted here is that of
an outsider, a neophyte, witnessing an event for the first
time. The structural formula for meal presentations, however, unfolds from an interior perspective in order to accentuate Emma's perceptions of and reactions to aristocratic
customs; moreover, meticulous documentation of the sumptuous
décor, the clothes of the guests, and the copious gastronomical delights seems only natural here since an initiate
would notice and attempt to digest all these novelties. The
social and economic sphere evoked in this description of
Vaubyessard stands in direct opposition to those spheres
portrayed at Emma's wedding feast: whereas the participants
at the latter event were rural peasants for the most part,
the guests at the ball belong to the provincial *haute-
bourgeoisie* and aristocracy. Their diversions, unlike the
feats of strength and the revelry at the wedding party, may
be classified among the parlour variety and reveal little
intermingling of the sexes. Their clothes and the furnishings of the chateau reflect their class affiliation, and
the ball, contrary to the wedding, has no institutionalized
ceremonial function but rather represents an indulgence of
the gentry, a social rite without ritual aspects other than
the formally vacant *etiquettes*, *protocoles*, and *formules de
politesse*. Even the banquet, as may be expected, follows a

different gastronomical pattern from the wedding: at Vaubyessard the evening begins and ends with a meal. During the interval between the *dîner* and the *souper* the ball occurs. Finally, whereas time was suspended at the wedding feast so as to produce an archetypal ambience, it is here highly structured and codified in order to capture and reinstate, if only for a few hours, the lost and cherished times of the *Ancien Régime*.

In the initial passages of the meal context the narrator presents the festivity entirely through Emma. Evoking the emotional impact of Vaubyessard on her, he uses a lexicon rich with allusions to sensation:

> Emma se sentit, en entrant, enveloppée par un air chaud, mélange du parfum des fleurs et du beau linge, du fumet des viandes et de l'odeur des truffes. Les bougies des candélabres allongeaient des flammes sur les cloches d'argent; les cristaux à facettes, couverts d'une buée mâte, se renvoyaient des rayons pâles ...
>
> (*Madame Bovary*, 45)

This description is characteristic of the formula employed for most banquet scenes: the effect of Emma's excitement is communicated by the narrator's sensorial approach to description, for he begins the episode with the verb *se sentir* and then relates everything to the other senses stimulated. This technique results in a sensory blend that relies heavily on the harmonious mixture of the scents of flowers, linen, meats, and truffles along with the brilliant effects produced by the reflections of candlelight on the silverware and crystal.

Then, having titillated the reader's senses with light and delicate aromas, the narrator concentrates on the table setting and the delicacies displayed before Emma. This gastronomically stylized vignette creates an impression of elegance and opulence:

> ... des bouquets étaient en ligne sur toute la longueur de la table, et, dans les assiettes à large bordure, les serviettes, arrangées en manière de bonnet d'évêque, tenaient entre le baillement de leurs deux plis chacune un petit pain de forme ovale. Les pattes rouges des homards dépassaient les plats; de gros fruits dans des corbeilles à jour s'étageaient sur la mousse; les cailles avaient leurs plumes, des fumées montaient ...
>
> (*Madame Bovary*, 45)

This dinner surpasses the wedding feast in every way: the
sensuous atmosphere, the table arrangement, the exquisite
dishes all contribute to a feeling of distinction. Emma
visually devours the sumptuous fare so characteristic of
classic cuisine and realizes that the dishes, like the
guests, are emblematic of superiority.[13] For the heroine
and for the reader, this meal epitomizes culinary stylization: the food comprises an elite repertory of dishes from
the world of gastronomy just as the amphytrions figure as
the cream of society. The impression of epicurean splendour
becomes even more vivid in Emma's mind as she watches the
maître d'hôtel at work: '... et, en bas de soie, en culotte
courte, en cravate blanche, en jabot, grave comme un juge,
le maître d'hôtel, passant entre les épaules des convives
les plats tous découpés, faisait d'un coup de sa cuiller
sauter pour vous le morceau qu'on choisissait' (*Madame
Bovary*, 45). *Bovarysme*, though somewhat couched in the
connotative language of these passages, is made evident in
the narrator's emphasis on witnessing, on speechlessness, on
non-participation. Emma decodes the gastronomical signs and
markers but nowhere is her actual distance from food more
apparent: she sees surfaces only, never once penetrating
the veneer to delight, as did Rabelaisian heroes, in the
epistemological ecstasy of the *substantifique moelle*:

> Tout se trouve ici gâché par l'immédiateté du contract;
> et c'est bien l'un des aspects de la maladie bovaryste
> que ce marque fondamental de *retenue*: ... L'artiste se
> détache du paysage: il le tient à bout de bras ou de pin-
> ceau pour le laisser s'établir devant lui dans la vérité
> de son équilibre. Mais Emma se jette goulûment sur toutes
> les proies et voulant tout immédiatement consommer, elle
> ne peut rien retenir.
>
> (Richard, 124)

Throughout the remainder of the meal Emma drifts in and
out of reveries. Ironically, one fantasy episode finds her
aggrandizing the marquis' father-in-law, who because of his
advanced age and unrefined table manners is somewhat alienated from the rest of the company but who, in Emma's estimation, must have enjoyed many amorous moments in the arms
of noble ladies. The contrast between the vulgar reality
of the old man's eating habits as described by the narrator
('... un vieillard mangeait, laissant tomber de sa bouche
des gouttes de sauce,' *Madame Bovary*, 46), and the sublime
illusion into which Emma projects him ('Il avait vécu à la

Cour et couché dans le lit des reines!' *Madame Bovary*, 46),
once again reveals her capacity for self-deception, for
even when her desire to be in the presence of the aristocracy is realized she escapes to revery in still another
attempt to surpass the unsurpassable. However, the advent
of the champagne course recalls Emma to the realities of
the world surrounding her and, for the first and only time
in the novel, the narrator describes an ephemeral but au-
thentic correspondence between food-as-sign and food-as-
substance: 'On versa du vin de Champagne à la glace. Emma
frissonna de toute sa peau en sentant ce froid dans sa
bouche. Elle n'avait jamais vu de grenades ni mangé d'an-
anas. Le sucre en poudre même lui parut plus blanc et plus
fin qu'ailleurs' (*Madame Bovary*, 46). The tingling chill of
the champagne and the visual exoticism of the tropical fruits
strike Emma by their novelty; the fact that she experiences
them, that she *tastes* them, for the first time impresses
them more indelibly on her palate where they will leave
their traces for years to come.

The ball forms the penultimate link in the chain of events
occurring during this fabulous evening. As the sound of horns
and music announces the beginning of the dance Emma witnesses
another spectacular scene which the narrator describes as
it affects her senses. Indeed, the entire evening takes on
the character of an initiation ceremony in which Emma, the
neophyte, is introduced to the rituals of the gentry. She
wanders about the room, observing and listening as she goes.
Noble ladies and gentlemen speak of faraway lands which Emma
knows only vicariously through her reading. At this point
in the evening her rural background seems very remote, but
just as her present illusion reaches its zenith she notices
some peasant faces peering through the window, and her
thoughts return abruptly to her father's farm. The fragile
world in which she has been moving for the past few hours
is momentarily shattered by the force of reality.

Fortunately for Emma, the illusion prevails. Before retiring, she is treated to one more delight: in conformity with
aristocratic tradition that had begun to disappear by midcentury, the *souper* is served at midnight. Once again the
descriptive context becomes dense with the narrator's allusions to the alimentary, once more exotic and delicate foods
abound: 'Après le souper, où il y eut beaucoup de vins
d'Espagne et de vins du Rhin, des potages à la bisque et au
lait d'amandes, des puddings à la Trafalgar et toutes sortes
de viandes froides avec des gelées alentour qui tremblaient
dans les plats ...' (*Madame Bovary*, 49). Shortly after the

souper the evening activities begin to subside, but not before 3:00 a.m. when the final waltz is played and Emma, astonished that a viscount invites her to dance, is swept away in the rapturous whirlwind motion of the waltz: 'Ils tournaient; tout tournait autour d'eux, les lampes, les meubles, les lambris, et le parquet, comme un disque sur un pivot' (*Madame Bovary*, 50).

The principal impact of the evening's activities, which include the prelude to the banquet, the *dîner*, the ball, and the *souper*, results from the impressionistic rendering the events make on Emma's sensibilities. She is overwhelmed by the brilliance of the exterior, yet, expectedly, the character of the aristocrats escapes her. Emma notices only the material symbols of the good life; for this reason the entire ceremony is highly stylized. The importance of food for Emma lies in what it signifies not in what it is. This infatuation with the sign becomes most apparent at the table: the meal is set in a romantic ambience, the courses are sumptuous and exotic. The entire episode may be interpreted as an oneiric sequence in which the noblemen become little more than the symbolic projections of their clothes, their jewellery and, appropriately, their food: 'Ils avaient le teint de la richesse, ce teint blanc que rehaussent la pâleur des porcelaines, les moires de satin, le vernis des beaux meubles, et qu'entretient dans sa santé un régime discret de nourritures exquises' (*Madame Bovary*, 48). The reader can well detect a total absence of intellectual interactions on Emma's part in the Vaubyessard sequence: she does not engage in conversations, she overhears them; she does not notice the taste of food but rather its splendour and elegance; ultimately, she is absent even *in praesentia*.

At the conclusion of this spectacular event Emma attempts to sustain the illusion. As she and Charles make their return journey home, she sits in total silence until, suddenly, a group of cavaliers appears; the sight of these gentlemen projects her back into the mood of the previous day: 'Emma crut reconnaître le vicomte ...' (*Madame Bovary*, 51). This lingering illusion abruptly disappears when Emma and Charles arrive home, for the fact that the maid has not yet completed preparations for the evening meal reminds Emma of the hiatus between her normal life and the special aristocratic revel she has just attended. Under the present circumstances, Emma cannot contain herself: the tension between reality and dream now becomes a source of discomfort for her. Although this minor neglect on the part of her servant is not unusual in her home, Emma subconsciously transposes social codes and expects her maid to perform as graciously as the domestics at Vaubyessard. The meal that she and Charles are now about to eat further enhances her feelings of inferiority. The main course, which consists of onion soup and veal, makes the semiotic apparatus of food transparent, since these particular aliments are staples of the provincial bourgeoisie. The narrator's irony becomes evident in his allusion to the dishes served and in Charles' reaction to them:

> Il y avait pour dîner de la soupe à l'oignon, avec un morceau de veau à oseille. Charles, assis devant Emma, dit en se frottant les mains d'un air heureux:
> - Cela fait plaisir de se retrouver chez soi!
>
> (*Madame Bovary*, 52)

Gradually releasing the reader from the hyperbolic context of the Vaubyessard banquet, the narrator reports the effects of the ball on Emma two days after its termination. The evening at Vaubyessard was, in the eyes of Emma Bovary, the most blissful moment in her life; nothing will equal it in her memory. So overwhelming was Vaubyessard upon her senses and sensibilities that she uses it to measure the passage of time: it thus becomes a point of reference, an emotional barometer for all past and future events in her life: 'Son voyage à la Vaubyessard avait fait un trou dans sa vie, à la manière de ces grandes crevasses qu'un orage, en une seule nuit, creuse quelquefois dans les montagnes' (*Madame Bovary*, 53). The image of the *creux* underscores the appetite motif, or that social and psychological distance which Emma establishes between herself and the world. Her main occupation henceforth will be to relive this grand evening in memory and revery, to recreate its mystique, to re-experience its magic: all future events, by comparison, will leave her filled with disappointment and regret. Never again will her appetite be sated; her first and only 'taste' of the genteel life will slowly dissolve in the sea of time: 'Ce fut donc une occupation pour Emma que le souvenir de ce bal. Toutes les fois que revenait le mercredi, elle se disait en s'éveillant: "Ah! il y a huit jours ... il y a quinze jours ... il y a trois semaines ... j'y étais!"' (*Madame Bovary*, 53).

The *comices agricoles* comprise the last major banquet scene in *Madame Bovary*. As before, the narrator utilizes a pastoral celebration in an attempt to contrast Emma's romantic temperament with the more prosaic personality of the peasant.

In typical fashion he begins the *comices* scene with a look
at the elaborate preparations made for the feast. The *comices*
figure as the most memorable day in the life of Yonville,
the village selected by the government as the site for the
nation's tribute to commerce, agriculture, and industry.
In this particular scene, for one of the few times in the
novel, the reader witnesses a shift in emphasis from food-
as-sign to food-as-function. For this reason, during the
unfolding of the preliminary events leading up to the banquet, the narrator rarely refers to Emma but rather focuses
his gaze on her counterpart, M. Homais, as he delivers a
pompous but appropriate tirade on the virtues of agronomy.
Homais' rather lengthy discourse conforms perfectly to the
occasion, since it entails an implicit commentary on food
and agriculture along with their close relation to the
physiological and scientific aspects of eating. In effect,
Homais' remarks, with their positivistic emphasis on the
interdependence of nature and science, with their many references to the substantial and the material, constitute the
antipole of *Bovarysme:*

> - Croyez-vous qu'il faille, pour être agronome, avoir
> soi-même labouré la terre ou engraissé des volailles?
> Mais il faut connaître plutôt la constitution des sub-
> stances dont il s'agit, les gisements géologiques, les
> actions atmosphériques, la qualité des terrains, des
> minéraux, des eaux, la densité des différents corps et
> leur capillarité! Que sais-je? Et il faut posséder à fond
> tous les principes d'hygiène, pour diriger, critiquer la
> construction des bâtiments, le régime des animaux, l'ali-
> mentation des domestiques!
> - Plût à Dieu que nos agriculteurs fussent des chimistes
> ...

(*Madame Bovary*, 125)

Although he is ironized by the narrator, Homais displays a
rather modern consciousness in his advocacy of a holistic
philosophy of the alimentary cycle. In fact his attitude
reflects the thinking of certain social theorists such as
Fourier and Cabet, who believed that gastronomy belongs to
a much larger category of activities beginning with the
scientific cultivation of crops, their distribution, their
manner of preservation and preparation, their use in medical
and allied sciences, and, finally, the process of ingesting
them.[14]

The *comices agricoles* is a very lengthy scene containing
much extraneous detail that does not always relate to the
topic of food. The initial stages of the description, for
example, are devoted to speeches extolling the virtues of
agriculture and of all that is 'natural.' According to one
of the speakers agriculture forms the basis of man's very
existence: we owe our first allegiance to the earth because
it provides us with our basic needs – food and clothing.
Significantly, these are the two elements that the narrator
accentuated at the wedding feast and at the Vaubyessard
ball, but from a different angle – as signs, not as substances. In the peasant mentality, especially, food and
clothing undergo fewer sign transformations than among the
more sophisticated classes, though that is not to say that
they lack semiotic status for simple folks but rather that
peasants tend to consider the content of the alimentary more
than its form. On the other hand, the functional nature of
food and clothing is somewhat perverted by the concept of
stylization; these two sign-substances acquire a connotation
of social distinction; they become contaminated, as it were,
or overdetermined by their value as signs. Emma's tragedy,
as we have seen, her divergence from the normal customs of
her class, results from her inability to see *things* as they
are, that is, without their ameliorative connotations. Instead, she transforms the functional into the semiotic, into
what she deems to be a superior set of signifying entities.
It is no wonder, then, that Emma and Rodolphe are depicted
as complete outsiders during the addresses honouring rural
agriculture; their own discourse is sprinkled with allusions
to the signs of their superiority and sophistication:

> – D'ailleurs, ajouta-t-il, quand on habite la campagne ...
> – Tout est peine, perdue, dit Emma.
> – C'est vrai! répliqua Rodolphe. Songer que pas un seul
> de ces braves gens n'est capable de comprendre même la
> tournure d'un habit!
> Alors ils parlèrent de la médiocrité provinciale, des
> existences qu'elle étouffait, des illusions qui s'y perd-
> aient.
>
> (*Madame Bovary*, 129)

The banquet itself, which forms an integral part of the
agricultural fair, does not receive nearly so much attention
from the narrator as did the two preceding banquets. Moreover, the narrator does not dwell on particular culinary or

alimentary details, nor on Emma's reaction to the meal; instead, he limits the eating sequence to a short paragraph, pointing out the unrefined and unsuccessful nature of the feast:

> Le festin fut long, bruyant, mal servi; l'on était si tassé que l'on avait peine à remuer les coudes, et les planches étroites qui servaient de bancs faillirent se rompre sous le poids des convives. Ils mangeaient abondamment.
>
> (*Madame Bovary*, 141-2)

In comparison with the other detailed descriptions of revels, this one reveals more by brevity than by what it recounts. The participants at this banquet eat abundantly but undoubtedly they eat poorly. The narrator's intentions are clearly ironical, with at least half the irony directed at the ruminations of the speakers and the remainder aimed at Emma and Rodolphe, whose pseudo-sophisticated rejoinders betray the fundamental split between the rural materialistic life of the peasant and the romantic illusory existence of more sensitive souls.

To a large extent the *comices agricoles* closes the cycle of major alimentary events which began with the wedding feast. This is because within the triadic structure of macro-meals the *comices* represent a descent from the peak-experience of Vaubyessard and a return to the less lofty plateau of rural revels. Ostensibly, the oscillation between the banal and the sublime has come full circle, and Emma can expect still another emotional abyss as had been the case following prior banquets. The narrator, however, delays but does not delete her doom. In this way he opens a new sequential pattern by offering Emma the promise of a new beginning, if an extra-marital love affair can be so considered. Thus Emma does not immediately relapse into boredom and depression after the *comices* episode; instead, in Rodolphe's embraces, she enjoys another privileged moment during which revery is momentarily transformed into reality. Deception, though, ultimately ensues. Rodolphe's affections had only been superficial. Even in love Emma never really attains that substantial communion which she eschewed at the level of the alimentary. Rather, her desire feeds on fantasy: for Emma Bovary felicity, satiation, and identification of self with the very essence of things can never be more than an ephemeral epiphany.

In assessing the gastronomical and alimentary discourse in
Madame Bovary I would contend that two structural patterns
emerge from the profusion of meal scenes in the novel. Those
centred around the thematic of *Bovarysme* fall into binary
groupings whereas those which are used as pivotal points in
the narrative follow a ternary principle. These two organizational patterns do not conflict but rather tend to comp-
lement each other. Indeed, we may speak of a kind of embed-
ding process in which the binary groups figure as structural
components of the ternary groups. In other words, the gastronomical and alimentary dichotomies inherent in *Bovarysme* are
signs belonging to the psychological coding mechanisms at
work in the novel while the semiotic apparatus of the major
banquets functions within a larger system of cultural and
ideological codes.

The coalescence of codes in the alimentary discourse of
Madame Bovary may best be illustrated at the anecdotal level
of the text, that is, as regards its principal actors and
actions. The actors, which are here defined according to
Greimas' system of *actants* or spheres of action,[15] ostensibly belong to two categories: those who conform to Emma's
vision of the world and those who do not. Thus binary oppositions modelled on the dichotomy of *Bovarysme* include character contrasts (the sublime vs the mediocre), class conflicts (aristocrats vs peasants), and thematic oppositions
(Romanticism vs Realism). On the other hand, the principle
of ternary structuration – the overriding ideology of aesthetic organization – governs the level of actions themselves:
there are three major banquets which are structured and presented in tripartite fashion and which, moreover, parallel and
reflect the three-stage evolution of Emma's life. The prevailing structure in the micro-sequences and the macro-sequences
of the novel follows a plateau-peak-plateau progression. It
is interesting to note that this structure corresponds perfectly, though perhaps inadvertently, with the actual stages
of a meal as it unfolds. The fundamental mimesis that occurs
at all the organizational levels of the alimentary discourse
in *Madame Bovary* may be schematized as follows:

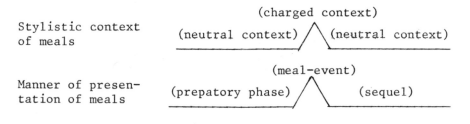

Stylistic context of meals

(charged context)

(neutral context) /\ (neutral context)

Manner of presentation of meals

(meal-event)

(prepatory phase) /\ (sequel)

Pivotal banquets marking the major stages in the evolution of Emma's life and corresponding to the manic/depressive syndrome

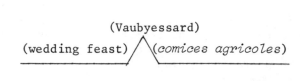

(Vaubyessard)

(wedding feast) / \ (*comices agricoles*)

The semiotic overlapping in the formal organization of the alimentary discourse in *Madame Bovary* demonstrates a balanced integration of binary and ternary structuring, for although each category above consists of a three-part paradigm, there is in each case a two-part progression from plateau-event to peak-event followed by a return to plateau-event.

The stylistic procedures used in meal descriptions and the manner of presenting the unfolding of a given dining episode form parts of the micro-sequences of the novel whereas the three pivotal meals demarcate the macro-sequences, at least as far as its alimentary discourse is concerned. Up to this point the reader has viewed the contrasts and oppositions among characters and events through the interpretative grid of *Bovarysme*; thus characters and events which conform to Emma's vision carry positive connotations whereas those which contrast with it tend to elicit negative responses. For example, Vaubyessard epitomizes elegant cuisine and company as opposed to the *repas de ménage* wherein Charles' mediocrity predominates. Similarly, Vaubyessard is equated with Emma's elation and the domestic meals with her despair. At the level of the fiction, then, the reader, who often perceives events through Emma, condescendingly accepts her reality as the psychological and, even more important, as the ideological norm of the text. Consequently, the pivotal meals of the novel appear to oppose only two actantial categories: the *Bovarystes* and the *non-Bovarystes*.

At the semantic core of the text, however, it is the ideological discourse of the novel which informs its other structural matrices, for the implicit message transmitted by the fiction, the synthesizing stream into which all subcodes of the text flow and coalesce, is the ostensibly pure ideology of *l'art pour l'art*. In this sense all of the polar oppositions and ternary groupings are harmonized and blended in the Work. It is also by means of this global structuration according to which the whole is greater than the sum of its parts that *Bovarysme*, which I have called

a binary principle and which I also discussed in relation
to ternary structure, is subsumed as an *idéologème* and in-
corporated into the very aesthetic core of the novel from
which reverberates the voice of a narrator who has himself
become the principal actant in his own narrative. *Bovarysme*
as a psycho-textual norm against which other actors and actions are measured, events, feelings, fantasies as related
through Emma, reality as dichotomized by the manic/depressive
– all are ultimately focalized in the narrator's ironic
voice, for he is there to remind us that Emma's pseudo-
aestheticism is just as hideous as Charles' mediocrity,
Homais' pomposity, and Rodolphe's duplicity. Indeed, the
narrator as supreme aesthete, as impassible observer, as
hero, surpasses all mundane ideologies in his aesthetic
idealism: *Madame Bovary*, by virtue of a meticulous artistic
structuration, exhibits the coherence and consistency of an
exquisitely prepared meal.

CONCLUSION

Food has stirred the imagination of writers from the very
inception of the verbal arts. It would hardly be an exaggeration to say that no period in the history of Western
literature has been unaffected by alimentary discourse in
its multiple forms. Food and its representation in literature characterize the cultural ethos of a people to such
an extent that whether its presence in a text be oriented
toward poetic evocation or realistic depiction it serves
as a marker, or rather a metonym, of a society at a given
moment in its evolution. To endeavour to uncover the role
that food and eating have played in literature would demand
an enormous effort, all the more so when one considers that
even in a single national literature or a limited corpus of
texts the alimentary is omnipresent. These difficulties not-
withstanding, it is possible to extrapolate from a representative body of writings the underlying functions of food in
fiction. Moreover, since food operates in literary and cultural contexts simultaneously, it lends itself to semiotic
analysis by virtue of its double character as a sign and as
a functional entity: food both signifies and sustains life.
Given the circumstances stated above, it has been my intention in this book to examine the semiotic functions of the
meal complex in a corpus of texts characterized by a certain
density or pervasiveness of eating scenes and by an articu-
lation of the alimentary to such a degree that food and eating become a kind of language or discourse. For these reasons

the corpus consists of novels portraying life in France
roughly between 1830 and 1848, a period of French history
which also witness the rise, indeed the apotheosis, of
alimentary and culinary consciousness, gastronomy, and
gastronomical discourse.

It follows from what has been previously said that I have
had to impose certain limitations in order to arrive at a
coherent and concise analysis. First of all, whereas the
history of French letters is punctuated by writers with
more than just a passing interest in food and gastronomy –
Rabelais, Rousseau, Huysmans, Zola, and Proust to name but
a few prose writers who fictionalized *la bonne chère* – this
book includes only those novelists writing during the July
Monarchy period whose works or reputations have remained
monumental in French literature. Second, and this is a point
which will be taken up in more detail shortly, the present
study embraces the mimetic function of the meal primarily,
or those semiotic processes whereby the meal-as-historical-
phenomenon is transcoded to the meal-as-narrative-sign,
that is as a microcosm and a metonym of nineteenth-century
French culture. Germane to this concept of narrative transcoding is a semantic of systematicity according to which
the meal complex operates as a conventional cultural code:
that is, the narrative semiosis of fictional meals dupli-
cates, for the most part, the cultural semiosis, thus making
the fictional meal a mirror of the historical meal. Finally,
given the critical optic I have employed, individual or personal signifying practices have not been discussed in any
depth. Consequently, the reader will have discovered, perhaps to his dismay, the absence of that phantasmagoria of
fare of which Bachelardian and Richardian criticism so willingly avail themselves.

Despite the limitations under which this inquiry unfolds,
it is clear that my organizing principle governs the functions for the meal-sign in novels of the July Monarchy
period. Most readers will have undoubtedly noticed that the
chapters of this study follow a chronological progression
with respect to the individual careers of the authors discussed: it would be appropriate to note in this context that
the meal-sign, while existing primarily in a mimetic mode,
functions differently from author to author (i.e. inter-
textually) and, more often than not, functions similarly
within the works of the same author (i.e. intratextually).
Following this logic, chapters could have been organized
according to sign-functions of the meal rather than in conformity with historical chronology. Nevertheless, considering

the basic premise that meals reflect society and reveal its
internal organizational principles, it seemed more appropriate to attempt to discover whether the gastro-alimentary
sign evolves in a course and according to patterns which
parallel the actual history of the period. If so, then how
does the meal-sign function in the larger context? Does it
in fact acquire the status of an ideological phenomenon?
Does it enter into the arena of social praxis? Also, keeping
in mind the fact that the meal operates at the aesthetic
level of a given text or body of texts, one might well sup-
pose that it would mirror the evolution of French letters
during the period under consideration and would, therefore,
undergo modifications depending on what literary tradition
or current it belonged to. Clearly, the era which is under
analysis here is characterized by elements of Romanticism,
Realism, and Naturalism as well as by the influences of
these movements in the works of a specific author. This dichotomy between the extratextual and the textual is substan-
tially reduced in the mimetic mode of fiction wherein these
two entities overlap considerably: the fictional meal is in
large measure the historical meal transposed into *écriture*.
Since all of the novelists included in this study adhered
to the dictates of narrative realism it appeared unlikely
that the formal function of their fictional meals would
vary greatly; on the other hand, it would follow that the
semantic function of their meal scenes would show variations,
especially as one would expect literary messages to change
in response to changing social conditions. In point of fact
the semantic range of fictional dining episodes during the
July Monarchy period proves to be more extensive than their
formal range; however, the most interesting differences in
gastro-alimentary discourse for each author occur in terms
of the predominant type of sign-function each assigns to a
given meal complex. Essentially, the prevailing sign typology
for each specific author evolved out of social circumstances,
as a kind of response to society's ailments, as an ideological stance vis-à-vis the Bourgeoisie.

The organization of the chapters of this book thus conforms to the double exigency of historical chronology and
sign typology, at least to the extent that such a progression is possible. Since all of the novelists I have discussed used many different types of food signs, it was my central concern to discover what kind of gastro-alimentary sign
predominates in their individual discourses and why it prevails: in this way it is possible to conclude that for any
given author the sign is an ideolect and an ideological

entity while, at the same time, within the body of novels
written during the July Monarchy period, it reveals a typo-
logical evolution which corresponds with social and aesthetic history. Beginning with Balzac, then, whose stated purpose as we know was to 'faire concurrene à l'état civil,'
that is, to reproduce society rather than to restructure it,
the meal sign functions primarily as a metonym and an index
of extant socio-economic spheres. Balzac's discourse tends
to perpetuate the status quo: this conservative position
explains why there are numerous eating scenes in his novels
(it was earlier mentioned that the table and eating codes
are stabilizing forces par excellence), and it accounts for
the high incidence of scenes depicting differentiation at
table. Because there exists a one-to-one correspondence between authorial and social ideologies in *La Comédie humaine*,
Balzac's meal thematic represents the very system, social
and gastronomical, against which novelists like Sand, Sue,
and Hugo react so vehemently in their own gastro-alimentary
discourse.

George Sand, on the other hand, perceived the importance
of using the meal sign to reform society. She was one of
the first novelists to recognize that if the table can maintain the status quo, then it might also be the logical place
to start if one wants to change prevailing ideologies. While
remaining largely within a mimetic mode, she attempted to
undermine the status quo by introducing new gastro-alimentary
models to the contemporary public, which would minimize the
importance of food and dining as a differentiating sign and
enhance their commensal capacity. Sand's strategy was to
use meals of the past as prototypes for her contemporaries
to emulate. In effect, Sand reintroduced the meal ethic and
symbolism associated with early Christian agapes and communal repasts: within this particular ideology, which coincided
nicely with the ideas emerging from the Christian Socialist
movement, equality, fraternity, and solidarity are reinforced
in both an agricultural and an alimentary context: all men
labour and eat together; their community is confirmed, con-
solidated, and symbolized at the table where they break
bread together. Sand's gastro-alimentary discourse centres
on a sign typology which tends to privilege the symbolic,
most specifically that symbolism associated with ancient
Christian eating practices or their modern counterparts
which have best been preserved in peasant tradition.

Continuing in the ideological mould of George Sand and in
the literary mode of a committed literature, Sue and Hugo
advanced the evolution of the food sign by stressing its

experiential and existential immediacy. They represent the
first major effort to portray the effects of starvation on
society; consequently, food, or rather the absence of food,
introduces a motive for action, an inducement for change,
a reason for revolution. Their gastro-alimentary sign is
made to operate in and upon contemporary history; it is the
recoding of literary discourse into social praxis rather
than the transcoding of the cultural into the aesthetic.
Food functions in their works as a problematic, indeed as
the major problem facing an industrialized urban society
run by bourgeois capitalists. Sue and Hugo were quite per-
spicacious in making the connection, which later became a
social thesis among many theorists, between indigence, starvation, and crime. According to this cause-effect hypothesis,
the food sign is transformed into a signal in the works of
Sue and Hugo: the signalling function is certainly the most
elementary and perhaps the most efficacious type of semiotic
discourse because it demands an immediate response rather
than a reasoned interpretation. Sue and Hugo, by means of
the urgency which the gastro-alimentary sign acquires in
their novels, entreat the reader to collaborate in the process of social reform.

Flaubert's gastro-alimentary discourse is by far the most
aesthetically original and the most structurally cogent
when compared with that of the other novelists examined in
this essay. According to the anti-ideological posture implied in his doctrine of *l'art pour l'art*, Flaubert would
attempt to undermine the bourgeoisie, or rather transcend
and subsume all ideologies, in the sanctification of the
Work. However, at the level of ideological semiotics, even
those meal scenes which have the organic function of ampli-
fying the aesthetic quality of the message, as do many dining episodes in *Madame Bovary*, presuppose the existence of
social, economic, and ideological affinities between the
author and his contemporary readers. For writers like Flaubert, who accentuate the poetic function of the message,
the practicality of the gastro-alimentary sign and its po-
tentiality as praxis are minimized. Only the super-reader
will appreciate the aesthetics of the message, for it is
addressed only to him: other virtual readers within the
society are thus excluded. Flaubert's *l'art pour l'art* perpetuates actual social distinctions within nineteenth-century
French society precisely because it is addressed to an elite:
its *raison d'être* is above all artistic - message becomes
counter-message. Conversely, if the sign is to acquire a
practical purpose, i.e. if it is designed to function not

only within the fiction but also within the historical text,
then it must become transparent and accessible to everyone.

In essence, the history of the gastro-alimentary sign from
Balzac to Flaubert corresponds with the more general evolution in narrative from mimesis to poiesis, though it must
be kept in mind that Flaubert, too, wrote in a mimetic mode
especially as regards the structure of his eating scenes,
all of which are modelled on the paradigm of a three-course
service. Vis-à-vis the predominant characteristics of the
historical meal seized upon by July Monarchy novelists, it
would be accurate to say that Balzac endeavoured to represent it faithfully to his readers, that Sand, Sue, and Hugo
attempted to restructure it according to the commensal principle, and that Flaubert sought to reify it in the text.

Now that we have reached these conclusions about the typo-
logical evolution of the gastro-alimentary sign, it would
be appropriate to elucidate its underlying semantic. If one
considers the fact that July Monarchy novelists were above
all critics of the bourgeoisie, it becomes clear, in view
of the preponderance of that bourgeois phenomenon known as
la gastronomie, that anyone attempting to subvert the bourgeois ideology would *ipso facto* be compelled to embark upon
a critique of bourgeois eating practices and mythologies.
Certainly, the pervasiveness of gastronomy in the culture
at large and its concentration in Paris, not to mention the
pleasures it offers to the artistic imagination, help to
account for the disproportionately high incidence of eating
scenes and descriptions of fare in novels of the July Monarchy period, but these factors alone do not explain the
proliferation of literary feasts and banquets. Ironically,
even those fundamental metaphors and metonymies by means
of which the culinary and alimentary reveal essential con-
fluences and parallels with the very act of artistic creation often find their generative bases in the bourgeois
ideology itself. Gastronomy is perhaps the most original
artistic invention of the bourgeoisie, and certainly novelists would have apprehended the exquisite aesthetic properties of a perfectly orchestrated repast, but gastronomy is
also an economic phenomenon, an element of the mythology of
consumption. Indeed, food and eating are metaphors of art,
writing, and reading, yet even art was subsumed in the bourgeois capitalist system to the extent that the artist depen-
ded upon the Bourgeois to produce and disseminate his works,
which thus became parts of - while remaining reactions to -
the production/product mentality of the bourgeoisie.[1]

It is no wonder that this ambivalent phenomenon known as
la gastronomie, artistic endeavour on the one hand and economic enterprise on the other, produced a tension within the
ideological constructs of July Monarchy novelists and also
within the gastro-alimentary sign itself, where it is reflected as a dislocation between the signifier and the signified. With respect to the new meal semiosis in nineteenth-
century France, the novelist is torn between the desire to
uphold the meal's conventional structure with its connotations of stability, security, and solidarity (particularly
during the era of social changes in which he lived) and the
need to destroy it if he wishes to transform society (revolutions begin at table). In spite of the general evolution
from mimesis to poiesis, which concerns itself with aesthetics rather than ideological praxis, the form that the fictional meal acquires in the contemporary novel shows very
little development from Balzac to Flaubert: for these two
novelists as well as for Sand, Sue, and Hugo, the structural
similarity between the historical meal and the fictional
meal remains intact. On the contrary, the content of the
meal sign undergoes a semantic bifurcation, since meals in
nineteenth-century French literature convey both content
units of the culture at large (e.g., social and economic
differentiation or assimilation, sexuality, temperament,
or, in general, those codes that we have examined in this
study) and a desire to nullify and transform these same
content units into undifferentiated spheres of human interaction based on Christian, socialist, utopian, and, in the
case of Flaubert, aesthetic models. There is thus a code-
reinforcing and a code-breaking tendency at work in the
fictional meal semiosis which can only serve to create a
semantic disequilibrium that threatens to undermine the
novelists' critical position with respect to the bourgeoisie.
   Finally, bringing this tension to the personal and experiential level of July Monarchy novelists themselves, Balzac,
Sand, Sue, Hugo, and Flaubert were all somewhat renowned
as epicures. So if novelists created the myth of the bourgeoisie, it is no less true that the bourgeoisie created
the gastronomical myths to which these same novelists suc-
cumbed, consciously but enthusiastically: they found themselves in the paradoxical position of critizing the bourgeois
meal structure while discoursing and delecting on *la cuisine
bourgeoise*. Even Sand, who idealized peasant eating customs
and sang paeans to equality at table, served magnificently
sumptuous meals at Nohant, and we seriously doubt that her

domestics and the neighbouring peasants supped in her dining room despite the descriptions of those practices in her novels. Whatever one's ideological penchants may be, one does not bite the hand that feeds. These writers must have taken enormous delight in evoking the pleasures of the table, for even in the most utopian of societies described by nineteenth-century theorists the aim was to enable everyone to 'eat like a king,' not like a peasant. The dilemma faced by July Monarchy novelists centres not on food as substance, not on food as ceremony, not on food as art, but rather on food as social, economic, and ideological sign. And it is not so much the *embourgeoisement de la cuisine* that revolts these novelists as the *embourgeoisement de la culture*. How to have one'c cake and eat it too? How to deconstruct the bourgeoisie and simultaneously retain its greatest artistic enterprise – gastronomy?

It should be evident at this point that novelists writing in the second quarter of the nineteenth century faced an essential paradox: in so far as the meal-sign is concerned they remained formally supportive of the bourgeoisie in their espousal of realism and a mimetic mode of discourse, yet they also pretended to be ideologically critical of the Bourgeois in their semantic discourse. More specifically, at the level of the signifier (here defined as the fictional depiction of the meal, its textual representation) virtually no attempt was made to invent a new semiotic structure or to create a new semiosis: on the contrary, the predominance of the mimetic meal tends to reinforce and confirm the very social organization which the novelists purported to change. On the other hand, because the signifier tended to perpetuate the bourgeois ethos – for meal codes are among the most inflexible in any culture – novelists were forced to carry on the battle at the level of the signified; that is, they attempted to transform the content-plane of the sign without altering the expression-plane. For any given fictional account of a meal, then, the reader had to go beyond the surface structure of the description to its deeper significations: he had to make use of his capacity to detect and decode the gastro-alimentary sign in all of its manifestations, and, moreover, he had to become aware of the fundamental irony which is operative in any interpretation of a sign whose components communicate opposing messages.

Even in those meal ethics which are meant to supplant the bourgeois ideology, namely the pastoral, communal, Christian models proposed by Sand, Sue, and Hugo, or in those which are meant to submit food and meals to an aesthetic transformation, as in the novels of Flaubert, the historico-mimetic

model remains intact: the author either returns to Christian
prototypes or recommends their permutation into modern forms.
Whereas a radical transformation was called for at the level
of the signifier, such as the introduction of taboo foods or
socially 'revolting' table practices, in order to bring
about a concomitant change at the level of the signified,
only the most benign forms of gastro-alimentary restructura-
tion were suggested by theorists and novelists alike. In the
works of Cabet, Leroux, and Fourier, for instance, the principal aim was to find the most equitable means of feeding
the masses in an ambience uninhibited by social stigmas and
prejudices: hence, a combination of the communal model,
wherein everyone functions as both provider and consumer,
and the commensal principle, according to which all are
equals at table.

Fourier was the most visionary and perhaps the most revolutionary theorist of *la gastrosophie*, as he calls the
gastro-alimentary complex when it is raised to the level of
a science, for he understood that gastronomical fulfilment
is man's most basic pleasure and thus might well serve as
the point of departure in the process of social transformation.[2] Like Rousseau before him, Fourier perceived the enormous pedagogical potential of alimentary desire in regulating and in fact programming the education and development
of children, since the latter are so often governed by their
gluttony and may be easily moulded by sages intent upon re-
forming society in a non-violent, gradual manner.[3] Although
there is an enormous amount of play in his gastrosophical
theories, Fourier realized the need to alter contemporary
eating practices and prejudices by creating a new gastro-
alimentary semiosis; that is, by changing the 'grammar' of
the meal and introducing heretofore untried, often unpalat-
able, combinations of foods or infantile aliments such as
lemonade and melons. His system was truly visionary, containing as it did all the creative/destructive virtualities capable of effecting a transformation in the meal semantic by
liquidating its surface structure. Fourier's system, if
adopted as a social or fictional model, would have had an
enormous impact on the bourgeois meal ethos, more indeed
than the mimetic modes of discourse employed in the novels
of Balzac, Sand, Sue, Hugo, and Flaubert, were it not for the
fact that few readers could really take Fourier's often ironic
and ludicrous discourse seriously. Perhaps Fourier was merely
toying with his readers, but one must not lose sight of the
fact that from a semiotic standpoint, everything is a system
of arbitrary and conventionalized rules, and that Fourier, half
in earnest, half in jest, was inventing the rules of a new game.

Our novelists pose the paradox of a critique which takes heed of substance at the expense of form. Obviously, the sign is a binary phenomenon consisting of a signifier and a signified, but implicit in this definition is a relation or a process between the signifier and the signified which may be called signification or semiosis. In short, signifier and signified are inseparable, mutually dependent, both terms of the sign structure: an alteration in one of the terms entails a concomitant modification in the other. July Monarchy novelists wanted to subvert the semantic of the bourgeois meal phenomenon but they did not radicalize its formal structure. Consequently, no new semiosis was engendered. This is not to say, however, that these novelists were not effective as critics of the bourgeoisie; only that they failed to utilize the meal complex to its full revolutionary potential. In this regard it is interesting to note that possibly the most ironic example of this failure occurs in Flaubert's *L'Education sentimentale*, which treats the social turmoil prior to 1848. Amidst all the turbulence recounted in this narrative, the meal scenes that are profusely interspersed throughout mark the solidarity among the adherents of the various political factions. At the beginning of the reaction to the Republican tide, one of the guests who has been invited to a splendid dinner offered by the bourgeois incarnate, M. Dambreuse, exclaims: ' - Ah! espérons que MM. les Républicains vont nous permettre de dîner!' (*ES*, 342).[4] This meal is all the more precious precisely because it is so tenuous; the guests at the Dambreuse table are appreciative of the contingencies which have momentarily allowed them to maintain their standard of living. The narrator, cognizant of the significance the meal has for the guests at the Dambreuse table, transmits to the reader this sense of security and stability that the meal so often connotes: 'Tout cela semblait meilleur après l'émotion des jours passés. On rentrait dans la jouissance des choses que l'on avait peur de perdre' (*ES*, 342).

Social transformation was one of the basic objectives of July Monarchy novelists, but unfortunately the means by which they sought to reform society were insufficient because these writers so often lacked insight into code-making and code-breaking mechanisms. Essentially, they operated from within an aesthetics of identification instead of imposing an aesthetics of opposition, or, more often than not, their critique took the form of a mixed aesthetics consisting of a formal identification alongside of a semantic opposition. This is surprising, since some very important writers prior

to the July Monarchy period understood the revolutionary
potential of the transgressional space of alimentary signifying practices. From the physical and anthropological
perspectives, cooking equates with metamorphosis; the kitchen is the symbolic locus of transformation. Alimentary,
culinary, and gastronomical practices, as some very clever
theorists of education learned, might well form the basis
of a pedagogy of indoctrination (assimilation and initiation into the established order and the maintenance of its
codes) or a pedagogy of transgression (an asystematic or
chaotic tendency whose purpose is to introduce anarchy or
revolution by nullifying extant codes and thereby opening
the system to new possibilities).

Jean-Jacques Rousseau may be classified as a particularly
keen observer of the transgressional virtualities implied
in the act of eating. In the first place, Rousseau's romanticism, to the extent that it emphasized the solitary individual and his natural instincts, contrasts with so-called
socialized and civilized eating customs and practices. Romanticism, by its very nature, imposes new gastro-alimentary
codes and attitudes because it tends to attenuate the conventional rituals associated with eating: 'Si dans l'état
de nature l'homme se nourrit solitairement, manger implique
dans l'état de société tout un système de relations dont la
première est affective.'[5] In this sense romanticism contains
an anticultural, antisocial component. Rousseau knew that
if eating is the equivalent of learning a social system,
and constitutes a form of acculturation, then by modifying
the eating complex one modifies the system: 'Hors du code
des repas fixes Rousseau institue des rites personnels, une
dispersion de cérémonies intimes, de jeux, de fêtes où il
réorganise la pratique sociale' (Bonnet, 255). In both *la
Nouvelle Héloïse* and *Emile*, Rousseau attacks contemporary
cultural ideologies by transgressing the prevailing gastro-
alimentary norms.

Whatever the reasons may be, nineteenth-century novelists
borrowed little from Rousseau's thoughts on the alimentary,
the culinary, and the gastronomical. But they owe him a
large debt as regards the social (socializing) space in
which the meal unfolds. Rousseau advocated an open, outdoor,
pastoral locus for the ingestion of meals because of the
salutary effects of nature upon the individual: 'Chez
Rousseau c'est toujours à l'extérieur que s'effectue la
communion sociale car on peut y improviser des relations
nouvelles tandis que l'espace intérieur des habitats fige
les pratiques sociales' (Bonnet, 254). Implicit in this

notion of an outdoor meal is the transition from a fixed
social structure (a highly codified, differentiating space)
to a more fluid contour (an open, creative, non-differen-
tiating space). In the novels of George Sand and Eugène Sue
especially, the reader will remember the overwhelming importance both writers attached to establishing communes in
the country and partaking of meals in a more primitive,
natural, equalizing space.

The particular forms of transgression appearing in the
writings of Rousseau reveal a fundamental ideology which
is shared by many nineteenth-century novelists: namely, the
individual worth of the human being in an ever-depersonalizing
social structure. Rousseau's gastro-ethic, however, unlike
that of many nineteenth-century novelists, constitutes a
veritable ideosemiotics, a personal alimentary system designed to offset the evils of modern civilization, one of
which is man's failure to follow his natural instincts (appetites) because he has been led astray by the artifices of
gastronomy:

.. l'appétit, instinctif mais raisonnable, doit le con-
duire vers le bonheur du désir assouvi sans recherche et
sans fioriture. Le plaisir du corps réside dans la simp-
licité de cet assouvissement et aux yeux de l'auteur de
l'*Emile* ou de *la Nouvelle Héloïse*, tout ce qui pourrait,
par un excès de luxe ou de raffinement, dévier ce plaisir
vers l'artifice de la gastronomie est jugé avec le plus
grand mépris.

(Châtelet, 127)

Rousseau's culinary system constitutes an applied semiotic
of alimentary purity and naturalism. Basing this system on
codes of privation rather than on codes of gourmandise,
Rousseau refutes the notion of pleasure and excessive indulgence (an image of the body and the psyche which is antithetical to the carricature of the gluttonous eroticism of
the *bon bourgeois* of the nineteenth century) and advances
instead an ethic of eating which would supply nineteenth-
century novelists and theorists with anti-bourgeois arma-
ments. Noëlle Châtelet, in her excellent analysis of Rousseau's culinary philosophy, describes his major contributions
to this domain as follows:

Pourquoi cette insistance tout d'abord sur la philosophie
de Rousseau en matière culinaire? Sans doute parce qu'il
demeure à nos yeux l'un des rares théoriciens - et non

pas seulement romancier – à penser et écrire les turbu-
lences du corps (rivé aux pulsions de l'âme) à l'époque
stratégiquement décisive où celui-ci se cherchait à
travers la médecine et la physiologie ...; enfin et sur-
tout, parce que, d'une manière naïve il est vrai, roman-
tiquement, il échafauda les fondations, la charpente idéo-
logique d'une conception du corps qui nous sert encore de
modèle, le modèle d'un corps naturellement sain, menacé
par une civilisation toujours plus contraignante.

(Châtelet, 130)

Rousseau's transgression of the established eating ethic
is in fact aimed at creating a new, more natural approach
to eating and hygiene: it offers an alimentary and culinary
model for all of society, and in this sense it transgresses
in order to restructure and to integrate. It has the wel-
fare of mankind at heart; it is indeed a vision and an objective which has been at least partially actualized in
contemporary eating practices. However, in spite of its obvious salutary value, it did not, as Rousseau had wished,
displace gastronomy or replace its semiosis.
At the opposite extreme from Rousseau, though still operating within the transgressional mode, is the Marquis de
Sade. His gastro-alimentary discourse was clearly too radical to serve as a model for nineteenth-century novelists.
Yet Sade, perhaps more than any novelist writing prior to
the nineteenth century, understood the revolutionary potential of the body as a desiring, devouring machine. Moreover,
he had both the insight and the temerity to violate social
norms by exposing, even flaunting, taboos associated with
alimentary and bodily functions, and thus creating in effect
the libertine body: 'Entre les mains de Sade, le corps a
enfin dit tout ce qu'il pouvait dire: il a fait des aveux
complets' (Châtelet, 63). In spite of Sade's proclivity for
exaggerating the desiring body beyond all measure, he recognized the need to alter the expression plane in order to
bring about transformations on the content plane: whether
he did so out of discontent, visionary zeal, or madness,
Sade's orgiastic feasts, his perverted and pernicious alimentary ethic, and his flagrant promotion of the lower-body
principle introduce a disturbing language and a language of
disturbance into French letters. Only in Rabelais does one
witness such corporeal *démesure*, but in the latter's discourse corporality and excess are celebrations of life,
exuberance for ingesting the knowable, oral assimilation –
whereas in the Sadian universe disproportion tends to

privilege a rejection of existence, perverse delights in excretion, and fixation on the anal. Sade even goes so far as to compose meals of fecal matter, extending eros beyond all reasonable limits and thereby converting it into thanatos.

This semiosis of excess culminates in the practice of cannibalism, which to society, as Sade well knew, represents the ultimate form of social transgression. Unlike the *corps sain* championed by Rousseau, the *corps libertin*, with its emphasis on an inverted, disintegrative orality, transgresses not only the norms of society at large but also the norms of the natural body. Metaphorically speaking, the *corps libertin* is a body devouring itself.[6]

Nineteenth-century novelists failed to exploit the transgressional possibilities of alimentary discourse introduced by Rousseau and Sade; moreover, they did not seem to perceive the inherent transformational capacities of this discourse or its non-fortuitous emergence at the time of the French Revolution. In a penetrating analysis of the social and gastronomical context in 1789, Frédéric Lange exposes the exhilarating dialectic between the ordinary table and the revolutionary table:

> Donc, révolutionnaires, les tables fleurissent en France comme des foyers subversifs pendant la Révolution. Engendrées, propagées et amplifiées par la table, les idées révolutionnaires séduisirent vite la France entière. Et c'est à table que, contaminé, on se conforta dans sa volonté de démocratie. Bonne conductrice, la table secoua l'Occident.
>
> Mais ce fut pour mieux le mater. Après la flambée, la Révolution mourut à table et par la table. Noyée sous les paroles échangées, étouffée par les propos de cafés du Commerce, la Révolution s'enlisa dans la velléité, puis philosopha avant de s'embourber définitivement dans le commerce relativisé.
>
> (Lange, 154)

The purpose of this digression on Rousseau and Sade has not been to suggest that their individual forms of transgression should have been adopted by nineteenth-century novelists, but rather to support the fundamental notion that the alimentary, by its inherent nature, equates with transformational processes whereas the gastronomical tends to systematize, to conventionalize, and to socialize alimentary phenomena. Alimentary activity is individualistic,

hedonistic, and idiosyncratic; in this sense it is at odds
with social norms and the imposition of fixed codes, it is
self-regulating and self-fulfilling. Gastronomical behaviour,
on the other hand, may be described as collective activity
– adherence to social constraints, identification with the
established order – and conforms to an ideology of the culture not to the logic of the self. In principle, alimentary
discourse is potentially capable of being in confrontation
with gastronomical discourse: in fact, and even more important, alimentary discourse has the capacity to transform
and transgress gastronomical discourse, to model new systems,
to usher in the revolution. This because it concerns itself
with a semiotics of the desiring individual. Gastronomical
discourse, however, or, strictly speaking, the discourse of
la gastronomie, represents the very antithesis of change
because it is a codified product of the society and not a
codifying process for the society: it concerns itself with
a semiotics of system. Nineteenth-century novelists, in
spite of their endeavour to undermine the bourgeois ideology, made the mistake of wanting to subvert the prevailing
eating ethos without concomitantly modifying the gastro-
alimentary system in which the ethos was actualized. Essentially they were attempting to maintain the system (*la gastronomie*) while, paradoxically, hoping to change values
within the system, that is, by making the *discours alimentaire*, which is governed by an anarchic, pleasure-seeking
principle, compatible with its opposite – *le discours gastronomique*. This attempt to make the gastronomical shape
the alimentary, rather than the contrary, accounts for the
extent to which our novelists were locked into a relatively
uniform pattern in their evocation of meals, for one finds
very few descriptions of characters actually engaged in
eating, reacting to, and talking about food itself: taste,
texture, and consistency go virtually unnoticed. From the
point of view of the characters in a given novel and of the
narrator himself, food is perceived and described as a sign
operating within the fixed system of gastronomy, not as an
alimentary substance capable of promoting good health and
moral character as in the works of Rousseau or charged with
an extreme transgressional tendency as in the novels of Sade.
   It is somewhat ironic that the supreme social transgression
which cannibalism constitutes often manifests itself in the
nineteenth-century French novel as a negative social metaphor according to which the rich devour the poor and, also,
as a positive cosmological metaphor in which all of life is
seen as a process of perpetual autophagy. The social metaphor

appears in most of the novelists included in this book and
is generally associated with capitalism as a form of endocannibalism. This image is particularly active in Sue's *Les
Mystères de Paris*, much of whose action unfolds in the
Parisian slums, for the ghetto is the veritable *ventre de
Paris*, the locus of an insidious social envelopment. Similarly, the character of l'Ogresse in *Les Mystères de Paris*
belongs to the cannibalistic motif in so far as she represents the unnatural and inverted practice of maternal assimilation or, to put it in social terms, the devouring of
les enfants de la patrie. Contrary to this image is the
Hugolian vision of universal consumption, which is benignly
beautiful in its connotations of cosmological infusion and
resigned in its unconditional surrender to the supramundane
order of things:

> La catégorie hugolienne de l'obscène doit sans doute être
> pensée en un tel carrefour de sens. Mail il existe, d'ail-
> leurs liée fantasmatiquement à celle-ci, une forme encore
> plus simple du mélange, c'est la voration: engloutisse-
> ment primitif d'un être par un autre, puis sa digestion,
> son assimilation. En une vue admirable l'interpénétration,
> prenant alors valeur cosmique, devient une des catégories
> de l'appétit: 'Toute la nature que nous avons sous les
> yeux est mangeante et mangée. Les proies s'entremordent ...'[7]

The irony arising from these two meatphorical networks
derives from the fact that nineteenth-century French novelists did not impose appropriate forms of gastro-alimentary
transgression in their narratives as had Rousseau and Sade
before them, but rather implicitly accepted the notion that
capitalism, which in part reveals its ideology in gastronomy,
transgressed the humanist ethic which had been part of their
education. They were reluctant to become transgressors in
their turn: their failure to radicalize gastro-alimentary
discourse in the nineteenth century results partly from the
novelists' incorporation in the very system of which they
were the critics. To eat or be eaten - that is the question!

NOTES

INTRODUCTION

1 In my discussion of the socio-historical evolution of
meals, food, and cuisine in nineteenth-century France
I am deeply indebted to the following: Jean-Paul Aron,
Le Mangeur du XIXe siècle (Paris: Robert Laffont, 1973);
Priscilla P. Clark, 'Thoughts for Food, I: French Cuisine
and French Culture,' *French Review*, 49 (October 1975),
32-41, and 'Thoughts for Food, II: Culinary Culture in
Contemporary France,' *French Review*, 49 (December 1975),
198-205; Christian Guy, *An Illustrated History of French
Cuisine*, translated by Elisabeth Abbott (New York:
Bramhall House, 1962); Reay Tannahill, *Food in History*
(New York: Stein and Day, 1973). Subsequent references
to these titles will appear in the text.
2 There is some disagreement as to the actual date of the
first restaurant in France. Guy claims that a man named
Beauvillier opened the first restaurant in 1782 (*An Illustrated History of French Cuisine*, 89) whereas Clark
gives 1765 as the date while qualifying her statement
with Brillat-Savarin's observation that the first restaurant opened in 1770 ('Thoughts for Food, I: French Cuisine and French Culture,' 37).
3 Jean-Paul Aron notes that in the nineteenth century there
are 'trois langages de la chère.' The first language,
called 'la parole du monde,' comprises the geographical
space evoked by certain foods: 'Au commencement de l'âge
d'or, la table semble un lexique de l'univers, des territoires proches et lointains, de l'Europe conquise et
de la France intégrée dont la commune capitale est Paris.'
Le Mangeur du XIXe siècle, 177.
4 D.W. Fokkema, 'Continuity and Change in Russian Formalism, Czech Structuralism, and Soviet Semiotics,' *PTL*, 1
(January 1976), 186.
5 Gerard Genette, *Figures III* (Paris: Editions du Seuil,
1972).
6 Segre defines the sign as a deliberate attempt to communicate something to someone in terms of a convention or
code which the addresser and addressee both accept. He

goes on to describe what is communicated by and in cuisine as belonging to the category of symptoms or indexes according to which culinary language corresponds to social categories, regional differences, and so on. Such indexes, he claims ' ... are part of the categories of customs, and, until they contain an *individual desire to express something*, they cannot be considered as meaningful in a linguistic sense; ...' Cesare Segre, *Semiotics and Literary Criticism* (The Hague: Mouton, 1973), 27-8. Barthes refines this distinction even more: 'Beaucoup de systèmes sémiologiques (objets, gestes, images) ont une substance de l'espression dont l'être n'est pas dans la signification: ce sont souvent des objets d'usage, dérivés par la société à des fins de signification: le vêtement sert à protéger, la nourriture sert à se nourrir, quand bien même ils servent aussi à signifier. On proposera d'appeler ces signes sémiologiques, des *fonctions-signes*.' Roland Barthes, *Eléments de Sémiologie* (Paris: Editions Gonthier, 1964), 113.

7 Jean-Claude Bonnet, 'Le Système de la cuisine et du repas chez Rousseau,' *Poétique*, 22 (1975), 245.

8 Norman O. Brown, *Love's Body* (New York: Random House, 1966), 169.

9 Frédéric Lange, *Manger ou les jeux et les creux du Plat* (Paris: Editions du Seuil, 1975), 61. Subsequent references will appear in the text.

10 In my remarks on the psychological and sociological dimensions of the act of eating I owe much to Frédéric Lange's penetrating study on the subject. Lange's comments on Christian ceremonies are particularly incisive: 'Tous les textes sacrés, toutes les mythologies témoignent que le repas fut un acte cosmique. La Cène, au cours de laquelle le Christ se présente comme un aliment et incite ses disciples, puis à travers eux tous les croyants, à refaire l'acte d'ingestion du pain et du vin en souvenir de lui, est pour les Occidentaux le modèle le plus évident de la sacralisation du repas. En fait, ce modèle est un avatar du festin d'immortalité dont partent toutes les mythologies indo-européenes.' *Manger ou les jeux et les creux du plat*, 61.

11 A.J. Greimas, *Sémantique structurale* (Paris: Larousse, 1966), 172-92.

12 Tzvetan Todorov, *Introduction à la littérature fantastique* (Paris: Editions du Seuil, 1970), 171.

13 Julia Kristeva, *Le Texte du roman* (The Hague: Mouton et Cie., 1970), 12.

CHAPTER ONE: BALZAC

1 P. Barbéris, 'La Pensée de Balzac: histoire et structure,' *Revue d'Histoire Littéraire de la France*, 1 (March, 1967), 18-54.

2 So important is the role of money in characterizing the Bourgeois that one sociologically oriented critic has been persuaded to write that 'The most current as well as the most useful definition of the bourgeoisie fixes on its originally distinct economic function.' Priscilla Clark, *The Battle of the Bourgeois, the Novel in France, 1789-1848* (Paris: Didier, 1973), 20.

3 Honoré de Balzac, *Eugénie Grandet* in *La Comédie humaine*, ed. Marcel Bouteron, vol. II (Paris: Bibliothèque de la Pléiade, 1951), 487. Hereafter cited in the text as *EG*.

4 For a thorough discussion of the concept of autophagy, see Norman O. Brown, *Love's Body* (New York: Random House, 1966), 169.

5 Honoré de Balzac, *La Rabouilleuse*, in *La Comédie humaine*, ed. Marcel Bouteron, vol. III (Paris: Bibliothèque de la Pléiade, 1951), 996. All subsequent references will appear in the text.

6 Honoré de Balzac, *La Peau de chagrin*, in *La Comédie humaine*, ed. Marcel Bouteron, vol. IX (Paris: Bibliothèque de la Pléiade, 1951), 51. Hereafter denoted in the text as *PC*.

7 Honoré de Balzac, *Le Père Goriot*, in *La Comédie humaine*, ed. Marcel Bouteron, vol. II (Paris: Bibliothèque de la Pléiade, 1951), 914. Subsequently cited in the text as *PG*.

8 Karl Menninger, *The Vital Balance* (New York: The Viking Press, 1963), 135

9 Honoré de Balzac, *La Physiologie du mariage*, in *La Comédie humaine*, ed. Marcel Bouteron, vol. X (Paris: Bibliothèque de la Pléiade, 1951), 713. Denoted in the text as *PM*.

10 As early as the eighteenth century, Rousseau had devised a culinary system which was not only salubrious but also morally edifying. See Jean-Claude Bonnet, 'Le Système de la cuisine et du repas chez Rousseau,' *Poétique*, 22 (1975), 250-53.

11 Frédéric Lange, *Manger ou les jeux et les creux du Plat* (Paris: Editions du Seuil, 1975), 61.

12 In *L'Education sentimentale*, Flaubert, using a similar style and technique, describes an orgiastic feast at the home of a courtesan, but whereas Balzac tends to emphasize

the moral – and almost mystical – aspects of the ritual of eating, Flaubert underlines the alliance between a degenerating ideology and a decadent morality. In his depiction, licentiousness is linked with political decay, and the entire sequence becomes a grotesque portrayal of the failure of human ambitions, an archetype of the Fall.

13 Honoré de Balzac, *L'Auberge rouge*, in *La Comédie humaine*, ed. Marcel Bouteron, vol. IX (Paris: Bibliothèque de la Pléiade, 1951), 956. Subsequently cited in the text as *AR*.

14 Honoré de Balzac, *Les Deux Rêves*, in *La Comédie humaine*, ed. Marcel Bouteron, vol. X (Paris: Bibliothèque de la Pléiade, 1951), 287. Hereafter cited in the text as *DR*.

15 'As in the ritual of dining, where the individual desire (hunger) is constrained by group norms, so too French cuisine, with its elaborate rules and regulations, applies its code like the *Code civil* to particular situations. The stylization of nature, its aesthetization and spiritualization, are the essence of French cuisine and an important part of French culture.' Priscilla P. Clark, 'Thoughts for Food, I: French Cuisine and French Culture,' *French Review* (October 1975), 35.

CHAPTER TWO: SAND

1 George Sand, *La Mare au diable* (Paris: Editions Garnier Frères, 1969), 10. Hereafter cited as *MD*.

2 Depictions of aristocratic meals are rare in Sand's pastoral novels, yet when they do occur they usually stand in contrast to the 'conventional' *Fête pastorale* to the extent that they represent artificiality of décor and ambience, i.e. nature corrupted by man and money. One such scene takes place in *Consuelo* when one of the characters, Count Hoditz, offers a dinner party in the grotto attached to his alpine home. The meal episode is focused through Consuelo, whose perception of the perversion of nature clearly reflects Sand's own feelings about sign effacing substance in contemporary society: 'Mais Consuelo s'aperçut bientôt des bizarres recherches par lesquelles le comte avait réussi a gâter cette sublime nature. La grotte eût été charmante sans le vitrage, qui en faisait une salle à manger intempestive. Comme les chevrefeuilles et les liserons ne faisaient encore que bourgeonner, on avait masqué les chassis des portes et des croisées avec des feuillages et des fleurs artificielles, qui faisaient là une prétentieuse grimace.

Les coquillages et les stalactities, un'peu endommagés
par l'hiver, laissaient voir le plâtre et le mastic qui
les attachaient aux parois du roc ...' George Sand,
Consuelo, in *Œuvres illustrées de George Sand*, ed. J.
Hetzel (Paris: Librairie Blanchard, 1855, 279).
3 George Sand, *Le Meunier d'Angibault*, in *Œuvres de George
Sand* (Paris: Calmann-Levy, n.d.), 332. All subsequent
references appear in the text as *MA*.
4 George Sand, *François le Champi* (Paris: Editions Garnier
Frères, 1969), 264. Hereafter cited as *FC*.
5 George Sand, *Les Maîtres Sonneurs* (Paris: Editions Garnier Frères, 1958), 378-9. Subsequently designated as *MS*.
6 George Sand, *Jeanne*, ed. Cecile Hugon (Oxford, 1907), 133.
7 George Sand explains this *Berrichon* feast in a footnote -
'*Jaunée*: feu de Saint-Jean: "Dans nos villages, la veille
de la Saint-Jean (23 juin) à la tombée de la nuit, chaque
famille fournit, selon ses facultés, un ou plusieurs
fagots pour faire la jonée. On empile ces fagots au pied
et le long d'une perche fichée en terre sur le lieu le
plus éminent des environs ... A peine les fagots commen-
cent-ils à pétiller et à se tordre sous l'étreinte des
flammes, que tous les assistants, jeunes ou vieux, se
prennent par la main et se mettent à danser des rondes
autour de la jonée." Laisnel de la Salle, *Croyances et
légendes du centre de la France*, t. I, pp. 78-80. - Ici
la fête de la jaunée a lieu non pas la veille, mais le
jour même de la Saint-Jean' (*MS*, 112-13).
8 In the first phase of the Dionysian rite the sheaf must
be broken apart (sparagmos) and scattered, symbolizing
the death of the god, the preparation for the new season,
and the reviving of the god. The second phase of the
ceremony corresponds to the carrying of the new sheaf
(anagnorisis and epiphanos), thus beginning a new cycle.
9 Edith Hamilton, *Mythology* (New York: The New American
Library, 1940, 1942), 45.
10 I am using the term 'code' not so much in a rigorous
semiotic sense - see Umberto Eco's 'Theory of Codes' in
A Theory of Semiotics (Bloomington, London: Indiana University Press), 48-150 - but rather in reference to what
are commonly considered 'codes of behaviour.' For further
clarification of this terminological problem I call the
reader's attention to the elucidating remarks of Leo
Zawadowski: '... many "semiotic" descriptions of rites
and customs have little really semiotic in them; they
relate and interpret "codified" behavior, much of which
has no informative function, and while being an interesting

topic for ethnography has not much to do with semiotics in the proper sense. If "semiotics" came to be considered as a science of *all codes of behavior*, it would be a sub-discipline of ethnology and should not be called semiotics.' Leo Zawadowski, 'Semiotics and Linguistics: Fruitful Interdependence – in search of semiotic identities,' *Canadian Journal of Research in Semiotics*, 4 (Winter 1976-7), 68.

11 George Sand, *Consuelo*, in *Œuvres illustrées de George Sand*, ed. J. Hetzel (Paris: Librairie Blanchard, 1855), 163.

12 The discussion in this essay of *Procope le Grand* and *Consuelo* might seem unjustifiable in terms of the criterion for analysis set out in the Introduction (i.e. inclusion of French novels whose plots unfold in France roughly between 1789 and 1848). Nevertheless, given the importance of Christian meal symbolism in Sand's opus, it is appropriate to allow this digression in order that the reader may better comprehend the ideological parameters of the meal which Sand establishes for her contemporaries.

13 George Sand, *Procope le Grand*, in *Œuvres illustrées de George Sand* (Paris: Librairie Blanchard, 1854), 10. Subsequently referred to as *PG*.

14 George Sand, *Le Compagnon du Tour de France* (Paris: Editions Montaigne, 1928), 38. Hereafter cited as *CTF*.

15 Similarly, at a later Bricolin dinner at which Marcelle requests Grand-Louis' presence, Mme Bricolin uses the table as a social weapon to thwart off the miller. She aligns her relatives against Grand-Louis in an effort to ridicule him for aspiring to marry a Bourgeoise. Grand-Louis' public derision illustrates the most extreme form of social differentiation encountered in Sand's novels.

16 George Sand, *Le Marquis de Villemer*, ed. Charles D. Young (New York: Oxford University Press, 1917), 212.

CHAPTER THREE: SUE AND HUGO

1 Jean-Louis Bory, *Eugène Sue: le roi du roman populaire* (Paris: Hachette, 1962), 264.

2 Jean-Paul Aron, *Le Mangeur du XIXe siècle* (Paris: Robert Laffont, 1973), 249. Subsequent references to this work will appear in the text and are designated by the author's name.

3 For clarification of the terminology the reader may consult the section of the introduction entitled 'Types of Meal Signs,' pp. 19-21.

4 Among the many types of discourse centring on food and
gastronomy in nineteenth-century France, one might classify utopian works (e.g., Cabet's *Voyage en Icarie*,
Fourier's *Nouveau Monde amoureux et al.*, and Leroux's *De
l'humanité, de son principe et de son avenir*) as non-
realistic texts in so far as their ideologies are projections into the future. Their solutions to the problem of
starvation, for example, are sought at the non-existent,
theoretical level and are, at best, what society can become. Realistic types of discourse, on the other hand,
focus on what is or on what has been: they signal inequity and injustice in practice, thereby advocating
immediate responses to extant problems. Novelists such
as Sue, and even Hugo to a certain extent, demand a 'gut
reaction' from their readers and involve them in a praxis
which will eventually implement change.
5 Eugène Sue, *Les Mystères de Paris* (Paris: G. Charpentier
et Cie., n.d.), I, 7. All other references appear in the
text as *Les Mystères*.
6 Jean-Louis Bory maintains, probably justifiably, that
Sue was still enamoured of fashionable society when he
wrote this passage. According to Bory, Sue was accustomed
to luxury, especially of a gastronomical sort, at least
prior to and just after his conversion to socialism in
1842. A friend of Brillat-Savarin, Sue was still dining
Chez Tortoni and at the *Café de Paris* when he criticized
the *arlequin* in his footnote.
7 In a section of his book entitled 'Débris,' Jean-Paul
Aron emphasizes the implicit metonymical character of
ghetto food in his own description of the *arlequin*. Such
foods are, he says, 'Produits du système hiéarchisé dont
nous dévalons la pente de plus en plus hallucinante, les
résidus se subordonnent comme des hypostases: les restes
des restes; leurs restes encore, et ainsi de suite. Autant de degrés, autant de niveaux d'exploitation. Pour
saisir le processus à sa source, point n'est utile de
sortir des Halles. Contemplez dans ce coin un pavillon,
soi disant contrôlé par les inspecteurs, en fait abandonné à son trafic sordide. On y entasse, attendant le
client, des têtes de poisson, des côtelettes mal rongées,
des bouts de gigot, des fragments de pâtisserie, le tout
pêle-mêle, imprégné de vingt sauces différentes, rejeton
du *bijou*, vieux de cinq jours, pas encore complètement
corrompu. On appelle cet amalgame l'*arlequin*, sans doute
à raison de sa bigarrure.' Aron, 297.
8 Victor Hugo, *Les Misérables*, ed. Maurice Allem (Paris:

Bibliothèque de la Pléiade, 1951), 510. All subsequent
references to this edition appear in the text.

9 Jean-Louis Bory mentions a pertinent event in Sue's life
which led to the former dandy's conversion to socialism.
On the evening of 26 May 1841 his friend Félix Pyat invited him to dine at the home of a Parisian worker-
intellectual, M. Fugères. Bory recounts how Sue quickly
took to 'les capacités culinaires de la classe ouvrière'
and 'la religion positive qui ramène tout à la question
humaine.' Bory, *Sue*, 230-34.

10 According to Jean-Paul Aron such fictionalized accounts
of horrifying eating conditions have a basis in reality.
In a section of his book aptly titled 'Abysses,' he describes the degrading quest for food by the poor: 'Deuxième
temps: on ne paie plus; toute organisation vacille; la
nourriture est aléatoire, tributaire des circonstances
ou des sursauts de l'instinct de vie. Paris est le champs
d'aventures dégradantes: poubelles assiégées; enfants
guêtant les détritus comme des trésors; affamés qui sui-
vent à la trace les mangeurs à 4 sous. Vous vous doutez
que ces chanceux ne font pas les difficiles ou des
cadeaux aus *bijoutiers* en vadrouille. Cependant, si bien
qu'ils nettoient leurs plats, "vous verrez encore, à
l'heure du service, de pauvres diables qui, la poche
vide et l'estomac creux, se tiennent debout près des
tables et guettent les assiettes où quelque dîneur aura
laissé des bribes de viande. Ils se précipitent souvent
à cinq ou six à la fois sur un os abandonné. C'est le
côté navrant du curieux spectacle de la Californie."'
Aron, 299.

CHAPTER FOUR: FLAUBERT

1 In his well-known essay, *Littérature et sensation* (Paris:
Editions du Seuil, 1954), Jean-Pierre Richard pointed
out the relation between the gastro-alimentary and the
aesthetic in Flaubert's vision of life and art. Speaking
of the novelist's very posture before existence, Richard
comments: '... Flaubert est devant les choses comme un
géant attablé' (120). Yet, unlike writers such as Eugène
Sue and Victor Hugo, who, as we have seen, exploit the
metaphorical dimension of life, more precisely society,
as a devouring machine, Flaubert tends to privilege the
pre-alimentary act, the excitement generated by viewing
the finest of fare: 'Etre en verve c'est avoir envie de
se mettre à table, sans céder tout de suite à cette envie'

(ibid.). And, similarly: 'Flaubert est voué à la *dégus-tation* plutôt qu'à l'engloutissement' (121). Furthermore, according to Richard, the artistic enterprise itself, and especially Flaubert's conception of it, corresponds with the process of ingestion: 'L'artiste pompe la na-ture: il s'ouvre à elle de toutes ses forces pour la laisser s'introduire en lui plus totalement que ne fait le commun des hommes' (122).

So extensive is the presence of the alimentary that it pervades all the works of Flaubert. Richard's short but brilliant analysis of the subject offers many in-sights to the interested reader while suggesting possible avenues of future studies. Although I have limited my analysis to *Madame Bovary* for purposes of economy, it should be made apparent that virtually all of Flaubert's writings, his *Correspondances* included, provide a plen-titude of gastronomical references: 'On mange beaucoup dans les romans de Flaubert; peu de tableau plus familier chez lui que celui de la table garnie sur laquelle s'am-oncellent les nourritures, autour de laquelle s'aiguisent les appétits' (119). All subsequent references will be indicated in the text by the author's name.

2 It may be helpful to point out that *la gastronomie* takes on new ideological connotations in the nineteenth century because of the shifts in social structure occasioned by the Revolution. Prior to 1789 a gastronome partook of *la grande cuisine*, that is, he was generally an aristocrat who had been raised on France's finest fare. *La gastro-nomie*, on the other hand, is a cultural mythology created and perpetuated by the bourgeoisie as it begins to gain ascendancy over the other social spheres. *La gastronomie*, then, acquires a new semiotic value as a sign of demo-cracy since the *bon bourgeois* could now rub elbows with aristocrats in fashionable restaurants, and as a marker of economic status: 'For the nineteenth-century bourgeois this, the most conspicuous of consumptions, could become a means of legitimizing a social status newly acquired.' Priscilla P. Clark, 'Thoughts for Food, I: French Cuisine and French Culture,' *French Review*, 1 (October 1975), 39. I should like to call attention to another observa-tion from the same article by Professor Clark which helps to elucidate, albeit indirectly, Emma Bovary's infatua-tion with the gastro-sign: 'If, as Thorstein Veblen ar-gued in *The Theory of the Leisure Class* (1899), conspicu-ous consumption generally marks efforts to stabilize high social status, the forms it takes vary considerably. The

French bourgeoisie turned to cuisine. By virtue of its long-standing association with the aristocracy, *la grande cuisine* conferred prestige upon the parvenue bourgeoisie. The bourgeois at the table participated in the leisure ethos associated with the aristocracy of times past.'

3 Victor Brombert, *The Novels of Flaubert: A Study of Themes and Techniques* (Princeton: Princeton University Press, 1966), 49.

4 Because of the all-pervasiveness of gastronomical and alimentary discourse in *L'Education sentimentale*, it will be helpful from time to time to make references to this novel, particularly as regards similarities and differences between the two works. The functions of dining scenes in *L'Education sentimentale*, for instance, are analogous in many ways to those in *Madame Bovary*, but meals in *L'Education sentimentale* occur more frequently and their structural organization is more complex. In part, the high frequency of eating episodes may be explained by the Parisian setting of the novel: in a large city there are numerous restaurants and cafés, and dinner parties are given more often than in the provinces. The meals in *L'Education sentimentale* differ from those in *Madame Bovary* to the extent that they belong to the life of the capital and thus serve to expose and emphasize the various social groups which Frédéric Moreau, the protagonist, encounters. Naturally, the reader will expect to find an abundance of various social spheres and political factions in a novel which depicts such a vast historical canvas. These heterogeneous groups would not ordinarily come into contact were there no narrative device designed to unite them, and with them their sociological, economic, and ideological characteristics, in a single and plausible locus. The primary function of the meal, then, in *L'Education sentimentale* is that of a structuring agent, for it is at table that characters meet, interact, and resolve or perpetuate their differences. As in *Madame Bovary*, the entire narrative evolves through carefully distributed eating scenes to such an extent that each meal episode enables the reader to situate its significance either on the sentimental and aesthetic plane or on the social and economic level. And, as with *Madame Bovary*, this novel, too, could be explicated on the basis of its gastro-alimentary discourse.

5 Jules de Gaultier, *Le Bovarysme*, third edition (Paris: Société du Mercure de France, n.d.), 14. Subsequently denoted by the author's name.

6 Gustave Flaubert, *Madame Bovary* (Paris: Editions Garnier Frères, 1961), 20. All references are to this edition, which will appear in the text as *Madame Bovary*.

7 Noëlle Châtelet has written a highly original and fascinating account of the symbolism of kitchens in what is perhaps the best recent study to appear in French on the social anthropology of food and cooking. See especially her chapter entitled 'Du sacré au sacrum' in *Le corps à corps culinaire* (Paris: Editions du Seuil, 1977), 21-32.

8 In *L'Education sentimentale* Flaubert uses the table or a meal setting for the introduction of nearly every major character in the novel. Although the kitchen itself does not have the same function in *L'Education sentimentale* as in *Madame Bovary* (i.e. serving as the locus for first encounters), it would be appropriate to note that Frédéric Moreau gets his first glimpse of Mme Arnoux, the woman he will always love, while she is eating lunch aboard a riverboat. Similarly, Frédéric makes most of his acquaintances at table or in Parisian restaurants and bistros, and, generally, learns the character and whereabouts of his friends by their eating habits.

9 In *L'Education sentimentale*, a novel which largely depicts bourgeois life, the kitchen sometimes serves this double purpose, but with a reversal in connotations occasioned by an emphasis on the male's role in the kitchen. The bourgeois male in nineteenth-century France took great pride in his gastronomical savoir-faire, so it is no wonder that the narrator has Jacques Arnoux, an eminent Parisian bourgeois, demonstrate his culinary artistry to Frédéric Moreau as part of the latter's initiation into *le beau monde*: 'Arnoux commandait aux domestiques en les tutoyant, battait la remoulade, goûtait les sauces, rigolait avec la bonne.' Gustave Flaubert, *L'Education sentimentale* (Paris: Editions Garnier Frères, 1964), 122. That Arnoux is preparing this meal in the kitchen of his mistress further attests to the relation between kitchens and lovers in the novels of Flaubert.

10 Christian Guy, *An Illustrated History of French Cuisine*, trans. Elisabeth Abbott (New York: Bramhall House, 1962), 160-1.

11 Describing Rousseau's aversion to the 'pharmaceutical' dangers inherent in nature - 'La plante vénéneuse est comme un scandale de la nature,' and, similarly, 'La "pharmacie" ne doit pas venir souiller les images champêtres' - Jean-Claude Bonnet makes some rather incisive and insightful remarks on the psychology of *l'empoisonement*

which are not without relevance to Emma's malady: 'Il n'est pas indifférent que le trouble de la relation à autrui passe par l'obsession du poison, c'est-à-dire une névrose alimentaire. Le poison ... symbolise la rupture de la relation sociale avec un retour de la violence.' Jean-Claude Bonnet, 'Le système de la cuisine et du repas chez Rousseau,' *Poétique*, 24 (1975), 266-7. Victor Brombert, too, comments on the gastro-alimentary significance of Emma's suicide: 'Ironically, Emma's very death is provoked by *swallowing* poison, and the first symptoms of her agony are those of major indigestion.' Brombert, 52.

12 Among the novelists discussed in this book, George Sand evokes archetypal rituals of this kind with the greatest amount of sympathy for tradition and with the most elaborate ethnological detail. I refer the reader back to my chapter on Sand, which deals in part with ancient wedding practices in her native province of Berry. See especially pp. 66-70.

13 This theme of *voration visuelle* parallels Flaubert's own psychological and aesthetic predisposition toward *verve* and *dégustation* discussed by Jean-Pierre Richard (see note 1). Moreover, both Emma Bovary and Frédéric Moreau, in these scenes where they undergo an initiation into the culinary delights of fashionable society, react in the same way. During the first phase of the initiation rite they stand in awe before the objects of their adulation, looking at but not seeing the elements of the spectacle; during the second phase, they move about noticing, and then incorporating, the fine fragrances of *la noble chère* and the multitude of sensations in which they are immersed. Generally, the bedazzlement phase centres on the narrator's frequent use of the verb *regarder* whereas the passage phase corresponds with his use of the verb *sentir*. In essence, the object is ultimately, if only momentarily, assimilated: 'Percevoir, penser, aimer, c'est donc d'une certaine façon dévorer. L'objet se tient là, devant nous, dans sa distance et son étrangeté: pour le rendre nôtre il faudra le faire entrer en nous, nous pénétrer de lui, ou, comme dit encore Flaubert, l'*absorber*.' Richard, 122.

14 For further information on the theories of Cabet and Fourier see note 4 to chapter three. Jean-Jacques Rousseau also considered the total gastro-alimentary complex as a fundamental principle of education; Bonnet discusses at length Rousseau's concepts in his 'Le système de la cuisine ...' (see note 8 above).

15 For the theory of *actants*, see A.J. Greimas, *Sémantique structurale* (Paris: Larousse, 1966), 172-92.

CONCLUSION

1 Food as a metaphor of creation is a fascinating subject in itself, whether the creative act be artistic, social, or economic. Its metaphorical potentials in these domains are too vast to treat in this book; therefore, I refer the reader who is interested in the food-art alliance to Lange's brilliant analysis of the *manger-créer* paradigm. Frédéric Lange, *Manger ou les jeux et les creux du plat* (Paris: Seuil, 1975), 15-23. Subsequent references appear in the text. Concerning the relation between food and the capitalist mode of production, diffusion, and consumption the reader will kindly consult Priscilla P. Clark, 'Thoughts for Food, II: Culinary Culture in Contemporary France,' *The French Review*, II (December 1975), 198-205.
2 See especially Charles Fourier, *Théorie des quatre mouvements* in *Œuvres complètes* de Charles Fourier, vol. I (Paris: Editions Anthropos, 1967).
3 Noëlle Châtelet, *Le Corps à corps culinaire* (Paris: Seuil, 1977), 140. Hereafter cited as Châtelet in the text.
4 Gustave Flaubert, *L'Education sentimentale*, ed. Edouard Maynial (Paris: Editions Garnier Frères, 1964), 342.
5 Jean-Claude Bonnet, 'Le système de la cuisine et du repas chez Rousseau,' *Poétique*, 22 (1975), 247. Subsequent references will appear in the text following the author's name.
6 The best study of cannibalism to emerge so far in the works of Sade is Professor Fink's perceptive analysis of the anthropological, psychological, and social ramifications of the cannibalistic act. See Beatrice Fink, 'Sade and Cannibalism,' *L'Esprit Créateur* (Winter 1975), 403-12.
7 Jean-Pierre Richard, *Etudes sur le romantisme* (Paris: Seuil, 1970), 187.

GLOSSARY OF
METAFICTIONAL TERMS

Actant (actantial): an actant is a character or group of
characters responsible for a particular sphere of action
in a narrative.

Agape: early Christian feasts modelled on the Last Supper,
and symbolizing the principles of brotherhood and equality at table. Writers of social theory in nineteenth-
century France often used the agape model as the rationale for commensality and communal dining.

Alimentary (also alimentary codes, alimentary discourse and
alimentary sign): an act associated with eating which
centres on the praxis of ingestion. The alimentary, by
its inherent nature, coincides with transformational processes. In this sense alimentary activity is individualistic, hedonistic, and idiosyncratic. Unlike the gastronomical, the alimentary is at odds with social norms and
the imposition of fixed codes: it is self-regulating and
self-fulfilling.

Appetite (appetite motif): semiotically speaking, the degree zero of culinary consciousness. It is a basic biological signal for the organism, and as such it belongs to
the stimulus-response mechanism. Appetite attests to and
symbolizes the space existing between the subject and the
object. Its metonymic extension imposes itself upon man's
mental space in the form of desire and fulfilment.

Autophagy: refers literally or metaphorically to the act of
self-consumption. Metonymically speaking, cannibalism,
war, and even the entire life process may be considered
to be forms of autophagy.

Cannibalism (ecto-; endo-): Ectocannibalism denotes the actual or symbolic ingestion of humans by members outside
the family, clan, or tribe. Endocannibalism refers to the
actual or symbolic ingestion of humans by members of the
same family, clan, or tribe.

Chaleur-repos motif: pertains to the affective and phenomenological characteristics of the meal, the effects of
conviviality, security, and proximity resulting from
dining together in a reassuring ambience. Implicit in
this motif is the actual or symbolic presence of fire
for cooking or for warming.

Commensal dining: refers to the practice of dining with others, especially those belonging to a different social or economic group, though it may also pertain to banquets, communal meals or other feasts where homo- or heterogeneous grouping occurs. The prototype of commensality in the nineteenth-century French novel is the Last Supper. For this reason, commensal meals often symbolize brotherhood and, by extension, social equality.

Cuisine: in addition to its more conventional definitions, cuisine as cooking in general and cuisine as kitchen, the term here refers to the social and economic distinctions as may be exemplified by *la cuisine noble, la cuisine bourgeoise, la cuisine paysanne, et al.* It may also denote regional identity, e.g., *la cuisine normande, la cuisine parisienne, la cuisine bretonne.* The term *cuisine* may, therefore, carry ideological and/or geographical connotations. When cuisine is transformed from a usage into a sign, that is, when it acquires a semiotic status and is used to communicate cultural messages, we may say that it becomes part of a myth-making process (the mythologization of cuisine).

Culinary: anything pertaining to the preparation of food, its transformation by cooking, its preservation. Culinary practices are often rigidly codified as is the case in the standardization of a particular recipe or in the manner of preparing or serving a specific dish. In these instances we may speak of culinary codes and their role(s) within a given culture. Culinary stylization refers to the rendering of a particular food item into an artifact or a work of art. The nutritional aspect of the food item is subordinated to its aesthetic function; form predominates over substance.

Desire-appetite paradigm: biologically, appetite signals hunger or emptiness; its metaphorical counterpart is desire, or the need to fill up the space created by appetite. This often manifests itself in the form of excessive satiation.

Eating: ingesting or incorporating the world-object, either literally or symbolically.

Food thematic: refers to the use of food as a theme within a given corpus of texts. The food thematic is epitomized in the nineteenth-century French novel and corresponds largely with the advent of the bourgeoisie.

Food-work metonym: the peasant ethic whereby the purpose of food is to supply energy for work. Food is a means, not an end in itself: eating to live, not living to eat.

Food-as-function: the capacity of food to supply nourishment to the individual, its purely practical value in
sustaining life. As such, food is viewed as a substance.

Food-as sign: food, in addition to its function as sustenance, also signifies; it is invested with semantic properties within a specific culture and may, therefore, symbolize such things as social and economic status, regional
characteristics, and psychological and social phenomena,
among other things. In this capacity food becomes a kind
of praxis.

Gagner-son-pain motif: in simple terms, 'Eating to live'
rather than 'Living to eat'; specifically, this motif
belongs for the most part to the peasant/worker ideal of
the functional nature of food: it supplies energy for work.

Gastrology: that branch of medicine which studies the functions and diseases of the stomach. In the nineteenth-
century French novel there is often a pseudo-scientific
connotation associated with gastrology in so far as many
gastrologists believed that the stomach was the epicentre
of all illnesses: 'the stomach is the man.'

Gastronomy (la gastronomie): Conventionally, gastronomy denotes the art of good eating and an appreciation of the
pleasures of the table. In nineteenth-century France it
is transformed into a myth wherein food and taste are no
longer considered only as substances and markers of personal preference, but also as marketable products in the
economic circuit, symbols of social equality and socio-
cultural signs of enormous magnitude. Gastronomical discourse refers then to this whole complex of signs whereas
alimentary discourse centres around the individual act of
eating, not the social, and culinary discourse pertains
to any semiotic system in fiction describing the preparation and cooking of food.

Gastrosophie: a pseudo-science introduced partly in jest
by Charles Fourier. Understanding that gastronomical
fulfilment is man's most basic pleasure, he recognized
its pedagogical potential in regulating and programming
the education of children.

Gustatory (gustatory act): the act of eating itself, especially chewing and tasting. Unlike the alimentary, it is not
necessarily associated with desire; rather it denotes the
physical mechanics of eating and the pleasures related to it.

Hunger: a non-intentional, stimulus-response type of signal
in the organism. In fiction dealing with social problems
it often serves as a catalyst to action, either positive
or negative (e.g., working to eat vs stealing to eat).

Macro-meals/Micro-meals: terms used to describe Flaubert's elaboration of fictional meal scenes in *Madame Bovary*. Flaubert uses meals as semio-structural entities: macro-meals mark Emma Bovary's contentment in life and coincide with special occasions (wedding feasts, banquets, *la cuisine noble*) whereas micro-meals reflect her moments of despair and ennui (domestic meals).

Meal: the food served at table and, also, the meal structure or paradigm (preparation, service, courses, sequel). Since the meal consists of food, it enjoys the same semiotic status as the latter (see Food-as-function, Food-as-sign) and may be classified according to sign typologies as an index, a signal, a symptom, a symbol.

Meal-as-mirror-of-the-meal: the meal used as an inter- or intratextual reference to other meals.

Meal complex: the total semiotic discourse associated with food and the act of eating.

Meal semiosis: the relation between the meal-as-substance and the meal-as-sign; it is engendered both by cultural phenomena and fictional ideologies.

Nourishment principle: the correlation between food and work, food and physical activity (see Food-work thematic, *gagner-son-pain* motif).

Serenity syndrome: the state of rest and relaxation following ingestion in genial company; often associated with the pleasures of digestion, warmth, company, and conversation (see *chaleur-repos* motif).

SELECTED BIBLIOGRAPHY

Allemand, André. *Honoré de Balzac, creation et passion.*
  Paris: Librairie Plon, 1965
Aron, Jean-Paul. *Essai sur la sensibilité alimentaire à
  Paris au XIXe siècle.* Paris: Armand Colin, 1967
- *Le Mangeur du XIXe siecle.* Paris: Robert Laffont, 1973.
Auerbach, Eric. *Mimesis.* Translated by Willard R. Trask.
  Princeton: Princeton University Press, 1953
Bakhtin, Mikhail. *Rabelais and His World.* Translated by
  Helena Iswolsky. Boston: M.I.T. Press, 1965
Balzac, Honoré de. *L'Auberge rouge. La Comédie humaine.*
  Edited by Marcel Bouteron. Vol. IX. Paris: Bibliothèque
  de la Pléiade, 1951
- *Les Deux Rêves. La Comédie humaine.* Edited by Marcel Bou-
  teron. Vol. X. Paris: Bibliothèque de la Pléiade, 1951
- *Eugénie Grandet. La Comédie humaine.* Edited by Marcel Bou-
  teron. Vol. III. Paris: Bibliothèque de la Pléiade, 1951
- *Gobseck. Les Grands Ecrivains français.* Edited by Joseph
  D. Gaultier and Lewis A.B. Sumberg. New York: Holt,
  Rinehart and Winston, 1965
- *La Peau de chagrin. La Comédie humaine.* Edited by Marcel
  Bouteron. Vol. IX. Paris: Bibliothèque de la Pléiade, 1951
- *Le Père Goriot. La Comédie humaine.* Edited by Marcel Bou-
  teron. Vol. I. Paris: Bibliothèque de la Pléiade, 1951
- *Physiologie du mariage. La Comédie humaine.* Edited by
  Marcel Bouteron. Vol. X. Paris: Bibliothèque de la Pléiade,
  1951
- *La Rabouilleuse. La Comédie humaine.* Edited by Marcel
  Bouteron. Vol. III. Paris: Bibliothèque de la Pléiade,
  1951
Barberis, Pierre. 'La Pensée de Balzac: histoire et struc-
  tures.' *Revue d'Histoire de la Littérature de la France*
  (January-March, 1967)
Bardèche, Maurice. *Balzac romancier.* Paris: Librairie Plon,
  1940
Barthes, Roland. *Eléments de sémiologie.* Paris: Editions
  Gonthier, 1953 and 1964
- *Mythologies.* Paris: Editions du Seuil, 1957
- 'Pour une psycho-sociologie de l'alimentation contempor-
  aine,' *Annales*, 16, no. 5 (September-October, 1961)

Bertault, Philippe. *Balzac l'homme et l'oeuvre*. Paris: Boivin et Cie., 1946

Blond, Georges and Germaine. *Histoire pittoresque de notre alimentation*. Paris: Fayard, 1961

Bonnet, Jean-Claude. *Grimod de la Reyniere: Ecrits gastronomiques*. Paris: Editions Christian Bourgeois, 1978

- 'Le système de la cuisine et du repas chez Rousseau,' *Poétique*, 22 (1975)

Booth, Wayne C. *The Rhetoric of Fiction*. Chicago: University of Chicago Press, 1961

Bory, Jean-Louis. *Eugène Sue: Le Roi du roman populaire*. Paris: Hachette, 1962

Bourgin, Hubert. *Fourier. Contribution à l'étude du socialisme français*. Paris: Société Nouvelle de la Librairie et d'Edition, 1905

Bowman, Frank Paul. *Le Christ romantique: le sans-culotte de Nazareth*. Geneva: Droz, 1973

Brillat-Savarin, Jean Anthelme. *La Physiologie du goût*. Paris: Librairie Garnier Frères, n.d.

Brombert, Victor. *The Novels of Flaubert: A Study of Themes and Techniques*. Princeton: Princeton University Press, 1962

Brown, James W. 'A Note on Kitchens in *Madame Bovary*,' *USF Language Quarterly* (Fall-Winter, 1978)

- 'On the Semiogenesis of Fictional Meals,' *Romantic Review*, 64: 4 (November, 1978)

- 'The Ideological and Aesthetic Functions of Food in *Paul et Virginie*,' *Eighteenth-Century Life* (Spring, 1978)

- 'Theory for a Semiological Analysis of Fictional Meal Scenes.' Read at the *Modern Language Association* (December, 1974)

Brown, Norman O. *Love's Body*. New York: Random House, 1966

Burnand, Robert. *La Vie quotidienne en France en 1830*. Paris: Hachette, 1943

Cabet, Etienne. *Voyage en Icarie*. Paris: Au Bureau populaire, 1848

Charlety, Sébastien. *Histoire du Saint-Simonisme, 1825-1864*. Paris: Paul Hartmann, 1931

Châtelet, Noëlle. *Le corps à corps culinaire*. Paris: Editions du Seuil, 1977

Clark, Priscilla P. *The Battle of the Bourgeois: The Novel in France, 1789-1848*. Paris: Didier, 1973

- 'Thoughts for Food, I: French Cuisine and French Culture.' *The French Review*, 49 (October, 1975)

- 'Thoughts for Food, II: Culinary Culture in Contemporary France.' *The French Review*, 49 (December 1975)

Communications. 'La Nourriture.' 31 (1979)

Cortland, Peter. *Sentiment in Flaubert's 'Education senti-mentale.'* Muncie, Indiana: Ball State Monograph Number Four, 1966

Eco, Umberto. *A Theory of Semiotics*. Bloomington, London: Indiana University Press, 1976

Evans, David Owen. *Le Socialisme romantique: Pierre Leroux et ses contemporains*. Paris: Librairie Marcel Rivière et Cie., 1948

Félicien, Marceau. *Balzac et son monde*. Paris: Gallimard, 1955

Fink, Beatrice. 'Food as Object, Activity and Symbol in Sade.' *Romanic Review* (March, 1975)

- 'Sade and Cannibalism.' *L'Esprit Créateur* (Winter, 1975)

Fisher, M.F.K. and the editors of Time-Life Books. *The Cooking of Provincial France*. New York: Time-Life Books, 1968

Flaubert, Gustave. *Bouvard et Pécuchet*. Paris: Classiques Garnier, 1972

- *L'Education sentimentale*. Paris: Classiques Garnier, 1964
- *Madame Bovary*. Paris: Classiques Garnier, 1961
- *Salammbô*. Paris: Classiques Garnier, 1972
- *Trois Contes*. 'Un Coeur simple,' 'La Légende de saint Julien L'Hospitalier,' 'Hérodias.' Paris: Classiques Garnier, 1969

Fokkema, D.W. 'Continuity and Change in Russian Formalism, Czech Structuralism, and Soviet Semiotics,' *PTL*, 1 (January, 1976)

Fourier, Charles. *Manuscrits publiés par la Phalange Revue de la Science sociale, 1851-1852. Œuvres complètes de Charles Fourier*. Vol. X. Paris: Editions Anthropos, 1967

- *Le Nouveau Monde amoureux. Œuvres complètes de Charles Fourier*. Vol. VII. Paris: Editions Anthropos, 1967
- *Le Nouveau Monde industriel et sociétaire ou invention du procédé d'industrie attrayante et naturelle distribuée en séries passionnées. Œuvres complètes de Charles Fourier*. Vol. VI. Paris: Editions Anthropos, 1967
- *Théorie de l'unité universelle. Œuvres complètes de Charles Fourier*. Vol. IV. Paris: Editions Anthropos, 1967
- *Théorie des quatre mouvements et des destinées générales. Œuvres complètes de Charles Fourier*. Vol. I. Paris: Editions Anthropos, 1967

Frappier-Mazur, Lucienne. 'Texte métaphorique et réalité romanesque,' *L'Année Balzacienne*. Paris: Editions Garnier Frères, 1972

Frye, Northrop. *Anatomy of Criticism*. Princeton: Princeton University Press, 1957

Gaultier, Jules de. *Le Bovarysme*. 3rd ed. Paris: Société du Mercure de France, n.d.

Genette, Gérard. *Figures III*. Paris: Editions du Seuil, 1972

Godwin, Parke. *A Popular View of the Doctrines of Charles Fourier*. New York: J.S. Redfield, Clinton Hall, 1844

Graves, Robert. *The Greek Myths*. 2 vols. Baltimore: Penguin Books, 1955

Greimas, A.J. *Sémantique structurale*. Paris: Larousse, 1966

Groddeck, Georg. *La Maladie, l'art et le symbole*. Paris: Gallimard, 1969

Guiraud, Pierre. *La Sémiologie*. Paris: Presses Universitaires de France, 1971

Guy, Christian. *An Illustrated History of French Cuisine from Charlemagne to Charles de Gaulle*. Translated by Elizabeth Abbott. New York: Bramhall House, 1962

Hamilton, Edith. *Mythology*. New York: The New American Library, 1940

Hugo, Victor. *Les Misérables*. Edited by Maurice Allem. Paris: Bibliothèque de la Pléiade, 1951

Hunt, Herbert J. *Balzac's 'Comédie humaine.'* London: Athlone Press, 1959

Imbert, Patrick. 'Sémiostyle. La Description chez Balzac, Flaubert et Zola,' *Littérature*, 38 (1980)
- *Sémiotique et description balzacienne*. Ottawa: Editions de l'Université d'Ottawa, 1978

Jakobson, Roman. 'Closing Statements: Linguistics and Poetics,' in *Style in Language*. Edited by Thomas A. Sebeok. Cambridge, Mass.: M.I.T. Press, 1960

Johnston, James P. *A Hundred Years Eating*. Montreal: McGill-Queen's University Press, 1977

Journet, René and Guy Roberts, eds. *Mangeront-ils? Cahiers Victor Hugo*. Paris: Flammarion, 1970

Karénine, Wladimir. *George Sand, sa vie et ses oeuvres, 1838-1848*. Vol. III. Paris: Librairie Plon, 1912

Kempf, Roger. *Le Corps romanesque*. Paris: Editions du Seuil, 1968

Kristeva, Julia. *Le Texte du roman*. The Hague: Mouton, 1970

Lange, Frédéric. *Manger ou les jeux et les creux du plat*. Paris: Editions du Seuil, 1975

Le Breton, André. *Le Roman français au 19e siècle*. Paris: Société française d'Imprimerie et de Librairie, 1901

Le Huenen, Roland and Paul Perron. *Balzac. Sémiotique du personnage romanesque. L'Exemple d'Eugénie Grandet*. Paris: Didier-Erudition, 1980

Leroy, Maxime. *Histoire des idées sociales en France*. Vol.
  II. Paris: Bibliothèque des Idées, 1962
- *Histoire des idées sociales en France*. Vol. III. Paris:
  Bibliothèque des Idées, 1954
Lévi-Strauss, Claude. *Anthropologie structurale*. Paris:
  Plon, 1958
- *L'Origine des manières de table*. Paris: Plon, 1968
- *The Raw and the Cooked*. Translated by John and Doreen
  Weightman. New York: Harper Torchbooks, 1969
- 'Le Triangle culinaire,' *L'Arc*, 26 (1965)
Lubbock, Percy. *The Craft of Fiction*. New York: Viking
  Press, 1957
Magnolia, Robert. 'The Phenomenological Approach to Litera-
  ture: Its Theory and Methodology,' *Language and Style*,
  5 (Spring, 1972)
Martino, Pierre. *Le Roman réaliste sous le Second Empire*.
  Paris: Hachette, 1913
McVicker, Cecil D. 'Narcotics and Excitants in the *Comédie
  humaine*,' *Romance Notes*, 11 (1969)
Menninger, Karl. *The Vital Balance*. New York: Viking Press,
  1963
Montagné, Prosper. *Larousse Gastronomique, The Encyclopedia
  of Food, Wine and Cooking*. Edited by Charlotte Turgeon
  and Nina Froud. Translated by Nina Froud, Patience Gray,
  Maud Murdoch, and Barbara Macrae Taylor. New York: Crown
  Publishers, 1961
Mounin, Georges. *Introduction à la sémiologie*. Paris: Les
  Editions de Minuit, 1970
Oliver, Raymond. *The French at Table*. Translated by Claude
  Durrell. London: Wine and Food Society, 1967
Ponson du Terrail, Pierre Alexis. *Les Exploits de Rocambole*.
  6th ed. Paris: Librairie de la Société des Gens et Lettres,
  1868
Proust, Jacques. 'Sens et structure de "L'Education senti-
  mentale."' *Revue des Sciences Humaines*, fasc. 125 (1967)
Prudhommeaux, Jules. *Icarie et son fondateur: Etienne Cabet*.
  Paris: F. Rieder et Cie., 1926
Raimond, Michel. *Le Roman depuis la Révolution*. Paris:
  Armand Colin, 1967
Richard, Jean-Pierre. *Etudes sur le romantisme*. Paris: Edi-
  tions du Seuil, 1970
- *Littérature et sensation*. Paris: Editions du Seuil, 1954
- *Proust et le monde sensible*. Paris: Editions du Seuil,
  1974
- 'Proust et l'objet alimentaire,' *Littérature*, 6 (1972)

Riffaterre, Michael. 'Criteria for Style Analysis.' *Word*,
  15 (1959)
- 'Stylistic Context.' *Word*, 16 (1960)
Rossmann, Edward. 'The Conflict over Food in the Work of
  J.K. Huysmans,' *Nineteenth-Century French Studies* (Fall-
  Winter, 1973-4)
Sand, George. *Le Compagnon du Tour de France*. Paris: Edi-
  tions Montaigne, 1928.
- *La Comtesse de Rudolstadt*. *Œuvres complètes*. Paris:
  Calmann-Levy, n.d.
- *Consuelo*. *Œuvres illustrées de George Sand*. Edited by
  J. Hetzel. Paris: Librairie Blanchard, 1855
- *François le Champi*. Paris: Editions Garnier Frères, 1969
- *Jeanne*. Oxford, 1907
- *Les Maîtres Sonneurs*. Paris: Editions Garnier Frères, 1958
- *La Mare au diable*. Paris: Editions Garnier Frères, 1969
- *Le Marquis de Villemer*. New York: Oxford University Press,
  1917
- *Le Meunier d'Angibault*. *Œuvres de George Sand*. Paris:
  Calmann-Levy, n.d.
- *Procope le Grand*. *Œuvres illustrées de George Sand*.
  Paris: Librairie Blanchard, 1854
Saussure, Ferdinand de. *Cours de linguistique générale*.
  Paris: Payot, 1916
Schilling, Bernard N. *The Hero as failure: Balzac and the
  Rubempré Cycle*. Chicago: University of Chicago Press,
  1968
Segre, Cesare. *Semiotics and Literary Criticism*. The Hague:
  Mouton, 1973
Sherzer, Dina. 'Violence gastronomique dans *Moderato canta-
  bile*,' *The French Review*, 4 (March, 1974)
Soler, Jean. 'Sémiotique de la nourriture dans la Bible.'
  Annales, 4 (1973)
Sue, Eugène. *Les Mystères de Paris*. Paris: G. Charpentier
  et Cie., n.d.
Tannahill, Reay. *Food in History*. New York: Stein and Day,
  1973
Todorov, Tzvetan. *Introduction à la littérature fantastique*.
  Paris: Editions du Seuil, 1970
- 'Perspectives sémiologiques,' *Communications*, 7 (1966)
- 'Poétique,' in *Qu'est-ce que le structuralisme?* Edited
  by Oswald Ducrot. Paris: Editions du Seuil, 1968
Turnell, Martin. *The Novel in France*. New York: Vintage,
  1958
Ullmann, Stephen. *Style in the French Novel*. Oxford: Basil
  Blackwell, 1964

Wellek, René and Austin Warren. *Theory of Literature*. 3rd
 ed. New York: Harcourt, Brace and World, 1942
Wolitz, Seth L. 'The Multiple Functions of Food in Proust's
 Combray.' Read at the *Modern Language Association*
 (December, 1974)
Zawadowski, Leo. 'Semiotics and Linguistics: Fruitful Inter-
 dependence in Search of Semiotic Identities,' *Canadian
 Journal of Research in Semiotics*, 4 (Winter, 1976-7)
Żólkiewski, Stefan. 'Contribution au problème de l'analyse
 structurale,' *Fauna Linguarum*, 3 (October, 1966)

INDEX

UNIVERSITY OF TORONTO ROMANCE SERIES